Robert Browning

SELECT POEMS, VOL. II

Robert Browning

SELECT POEMS, VOL. II

[Edited with Introduction, Author's Background,
Complete Text and Select Criticism]

Aditya Nandwani
B.A. English (Hons) , Delhi University;
M.A. (English), IGNOU; Print Journalism (English) YMCA

ANMOL PUBLICATIONS PVT. LTD.
NEW DELHI - 110 002 (INDIA)

ANMOL PUBLICATIONS PVT. LTD.

H.O.: 4374/4B, Ansari Road, Darya Ganj,
New Delhi-110 002 (India)
Ph.: 23278000, 23261597

B.O.: No. 1015, Ist Main Road, BSK IIIrd Stage
IIIrd Phase, IIIrd Block
Bangalore - 560 085 (India)
Visit us at: www.anmolpublications.com

Select Poems, Vol. II

First Published, 2009

PRINTED IN INDIA

Printed at Mehra Offset Press, Delhi.

Contents

Preface

Robert Browning was an English poet and playwright whose mastery of dramatic verse, especially dramatic monologues, made him one of the foremost Victorian poets.

Browning's fame today rests mainly on his monologues, in which the words not only convey setting and action but also reveal the speaker's character. Unlike a soliloquy, the meaning in a Browning dramatic monologue is not what the speaker directly reveals but what he inadvertently "gives away" about himself in the process of rationalizing past actions, or "special-pleading" his case to a silent auditor in the poem. Rather than thinking out loud, the character composes a self-defense which the reader, as "juror," is challenged to see through. Browning chooses some of the most debased, extreme and even criminally psychotic characters, no doubt for the challenge of building a sympathetic case for a character who doesn't deserve one and to cause the reader to squirm at the temptation to acquit a character who may be a homicidal psychopath. One of his more sensational monologues (though not a dramatic monologue, by definition) is "Porphyria's Lover." The opening lines provide a sinister setting for the macabre events that follow. It is plain that the speaker is insanc, as hc strangles his lover with her own hair to try and preserve for ever the moment of perfect love she has shown him.

Ironically, Browning's style, which seemed modern and experimental to Victorian readers, owes much to his love of the seventeenth century poems of Robert Browning with their abrupt openings, colloquial phrasing and irregular rhythms. But he remains too much the prophet-poet and descendant of

Percy Shelley to settle for the conceits, puns, and verbal play of the Metaphysical poets of the seventeenth century. His is a modern sensibility, all too aware of the arguments against the vulnerable position of one of his simple characters, who recites: "God's in His Heaven; All's right with the world." Browning essentially endorses such a position because he sees an immanent deity that, far from remaining in a transcendent heaven, is indivisible from temporal process, assuring that in the fullness of theological time there is ample cause for celebrating life. Browning's is assuredly at once the most incarnate and dynamic of deities, in Christianity and perhaps in any of the world's great religions.

Author

Chapter 1

Introduction

It's past midnight in Florence's red-light district in the mid-15th century, and a man dressed as a monk has just been strong-armed by the police and questioned about his presence in such a place. Wait, he says, I can explain everything. That's where we find ourselves at the beginning of Browning's "Fra Lippo Lippi." What follows is a wild improvisation on assorted themes—lust, want, religion, art-making, and the nature of beauty. The good Fra Lippo—Carmelite Friar and in-house painter for Cosimo De' Medici—does explain his presence, explains in fact pretty much his entire life and art, over the course of nearly 400 lines. He is, like other of Browning's monologists, a world-class talker.

Browning wrote many kinds of poems, but the ones I like best and have been rereading for years are the dramatic monologues, in which the ventriloquist poet throws his voice and we hear a dummy (usually an actual historical personage) talk itself into existence. Although the speaker usually directs his gab to a particular person or persons, he may as well be talking to himself. The Duke of Ferrara in "My Last Duchess" is in love with the sound of his own voice and its homicidal menace. A dramatic monologue also lets the poet shape and set loose a voice that reveals something that matters not just to the speaker but to Browning, too.

The "unknown painter" whose voice we hear in "Pictor Ignotus" is soured by what he feels to be his contemporaries' indifference toward his work. In every monologue we hear the speaker (or what I think of as the consciousness of the poem) working through a crisis, conducting an argument, or rationalizing inclinations, actions, and beliefs. Some of these poems, such as "Fra Lippo Lippi" and "Pictor Ignotus," are about painting and are spoken by artists, which makes them ekphrastic poems; that is, they have to do with images—ekphrasis is Greek for description.

Even those not in artists' voices usually involve art. The dying ecclesiast in "The Bishop Orders His Tomb at Saint Praxed's Church," whose thoughts should be concentrated on last things and the afterlife, obsesses about architecture, stonemasonry, and sculpture.

Every Browning monologue discloses an idiosyncratic, preoccupied mind, and the imaginative arc that connects us to that mind is the same arc we make when reading Shakespeare: it's a character that speaks to us, not the poet, though it's the poet who gives spirit and voice to the character's passions. Browning, like Shakespeare, is everywhere and nowhere in the voices he creates. In "Fra Lippo Lippi," he has his character argue for the realistic style developed in Renaissance art because he wants to make a case for the vivid textures and psychological realism of his own poems, a prime instance of which is the very monologue we're reading. In this and other poems, we're suddenly made eavesdroppers to an already strung-out dramatic situation; it's like hearing one side of a telephone conversation we've tuned into after it has already started.

Browning takes nasty delight in dropping us into situations that engage moral questions attached to rough, unpleasant realities, though his tone is high-spirited and racy, not morose. "Andrea del Sarto," spoken by the 16th-century artist described by one of his contemporaries as "the faultless painter," starts with del Sarto's attempt to have a "relationship talk" with his wife: "But do not let us quarrel any more, / No, my Lucrezia; bear with me for once." A few years earlier, Lucrezia persuaded him to return from the Court of France (where he'd been invited and won acclaim and prosperity) to Florence—that is, to her and her claims on him—which he fears may have cost him the supreme fame of a Michelangelo or Raphael. We follow the movements of his mind as it dances through various subjects: good technique, nostalgia, fame, and covetousness. We learn that he's henpecked but loves his wife (in part because she's a reliable model), that he's sensitive to personal and professional slights, and that he's not entirely convinced that being a "perfect painter" is such a good thing after all.

In "My Last Duchess," the greatest modern poem I know about, the acidic, potentially murderous dynamics of jealousy, the duke of Ferrara is showing his art collection to the representative of a nobleman whose daughter the duke is betrothed to. The collection's centerpiece is a portrait of his lately deceased duchess, who in life—the duke lets the go-between (and us) know—distributed her attention to the world too indiscriminately to please the egomaniacal owner "of a nine-hundred-years-old name." Was the duchess superficial and flirty? Did she smile too much at everything alike? We have only the duke's word for it. There's no ambiguity about the duke's solution, though: "I gave commands; / Then all smiles stopped together." Listening to him, we're like Othello depending on an Iago for our intelligence.

To read these poems is to experience how a unique consciousness answers to reality. Whatever the monologist says about the world of circumstance is not a shared truth, it's a person-specific interpretation. Every detail he chooses to include reveals something essential about character. Fra Lippo's improvised self-defense becomes an eloquent, at times hilarious róumàof his orphaned, street-urchin beginnings and how those circumstances shaped his art. This painter, so gifted at rendering psychological subtleties in physiognomies, was once a starving kid who watched people's faces "to know who will fling / The bits of half-stripped grape-bunches he desires, / And who will curse him or kick him for his pains." Want taught him to value the pleasures of the flesh. The deprived child grew to become a man who, though a member of a religious order, chases girls. He's one of several clerics Browning loved to tease for their randy worldliness. The dying priest in "The Bishop Orders His Tomb" moans reverentially about the blue vein in the Blessed Virgin's breast.

It's not only the what of the monologues that wakes us into recognitions of character. The how matters just as much. Browning was vilified by critics for obscurity and abused as a language mangler. The speed of the thoughts that issue from his speakers' mouths sometimes blurs clarity. But the stream of consciousness is a crooked stream, and in the monologues Browning intentionally allows his speakers to indulge in interruptions and gnarly obliqueness.

We have to pay attention to his speakers' patterns of reasoning, however corrupted or manipulative. (Browning's speakers always represent their own interests, as we do when we conduct monologues in life.) He varies effects from poem to poem. "My Last Duchess," a viper of a poem, its beautifully reasoned discourse venomous with insinuation at every turn, is quite unlike the twisty confusions of the bishop's last thoughts on his deathbed, which snap back and forth from his envy of another cleric's tomb to his resentment toward his sons (don't ask) to his obsession with lapis lazuli and correct Latin.

The monologues are crafted to reveal the moral character of the speakers, and the crafting depends on the sonorities and rhythms of versification. Browning favored the blank-verse line—unrhymed iambic pentameter. In its stiffest form, with its ten syllable and alternating stressed/unstressed units, the line would sound like "I am, I am, I am, I am, I am." Gifted versifiers such as Browning work endless variations on this rudimentary pattern. When Fra Lippo gets serious about the relation of art-making to appetite, his meters turn blunt: "This world's no blot for us, / Nor blank; It means intensely, and means good: / To find its meaning is my meat and drink."

But when he describes how, while painting night after night all those saints and Madonnas, his attention was drawn by a sound outside his window, the meters dramatize the excitement and arrested attention he felt when he looked out and saw "Like the skipping of rabbits by moonlight—three slim shapes." The first half of the line prances toward those last three monosyllabic attention-stoppers. When he rhymed, he could do so to chilling effect. The rhyming couplets spoken by the smug, righteous duke in "My Last Duchess" growl with wounded vanity: "She liked whate'er / She looked on, and her looks went everywhere."

Selfhood in Browning is a mass of disheveled fragments of experience, and the monologues give form to what it feels like to actually live them, what it feels like to work at understanding meaning, with little more to go on than memory, desire, and circumstance. He loves to rake life's casual messiness across apparent certitude and aphoristic confidence. "Andrea del Sarto" contains Browning's most famous maxim: "A man's reach should exceed his grasp, / Or what's a heaven for." A sparkling nugget, that one. But all around it one hears about the dozens of tiny rips and rents in del Sarto's marriage, artistic practice, and worldly career. Readers like me who savor these poems go to them not for confirmation of what we already know but to experience the lurching, unstable process of making sense of things.

Chapter 2

Robert Browning Chronology

1812 Born in Camberwell, a London suburb. His father is a clerk at the Bank of England; his family are religious dissenters.

1820 Takes up school, as a weekly boarder in Peckham.

1826 Begins writing poetry, influenced largely by Shelley. Is tutored in French, Italian, Latin, and Greek.

1828 Attends London University for a semester; there he toys with atheism. Returns home, to study, write, and publish (at his father's expense) poetry. He will live at home until his thirties.

1833 Anonymously publishes his first work, the autobiographical Pauline, A Fragment of a Confession. It has almost no sales. Starts work on Sordello.

1834 Travels across Europe to Saint Petersburg, Russia; returns home.

1835 Publishes Paracelsus. which wins literary praise. Begins friendships with Carlyle, poet and critic W. S. Landor, and other men of letters.

1837 Strafford, the first of a series of unsuccessful plays, is produced and published.

1838 First visit to Italy.

1840 Publishes Sordello, a long narrative poem in dramatic monologue. It gains a reputation as "unintelligible" and "meaningless," establishing Browning as an obscure poet.

1841 Begins publishing a series of books under the title Bells and Pomegranates; composed mostly of plays. Publishes Pippa Passes.

1842 Publishes collection of poems called Dramatic Lyrics, including notably "My Last Duchess."

1843-44 Production of three now obscure plays. Visits Italy for a second time.

1845 Writes a letter to Elizabeth Barrett praising her poetry. Visits her and declares his love. Her father is against marriage, though. Publication of Dramatic Romances and Lyrics.

1846 Publication of A Soul's Tragedy, concluding the Bells and Pomegranates series. Marries Elizabeth Barrett, secretly. They settle in Florence, Italy, where they will live in a happy marriage for fifteen years.

1849 A son is born, Robert Barrett-Browning ("Pen").

1850 Publishes Christmas Eve and Easter Day.

1851-52 Visits Paris and London. Strikes friendships with literary and artistic figures of the day, including Dante Gabriel Rossetti, Charles Kingsley, and Tennyson.

1855 Publishes a two-volume poetry collection, Men and Women; it includes most of his best works, including "Fra Lippo Lippi" and "Andrea del Sarto."

1861 Elizabeth Barrett Browning dies; Browning moves to London with his son "Pen. "

1864 Publishes Dramatis Personae.

1868 Publishes The Ring and the Book, a long narrative poem of greed, deception, and murder; based on an Italian story. Though it was a popular success, it is now little read.

1869 Browning proposes marriage to Lady Ashburton, only to be rejected. This proposal, an example of Browning's propensity for social climbing, will continue to embarrass him in society and shame him over his infidclity towards his dead wife.

1871-87 Publishes over a dozen volumes of poetry during this period, which now reside in near-obscurity. They include narrative poems such as Red-Cotton Nightcap Country and the two collections of Dramatic Idyls, verse plays such as The Inn Album, and translations from Greek such as The Agamemnon of Aeschylus.

1880 Dr. F. J. Furnivall and others establish the Browning Society in London. They study his works and idolize him.

1889 Publishes Asolando, a last collection of poems, and an edition of his complete works. Dies in Venice of bronchitis; is buried in Poets' Comer of Westminster Abbey.

Chapter 3

Complete List of Works

- Pauline: A Fragment of a Confession (1833)
- Paracelsus (1835)
- Strafford (play) (1837)
- Sordello (1840)
- Bells and Pomegranates No. I: Pippa Passes (play) (1841)
- Bells and Pomegranates No. II: King Victor and King Charles (play) (1842)
- Bells and Pomegranates No. III: Dramatic Lyrics (1842) o "Porphyria's Lover" o "Soliloquy of the Spanish Cloister" o "My Last Duchess" o The Pied Piper of Hamelin o "Johannes Agricola in Meditation"
- Bells and Pomegranates No. IV: The Return of the Druses (play) (1843)
- Bells and Pomegranates No. V: A Blot in the 'Scutcheon (play) (1843)
- Bells and Pomegranates No. VI: Colombe's Birthday (play) (1844)
- Bells and Pomegranates No. VII: Dramatic Romances and Lyrics (1845) o "The Laboratory" o "How They Brought the Good News from Ghent to Aix" o "The Bishop Orders His Tomb at Saint Praxed's Church"
- Bells and Pomegranates No. VIII: Luria and A Soul's Tragedy (plays) (1846)
- Christmas-Eve and Easter-Day (1850)
- Men and Women (1855) o "Love Among the Ruins" "A Toccata of Galuppi's" o "Childe Roland to the

Dark Tower Came" o "Fra Lippo Lippi" o "Andrea Del Sarto" o "A Grammarian's Funeral" o "An Epistle Containing the Strange Medical Experience of Karshish, the Arab Physician"

- Dramatis Personae (1864) o "Caliban upon Setebos" o "Rabbi Ben Ezra"
- The Ring and the Book (1868-9)
- Balaustion's Adventure (1871)
- Prince Hohenstiel-Schwangau, Saviour of Society (1871)
- Fifine at the Fair (1872)
- Red Cotton Night-Cap Country, or, Turf and Towers (1873)
- Aristophanes' Apology (1875)
- The Inn Album (1875)
- Pacchiarotto, and How He Worked in Distemper (1876)
- The Agamemnon of Aeschylus (1877)
- La Saisiaz and The Two Poets of Croisic (1878)
- Dramatic Idylls (1879)
- Dramatic Idylls: Second Series (1880)
- Jocoseria (1883)
- Ferishtah's Fancies (1884)
- Parleyings with Certain People of Importance In Their Day (1887)
- Asolando (1889)

Chapter 4

The Spiritual Ebb and Flow Exhibited in English Poetry from Chaucer to Tennyson and Browning

Literature, in its most restricted art-sense, is an expression in letters of the life of the spirit of man co-operating with the intellect. Without the co-operation of the spiritual man, the intellect produces only thought; and pure thought, whatever be the subject with which it deals, is not regarded as literature, in its strict sense. For example, Euclid's 'Elements', Newton's 'Principia', Spinoza's 'Ethica', and Kant's 'Critique of the Pure Reason', do not properly belong to literature. (By the "spiritual" I would be understood to mean the whole domain of the emotional, the susceptible or impressible, the sympathetic, the intuitive; in short, that mysterious something in the constitution of man by and through which he holds relationship with the essential spirit of things, as opposed to the phenomenal of which the senses take cognizance.)

The term literature is sometimes extended in meaning (and it may be so extended), to include all that has been committed to letters, on all subjects. There is no objection to such extension in ordinary speech, no more than there is to that of the signification of the word, "beauty" to what is purely abstract. We speak, for example, of the beauty of a mathematical demonstration; but beauty, in its strictest sense, is that which appeals to the spiritual nature, and must, therefore, be concrete, personal, not abstract. Art beauty is the embodiment, adequate, effective embodiment, of co-operative intellect and spirit, "the accommodation," in Bacon's words, "of the shows of things to the desires of the mind."

It follows that the relative merit and importance of different periods of a literature should be determined by the relative degrees of spirituality which these different periods exhibit. The intellectual power of two or more periods, as exhibited in their literatures, may show no marked difference, while the spiritual vitality of these same periods may very distinctly differ. And if it be admitted that literature proper is the product of co-operative intellect and spirit (the latter being always an indispensable factor, though there can be no high order of literature that is not strongly articulated, that is not well freighted, with thought), it follows that the periods of a literature should be determined by the ebb and flow of spiritual life which they severally register, rather than by any other considerations.

There are periods which are characterized by a "blindness of heart", an inactive, quiescent condition of the spirit, by which the intellect is more or less divorced from the essential, the eternal, and it directs itself to the shows of things. Such periods may embody in their literatures a large amount of thought, thought which is conversant with the externality of things; but that of itself will not constitute a noble literature, however perfect the forms in which it may be embodied, and the general sense of the civilized world, independently of any theories of literature, will not regard such a literature as noble. It is made up of what must be, in time, superseded; it has not a sufficiently large element of the essential, the eternal, which can be reached only through the assimilating life of the spirit. The spirit may be so "cabined, cribbed, confined" as not to come to any consciousness of itself; or it may be so set free as to go forth and recognize its kinship, respond to the spiritual world outside of itself, and, by so responding, KNOW what merely intellectual philosophers call the UNKNOWABLE.

To turn now to the line of English poets who may be said to have passed the torch of spiritual life, from lifted hand to hand, along the generations. And first is "the morning star of song, who made His music heard below:

"Dan Chaucer, the first warbler, whose sweet breath
Preluded those melodious bursts that fill
The spacious times of great Elizabeth
With sounds that echo still."

Chaucer exhibits, in a high degree, this life of the spirit, and it is the secret of the charm which his poetry possesses for us after a lapse of five hundred years. It vitalizes, warms, fuses, and imparts a lightsomeness to his verse; it creeps and kindles beneath the tissues of his thought. When we compare Dryden's modernizations of Chaucer with the originals, we see the difference between the verse of a poet, with a healthy vitality of spirit, and, through that healthy vitality of spirit, having secret dealings with things, and verse which is largely the product of the rhetorical or literary faculty. We do not feel, when reading the latter, that any unconscious might co-operated with the conscious powers of the writer. But we DO feel this when we read Chaucer's verse.

All of the Canterbury Tales have originals or analogues, most of which have been reproduced by the London Chaucer Society. Not one of the tales is of Chaucer's own invention. And yet they may all be said to be original, in the truest, deepest sense of the word. They have been vitalized from the poet's own soul. He has infused his own personality, his own spirit-life, into his originals; he has "created a soul under the ribs of death." It is this infused vitality which will constitute the charm of the Canterbury Tales for all generations of English speaking and English reading people. This life of the spirit, of which I am speaking, as distinguished from the intellect, is felt, though much less distinctly, in a contemporary work, 'The Vision of William concerning Piers the Plowman'. What the author calls "KIND WIT", that is, "natural intelligence", has, generally, the ascendency. We meet, however, with powerful passages, wherein the thoughts are aglow with the warmth from the writer's inner spirit. He shows at times the moral indignation of a Hebrew prophet.

The 'Confessio Amantis' of John Gower, another

contemporary work, exhibits comparatively little of the life of the spirit, either in its verse or in its thought. The thought rarely passes the limit of natural intelligence. The stories, which the poet drew from the 'Gesta Romanorum' and numerous other sources, can hardly be said to have been BORN AGAIN. The verse is smooth and fluent, but the reader feels it to be the product of literary skill. It wants what can be imparted only by an unconscious might back of the consciously active and trained powers. It is this unconscious might which John Keats, in his 'Sleep and Poetry', speaks of as "might half slumbering on its own right arm", and which every reader, with the requisite susceptibility, can always detect in the verse of a true poet.

In the interval between Chaucer and Spenser, this life of the spirit is not distinctly marked in any of its authors, not excepting even Henry Howard, Earl of Surrey, whose sad fate gave a factitious interest to his writings. It is more noticeable in Thomas Sackville, Lord Buckhurst's 'Induction to the Mirror for Magistrates', which, in the words of Hallam, "forms a link which unites the school of Chaucer and Lydgate to the 'Faerie Queene'."

The Rev. James Byrne, of Trinity College, Dublin, in his lecture on 'The Influence of National Character on English Literature', remarks of Spenser: "After that dark period which separated him from Chaucer, after all the desolation of the Wars of the Roses, and all the deep trials of the Reformation, he rose on England as if, to use an image of his own,

"'*At last the golden orientall gate*
Of greatest heaven gan to open fayre,
And Phoebus, fresh as brydegrome to his mate,
Came dauncing forth, shaking his deawie hayre,
And hurled his glistering beams through gloomy ayre.'

"That baptism of blood and fire through which England passed at the Reformation, raised both Protestant and Catholic to a newness of life. That mighty working of heart and mind with which the nation then heaved throughout, went through every man and woman, and tried what manner of spirits they were of. What a preparation was this for that period of our literature in which man, the great actor of the drama of life, was about to appear on the stage! It was to be expected that the drama should then start into life, and that human character should speak from the stage with a depth of life never known before; but who could have imagined Shakespeare?"

And what a new music burst upon the world in Spenser's verse! His noble stanza, so admirably adapted to pictorial effect, has since been used by some of the greatest poets of the literature, Thomson, Scott, Wordsworth, Byron, Keats, Shelley, and numerous others; but none of them, except in rare instances, have drawn the music out of it which Spenser drew.

Professor Goldwin Smith well remarks, in his article on Mark Pattison's Milton, "The great growths of poetry have coincided with the great bursts of national life, and the great bursts of national life have hitherto been generally periods of controversy and struggle. Art itself, in its highest forms, has been the expression of faith. We have now people who profess to cultivate art for its own sake; but they have hardly produced anything which the world accepts as great, though they have supplied some subjects for `Punch'."

Spenser who, of all the great English poets, is regarded by some critics as the most remote from real life, and the least reflecting his age, is, nevertheless, filled with the spirit of his age its chivalric, romantic, patriotic, moral, and religious spirit. When he began to write, the nation had just passed through the fiery furnace of a religious persecution, and was rejoicing in its deliverance from the papistical rule of Mary. The devotion to the new queen with which it was inspired was grateful, generous, enthusiastic, and even romantic. This devotion Spenser's great poem everywhere reflects, and it has been justly pronounced to be the best exponent of the subtleties of that Calvinism which was the aristocratic form of Protestantism at that time in both France and England.

The renewed spiritual life which set in so strongly with Spenser, reached its springtide in Shakespeare. It was the secret of that sense of moral proportion which pervades his plays. Moral proportion cannot be secured through the laws of the ancients, or through any formulated theory of art. It was, I am assured, through his deep and sensitive spirit-life that Shakespeare felt the universal spirit and constitution of the world as fully, perhaps, as the human soul, in this life, is capable of feeling it. Through it he took cognizance of the workings of nature, and of the life of man, by direct assimilation of their hidden principles, principles which cannot be reached through an observation, by the natural intelligence, of the phenomenal. He thus became possessed of a knowledge, or rather wisdom, far beyond his conscious observation and objective experience.

Shakespeare may be regarded as the first and the last great artistic physiologist or natural historian of the passions; and he was this by virtue of the life of the spirit, which enabled him to reproduce sympathetically the whole range of human passion within himself. He was the first of the world's dramatists that exhibited the passions in their evolutions, and in their subtlest complications. And the moral proportion he preserved in exhibiting the complex and often wild play of the passions must have been largely due to the harmony of his soul with the constitution of things.

What the Restoration dramatists regarded or understood as moral proportion, was not moral proportion at all, but a proportion fashioned according to merely conventional ideas of justice. Shakespeare's moral proportion appeared to them, in their low spiritual condition, a moral chaos, which they set about converting, in some of his great plays, into a cosmos; and a sad muss, if not a ridiculous muss, they made of it. Signal examples of this are the 'rifacimenti' of the Tempest by Dryden and Davenant, the King Lear by Tate, and the Antony and Cleopatra (entitled 'All for Love, or the World well Lost') by Dryden.

In Milton, though there is a noticeable, an even distinctly marked, reduction of the life of the spirit (in the sense in which I have been using these words) exhibited by Shakespeare, it is still very strong and efficient, and continues uninfluenced by the malign atmosphere around him the last fifteen years of his life, which were lived in the reign of Charles II. Within that period he wrote the 'Paradise Lost', 'Paradise Regained', and

'Samson Agonistes'. "Milton," says Emerson, "was the stair or high table-land to let down the English genius from the summits of Shakespeare."

"These heights could not be maintained. They were followed by a meanness and a descent of the mind into lower levels; the loss of wings; no high speculation. Locke, to whom the meaning of ideas was unknown, became the type of philosophy, and his "understanding" the measure, in all nations, of the English intellect. His countrymen forsook the lofty sides of Parnassus, on which they had once walked with echoing steps, and disused the studies once so beloved; the powers of thought fell into neglect."

The highest powers of thought cannot be realized without the life of the spirit. It is this, as I have already said, which has been the glory of the greatest thinkers since the world began; not their intellects, but the co-operating, unconscious power IMMANENT in their intellects.

During the Restoration period, and later, spiritual life was at its very lowest ebb. I mean, spiritual life as exhibited in the poetic and dramatic literature of the time, whose poisoned fountain-head was the dissolute court of Charles II. All the slops of that court went into the drama, all the 'sentina reipublicae', the bilge water of the ship of state. The dramatic writers of the time, to use the words of St. Paul in his letter to the Ephesians, "walked in the vanity of their mind; having the understanding darkened, being alienated from the life of God through the ignorance that was in them because of the blindness of their heart; who, being past feeling, gave themselves over unto lasciviousness, to work all uncleanness with greediness." The age, as Emerson says, had no live, distinct, actuating convictions. It was in even worse than a negative condition. As represented by its drama and poetry, it may almost be said to have repudiated the moral sentiment. A spiritual disease affected the upper classes, which continued down into the reign of the Georges. There appears to have been but little belief in the impulse which the heart imparts to the intellect, or that the latter draws greatness from the inspiration of the former. There was a time in the history of the Jews in which, it is recorded, "there was no open vision". It can be said, emphatically, that in the time of Charles II. there was no open vision.

And yet that besotted, that spiritually dark age, which was afflicted with pneumatophobia, flattered itself that there had never been an age so flooded with light. The great age of Elizabeth (which designation I would apply to the period of fifty years or more, from 1575 to 1625, or somewhat later), in which the human faculties, in their whole range, both intellectual and spiritual, reached such a degree of expansion as they had never before reached in the history of the world, that great age, I say, the age of Spenser, Sidney, Marlowe, Shakespeare, Bacon, Raleigh, Hooker, Ben Jonson, Beaumont, Fletcher, Chapman, Dekker, Ford, Herbert, Heywood, Massinger (and this list of great names might be continued), that great age, I say, was regarded by the men of the Restoration period as barbarous in comparison with their own. But beneath all, still lay the restorative elements of the English character, which were to reassert themselves and usher in a new era of literary productiveness, the greatest since the Elizabethan age, and embodying the highest ideals of life to which the race has yet attained. We can account, to some extent, for this interregnum or spiritual life, but only to some extent. The brutal heartlessness and licentiousness of the court which the exiled Charles brought back with him, and the release from Puritan restraint, explain partly the state of things, or rather the degree to which the state of things was pushed.

In the middle of the eighteenth century, or somewhat earlier, the rise of the spiritual tide is distinctly observable. We see a reaction setting in against the soulless poetry which culminated in Alexander Pope, whose 'Rape of the Lock' is the masterpiece of that poetry. It is, in fact, the most brilliant society-poem in the literature. De Quincey pronounces it to be, though somewhat extravagantly, "the most exquisite monument of playful fancy that universal literature offers." Bishop Warburton, one of the great critical authorities of the age, believed in the infallibility of Pope, if not of THE Pope.

To notice but a few of the influences at work: Thomson

sang of the Seasons, and invited attention to the beauties of the natural world, to which the previous generation had been blind and indifferent. Bishop Percy published his 'Reliques of Ancient English Poetry', thus awakening a new interest in the old ballads which had sprung from the heart of the people, and contributing much to free poetry from the yoke of the conventional and the artificial, and to work a revival of natural unaffected feeling.

Thomas Tyrwhitt edited in a scholarly and appreciative manner, the Canterbury Tales of Chaucer. James McPherson published what he claimed to be translations from the poems of Ossian, the son of Fingal. Whether genuine or not, these poems indicated the tendency of the time. In Scotland, the old ballad spirit, which had continued to exist with a vigour but little abated by the influence of the artificial, mechanical school of poetry, was gathered up and intensified in the songs of him "who walked in glory and in joy, following his plow, along the mountain-side", and who is entitled to a high rank among the poetical reformers of the age.

It is not surprising that the great literary dictator in Percy's day, Dr. Samuel Johnson, should treat the old ballads with ridicule. The good man had been trained in a different school of poetry, and could not in his old age yield to the reactionary movement. Bishop Warburton, who ranked next to Johnson in literary authority, had nothing but sneering contempt to bestow upon upon the old ballads, and this feeling was shared by many others in the foremost ranks of literature and criticism. But in the face of all opposition, and aided by the yearning for literary liberty that was abroad, the old ballads grew more and more into favor. The influence of this folklore was not confined to England. It extended across the sea, and swayed the genius of such poets as Buerger and Goethe and Schiller.

Along with the poetical revival in the eighteenth century, came the great religious revival inaugurated by the Wesleys and Whitefield; and of this revival, the poetry of William Cowper was a direct product. But the two revivals were co-radical, one was not derived from the other. The long-suppressed spiritual elements of the nation began to reassert themselves in religion and in poetry. The Church had been as sound asleep as the Muses.

Cowper belongs to the Whitefield side of the religious revival, the Evangelicals, as they were called (those that remained within the Establishment). In his poem entitled 'Hope', he vindicates the memory of Whitefield under the name Leuconomus, a translation into Greek, of White field. It was his conversion to Evangelicism which gave him his inspiration and his themes. 'The Task' has been as justly called the poem of Methodism as the 'Paradise Lost' has been called the epic of Puritanism. In it we are presented with a number of pictures of the utterly fossilized condition of the clergy of the day in the Established Church (see especially book II., vv. 326-832, in which he satirizes the clergy and the universities).

Cowper has been truly characterized by Professor Goldwin Smith, as "the apostle of feeling to a hard age, to an artificial age, the apostle of nature. He opened beneath the arid surface of a polished but soulless society, a fountain of sentiment which had long ceased to flow."

The greatest things in this world are often done by those who do not know they are doing them. This is especially true of William Cowper. He was wholly unaware of the great mission he was fulfilling; his contemporaries were wholly unaware of it. And so temporal are the world's standards, in the best of times, that spiritual regenerators are not generally recognized until long after they have passed away, when the results of what they did are fully ripe, and philosophers begin to trace the original impulses.

"Only reapers, reaping early
In among the bearded barley,
Hear a song that echoes cheerly
From the river winding clearly
Down to towered Camelot:
And by the moon the reaper weary,
Piling sheaves in uplands airy,
Listening, whispers, 'Tis the fairy
Lady of Shalott."

John Burroughs, in his inspiring essay on Walt Whitman entitled 'The Flight of the Eagle', quotes the following sentence from a lecture on Burns, delivered by "a lecturer from over seas", whom he does not name: "When literature becomes dozy, respectable, and goes in the smooth grooves of fashion, and copies and copies again, something must be done; and to give life to that dying literature, a man must be found not educated under its influence."

Such a man I would say was William Cowper, who, in his weakness, was "Strong to sanctify the poet's high vocation", and who "Testified this solemn truth, while phrenzy desolated, Nor man nor angel satisfies whom only God created."

John Keats, in his poem entitled 'Sleep and Poetry', has well characterized the soulless poetry of the period between the Restoration and the poetical revival in the latter part of the eighteenth century, but more especially of the Popian period. After speaking of the greatness of his favorite poets of the Elizabethan period, he continues:

"Could all this be forgotten? Yes, a schism
Nurtured by foppery and barbarism,
Made great Apollo blush for this his land.
Men were thought wise who could not understand
His glories: with a puling infant's force
They sway'd about upon a rocking-horse,
And thought it Pegasus."

(Alluding to the rocking-horse movement of the Popian verse.)

"Ah dismal soul'd!
The winds of heaven blew, the ocean roll'd
It's gathering waves ye felt it not. The blue
Bar'd its eternal bosom, and the dew
Of summer nights collected still to make
The morning precious: beauty was awake!
Why were ye not awake? But ye were dead
To things ye knew not of, were closely wed
To musty laws lined out with wretched rule
And compass vile: so that ye taught a school

Of dolts to smooth, inlay, and clip, and fit,
Till, like the certain wands of Jacob's wit,
Their verses tallied. Easy was the task:
A thousand handicraftsmen wore the mask
Of Poesy. Ill-fated, impious race!
That blasphem'd the bright Lyrist to his face,
And did not know it, no, they went about,
Holding a poor, decrepid standard out
Mark'd with most flimsy mottoes, and in large
The name of one Boileau!"

It was these lines that raised the ire of Byron, who regarded them as an irreverent assault upon his favorite poet, Pope. In the controversy occasioned by the Rev. W. L. Bowles's strictures on the Life and Writings of Pope, Byron perversely asks, "Where is the poetry of which one-half is good? Is it the Aeneid? Is it Milton's? Is it Dryden's? Is it any one's except Pope's and Goldsmith's, of which ALL is good?"

In the first quarter of the nineteenth century, the spiritual flow which, as I have said, set in about the middle of the eighteenth century, and received its first great impulse from William Cowper, reached its high tide in Wordsworth, Coleridge, Shelley, Keats, Southey, and Byron. These poets were all, more or less, influenced by that great moral convulsion, the French revolution, which stirred men's souls to their deepest depths, induced a vast stimulation of the meditative faculties, and contributed much toward the unfolding of the ideas "on man, on nature, and on human life", which have since so vitalized English poetry.

"The agitation, the frenzy, the sorrow of the times, reacted upon the human intellect, and FORCED men into meditation. Their own nature was held up before them in a sterner form. They were compelled to contemplate an ideal of man, far more colossal than is brought forward in the tranquil aspects of society; and they were often engaged, whether they would or not, with the elementary problems of social philosophy. Mere danger forced a man into thoughts which else were foreign to his habits. Mere necessity of action forced him to decide."

Wordsworth exhibited in his poetry, as they had never

before been exhibited, the permanent absolute relations of nature to the human spirit, interpreted the relations between the elemental powers of creation and the moral life of man, and vindicated the inalienable birthright of the lowliest of men to those inward "oracles of vital deity attesting the Hereafter." Wordsworth's poetry is, in fact, so far as it bears upon the natural world, a protest against the association theory of beauty of the eighteenth century a theory which was an offshoot of the philosophy of Locke, well characterized by Macvicar, in his `Philosophy of the Beautiful' (Introd., pp. xv., xvi), as "an ingenious hypothesis for the close of the eighteenth century, when the philosophy then popular did not admit, as the ground of any knowledge, anything higher than self-repetition and the transformation of sensations."

Coleridge's 'Rime of the Ancient Mariner' is an imaginative expression of that divine love which embraces all creatures, from the highest to the lowest, of the consequences of the severance of man's soul from this animating principle of the universe, and of those spiritual threshings by and through which it is brought again under its blessed influence. In his 'Cristabel' he has exhibited the dark principle of evil, lurking within the good, and ever struggling with it. We read it in the spell the wicked witch Geraldine works upon her innocent and unsuspecting protector; we read it in the strange words which Geraldine addresses to the spirit of the saintly mother who has approached to shield from harm the beloved child for whom she died; we read it in the story of the friendship and enmity between the Baron and Sir Roland de Vaux of Tryermaine; we read it in the vision seen in the forest by the minstrel Bard, of the bright green snake coiled around the wings and neck of a fluttering dove; and, finally, we read it in its most startling form, in the conclusion of the poem, "A little child, a limber elf, singing, dancing to itself," etc., wherein is exhibited the strange tendency to express love's excess "with words of unmeant bitterness". This dark principle of evil, we may suppose, after dwelling in the poet's mind, in an abstract form, crept into this broken poem, where it lies coiled up among the choicest and most fragrant flowers, and occasionally springs its warning rattle, and projects its forked tongue, to assure us of its ugly presence. Both these great poems show the influence of the revival of the old English Ballads. Coleridge had drunk deep of their spirit.

Shelley and Byron were fully charged with the revolutionary spirit of the time. Shelley, of all the poets of his generation, had the most prophetic fervor in regard to the progress of the democratic spirit. All his greatest poems are informed with this fervor, but it is especially exhibited in the 'Prometheus Unbound', which is, in the words of Todhunter, "to all other lyrical poems what the ninth symphony is to all other symphonies; and more than this, for Shelley has here outsoared himself more unquestionably than Beethoven in his last great orchestral work.... The Titan Prometheus is the incarnation of the genius of humanity, chained and suffering under the tyranny of the evil principle which at present rules over the world, typified in Jupiter; the name Prometheus, FORESIGHT, connecting him with that poetic imagination which is the true prophetic power, penetrating the mystery of things, because, as Shelley implies, it is a kind of divine Logos incarnate in man a creative force which dominates nature by acting in harmony with her."

It is, perhaps, more correct to say of Byron, that he was charged with the spirit of revolt rather than with the revolutionary spirit. The revolutionary spirit was in him indefinite, inarticulate; he offered nothing to put in the place of the social and political evils against which he rebelled. There is nothing CONSTRUCTIVE in his poetry. But if his great passion-capital, his keen spiritual susceptibility, and his great power of vigorous expression, had been brought into the service of constructive thought, he might have been a restorative power in his generation.

The greatest loss which English poetry ever sustained, was in the premature death of John Keats. What he would have done had his life been spared, we have an assurance in what he has left us. He was spiritually constituted to be one of the subtlest interpreters of the secrets of life that the whole range of English poetry exhibits. No poet ever more deeply felt "the vital connection of beauty with truth". He realized in himself his idea of the poet expressed in his lines,

"'Tis the man who with a man
Is an equal, be he king,
Or poorest of the beggar-clan,
Or any other wondrous thing
A man may be 'twixt ape and Plato;
'Tis the man who with a bird,
Wren, or eagle, finds his way to
All its instincts; he hath heard
The lion's roaring, and can tell
What his horny throat expresseth,
And to him the tiger's yell
Comes articulate and presseth
On his ear like mother tongue."

"We often think of Shelley and Keats together, and they seem to have an attraction for minds of the same cast. They were both exposed to the same influences, those revolutionary influences in literature and religion which inaugurated a new period. Yet there is a great contrast as well as a great similarity between them, and it is interesting to remark the different spiritual results in the case of these two different minds subjected to conditions so similar in general, though different in detail. Both felt the same need, the need of ESCAPE, desiring to escape from the actual world in which they perceived more evil than good, to some other ideal world which they had to create for themselves.

This is the point of their similarity; their need and motive were the same, to escape from the limitations of the present. But they escaped in different directions, Keats into the past where he reconstructed a mythical Greek world after the designs of his own fancy, Shelley into a future where he sought in a new and distant era, in a new and distant world, a refuge from the present.

We may compare Keats's `Hyperion' with Shelley's `Prometheus', as both poems touch the same idea the dominion of elder gods usurped by younger, for Prometheus belonged to the elder generation. The impression Keats gives us is that he represents the dethroned gods in the sad vale, "far from the fiery noon", for the pleasure of moving among them himself, and creates their lonely world as a retreat for his own spirit. Whereas in the `Prometheus Unbound' we feel that the scenes laid in ancient days and built on Greek myths, have a direct relation to the destinies of man, and that Shelley went back into the past because he believed it was connected with the future, and because he could use it as an artistic setting for exhibiting an ideal world in the future.

"This problem of escape to rescue the soul from the clutches of time, `ineluctabile tempus', which Keats and Shelley tried to resolve for themselves by creating a new world in the past and the future, met Browning too. The new way which Browning has essayed the way in which he accepts the present and deals with it, CLOSES with time instead of trying to elude it, and discovers in the struggle that this time, `ineluctabile tempus', is really a faithful vassal of eternity, and that its limits serve and do not enslave illimitable spirit." From a Paper by John B. Bury, B.A., Trin. Coll., Dublin, on Browning's `Aristophanes' Apology', read at 38th meeting of the Browning Soc., Jan. 29, 1886.

Wordsworth, and the other poets I have named, Byron, Shelley, Keats, and Coleridge, made such a protest against authority in poetry as had been made in the 16th century against authority in religion; and for this authority were substituted the soul-experiences of the individual poet, who set his verse to the song that was within him, and chose such subjects as would best embody and articulate that song.

But by the end of the first quarter of the present century, the great poetical billow, which was not indeed caused by, but received an impulse from, the great political billow, the French Revolution (for they were cognate or co-radical movements), had quite spent itself, and English poetry was at a comparatively low ebb. The Poetical Revolution had done its work. A poetical interregnum of a few years' duration followed, in which there appeared to be a great reduction of the spiritual life of which poetry is the outgrowth.

Mr. Edmund W. Gosse, in his article 'On the Early

Writings of Robert Browning', in the 'Century' for December, 1881, has characterized this interregnum a little too contemptuously, perhaps. There was, indeed, a great fall in the spiritual tide; but it was not such a dead-low tide as Mr. Gosse would make it.

At length, in 1830, appeared a volume of poems by a young man, then but twenty-one years of age, which distinctly marked the setting in of a new order of things. It bore the following title: 'Poems, chiefly Lyrical. By Alfred Tennyson, London: Effingham Wilson, Royal Exchange, Cornhill, 1830.' pp. 154. The volume comprised fifty-three poems, among which were 'The Poet' and 'The Poet's Mind'. These two poems were emphatically indicative of the high ideal of poetry which had been attained, and to the development of which the band of poets of the preceding generation had largely contributed.

A review of the volume, by John Stuart Mill, then a young man not yet twenty-five years of age, was published in 'The Westminster' for January, 1831. It bears testimony to the writer's fine insight and sure foresight; and it bears testimony, too, to his high estimate of the function of poetry in this world an estimate, too, in kind and in degree, not older than this present century. The review is as important a landmark in the development of poetical criticism, as are the two poems I have mentioned, in the development of poetical ideals, in the nineteenth century.

In the concluding paragraph of the review, Mill says: "A genuine poet has deep responsibilities to his country and the world, to the present and future generations, to earth and heaven. He, of all men, should have distinct and worthy objects before him, and consecrate himself to their promotion. It is thus that he best consults the glory of his art, and his own lasting fame.... Mr. Tennyson knows that "the poet's mind is holy ground"; he knows that the poet's portion is to be

"Dower'd with the hate of hate, the scorn of scorn,
The love of love";

he has shown, in the lines from which we quote, his own just conception of the grandeur of a poet's destiny; and we look to him for its fulfilment.... If our estimate of Mr. Tennyson be correct, he too is a poet; and many years hence may be read his juvenile description of that character with the proud consciousness that it has become the description and history of his own works."

Two years later, that is, in 1832 (the volume, however, is antedated 1833), appeared 'Poems by Alfred Tennyson', pp. 163. In it were contained 'The Lady of Shalott', and the untitled poems, known by their first lines, 'You ask me why, tho' ill at ease', 'Of old sat Freedom on the Heights', and 'Love thou thy Land, with Love far brought'. In 'The Lady of Shalott' is mystically shadowed forth the relation which poetic genius should sustain to the world for whose spiritual redemption it labors, and the fatal consequences of its being seduced by the world's temptations, the lust of the flesh, and the lust of the eyes, and the pride of life.

The other poems, 'You ask me why', 'Of old sat Freedom', and 'Love thou thy land', are important as exponents of what may be called the poet's institutional creed. A careful study of his subsequent poetry will show that in these early poems he accurately and distinctly revealed the attitude toward outside things which he has since maintained. He is a good deal of an institutional poet, and, as compared with Browning, a STRONGLY institutional poet. Browning's supreme and all-absorbing interest is in individual souls. He cares but little, evidently, about institutions. At any rate, he gives them little or no place in his poetry.

Tennyson is a very decided reactionary product of the revolutionary spirit which inspired some of his poetical predecessors of the previous generation. He has a horror of the revolutionary. To him, the French Revolution was "the blind hysterics of the Celt", ['In Memoriam', cix.], and "the red fool-fury of the Seine" ['I. M.', cxxvii.]. He attaches great importance to the outside arrangements of society for upholding and advancing the individual. He would "make Knowledge circle with the winds", but "her herald, Reverence", must "fly

Before her to whatever sky
Bear seed of men and growth of minds."

He has a great regard for precedents, almost AS precedents. He is emphatically the poet of law and order. All his sympathies are decidedly, but not narrowly, conservative. He is, in short, a choice product of nineteenth century ENGLISH civilization; and his poetry may be said to be the most distinct expression of the refinements of English culture refinements, rather than the ruder but more vital forms of English strength and power. All his ideals of institutions and the general machinery of life, are derived from England. She is

"the land that freemen till,
That sobre-suited Freedom chose,
The land where, girt with friends or foes,
A man may speak the thing he will;
A land of Settled Government,
A Land of just and old Renown,
Where freedom broadens slowly down
From precedent to precedent:
Where faction seldom gathers head,
But by degrees to fullness wrought,
The strength of some diffusive thought
Hath time and space to work and spread."

But the anti-revolutionary and the institutional features of Tennyson's poetry are not those of the higher ground of his poetry. They are features which, though primarily due, it may be, to the poet's temperament, are indirectly due to the particular form of civilization in which he has lived, and moved, and had his culture, and which he reflects more than any of his poetical contemporaries.

The most emphasized and most vitalized idea, the idea which glints forth everywhere in his poetry, which has the most important bearing on man's higher life, and which marks the height of the spiritual tide reached in his poetry, is, that the highest order of manhood is a well-poised, harmoniously operating duality of the active or intellectual or discursive, and the passive or spiritually sensitive. This is the idea which INFORMS his poem of 'The Princess'. It is prominent in 'In Memoriam' and in 'The Idylls of the King'. In 'The Princess', the Prince, speaking of the relations of the sexes, says:

"in the long years liker must they grow;
The man be more of woman, she of man;
He gain in sweetness and in moral height,
Nor lose the wrestling thews that throw the world;
She mental breadth, nor fail in childward care,
Nor lose the childlike in the larger mind;
Till at the last she set herself to man,
Like perfect music unto noble words;
And so these twain, upon the skirts of Time,
Sit side by side, full-summ'd in all their powers,
Dispensing harvest, sowing the To-be,
Self-reverent each and reverencing each,
Distinct in individualities,
But like each other ev'n as those who love.
Then comes the statelier Eden back to men:
Then reign the world's great bridals, chaste and calm:
Then springs the crowning race of humankind."

To state briefly the cardinal Tennysonian idea, man must realise a womanly manliness, and woman a manly womanliness.

Tennyson presents to us his ideal man in the 109th section of 'In Memoriam'. It is descriptive of his friend, Arthur Henry Hallam. All that is most characteristic of Tennyson, even his Englishness, is gathered up in this poem of six stanzas. It is interesting to meet with such a representative and comprehensive bit in a great poet.

"Heart-affluence in discursive talk
From household fountains never dry;
The critic clearness of an eye,
That saw through all the muses' walk;
Seraphic intellect and force
To seize and throw the doubts of man;
Impassioned logic, which outran
The bearer in its fiery course;
High nature amorous of the good,
But touch'd with no ascetic gloom;
And passions pure in snowy bloom
Through all the years of april blood."

The first two verses of this stanza also characterize the King Arthur of the 'Idylls of the King'. In the next stanza we have the poet's institutional Englishness:

"A love of freedom rarely felt,
Of freedom in her regal seat
Of england; not the school-boy heat,
The blind hysterics of the celt;
And manhood fused with female grace
In such a sort, the child would twine
A trustful hand, unask'd, in thine,
And find his comfort in thy face;
All these have been, and thee mine eyes
Have look'd on; if they look'd in vain,
My shame is greater who remain,
Nor let thy wisdom make me wise."

Tennyson's genius was early trained by the skeptical philosophy of the age. All his poetry shows this. The 'In Memoriam' may almost be said to be the poem of nineteenth century scepticism. To this scepticism he has applied an "all-subtilizing intellect", and has translated it into the poetical "concrete", with a rare artistic skill, and more than this, has subjected it to the spiritual instincts and apperceptions of the feminine side of his nature and made it vassal to a larger faith. But it is, after all, not the vital faith which Browning's poetry exhibits, a faith proceeding directly from the spiritual man. It is rather the faith expressed by Browning's Bishop Blougram:

"With me faith means perpetual unbelief
Kept quiet like the snake 'neath Michael's foot,
Who stands firm just because he feels it writhe."

And Tennyson, in picturing to us in the Idylls, the passage of the soul "from the great deep to the great deep", appears to have felt it necessary to the completion of that picture (or why did he do it?), that he should bring out that doubt at the last moment. The dying Arthur is made to say:

"I am going a long way
With these thou seest if indeed I go
(For all my mind is clouded with a doubt)
To the island-valley of Avilion"; etc.

Tennyson's poetry is, in fact, an expression of the highest sublimation of the scepticism which came out of the eighteenth century, which invoked the authority of the sensualistic philosophy of Locke, and has since been fostered by the science of the nineteenth; while Browning's poetry is a decided protest against, and a reactionary product of, that scepticism, that infidel philosophy (infidel as to the transcendental), and has closed with it and borne away the palm.

The key-note of his poetry is struck in 'Paracelsus', published in 1835, in his twenty-third year, and, with the exception of 'Pauline' published in 1833, the earliest of his compositions: Paracelsus says (and he who knows Browning knows it to be substantially his own creed):

"Truth is within ourselves; it takes no rise
From outward things, whate'er you may believe:
There is an inmost centre in us all,
Where truth abides in fulness; and around
Wall upon wall, the gross flesh hems it in,
This perfect, clear perception which is truth;
A baffling and perverting carnal mesh
Blinds it, and makes all error: and 'TO KNOW'
Rather consists in opening out a way
Whence the imprisoned splendour may escape,
Than in effecting entry for a light
Supposed to be without. Watch narrowly
The demonstration of a truth, its birth,
And you trace back the effluence to its spring
And source within us, where broods radiance vast,
To be elicited ray by ray, as chance
Shall favour: chance for hitherto, your sage
Even as he knows not how those beams are born,
As little knows he what unlocks their fount;
And men have oft grown old among their books
To die, case-hardened in their ignorance,
Whose careless youth had promised what long years
Of unremitted labour ne'er performed:
While, contrary, it has chanced some idle day,
That autumn-loiterers just as fancy-free

As the midges in the sun, have oft given vent
To truth produced mysteriously as cape
Of cloud grown out of the invisible air.
Hence, may not truth be lodged alike in all,
The lowest as the highest? some slight film
The interposing bar which binds it up,
And makes the idiot, just as makes the sage
Some film removed, the happy outlet whence
Truth issues proudly? See this soul of ours!
How it strives weakly in the child, is loosed
In manhood, clogged by sickness, back compelled
By age and waste, set free at last by death:
Why is it, flesh enthralls it or enthrones?
What is this flesh we have to penetrate?
Oh, not alone when life flows still do truth
And power emerge, but also when strange chance
Ruffles its current; in unused conjuncture,
When sickness breaks the body hunger, watching,
Excess, or languor oftenest death's approach
Peril, deep joy, or woe. One man shall crawl
Through life, surrounded with all stirring things,
Unmoved and he goes mad; and from the wreck
Of what he was, by his wild talk alone,
You first collect how great a spirit he hid.
Therefore set free the spirit alike in all,
Discovering the true laws by which the flesh
Bars in the spirit!...
I go to gather this
The sacred knowledge, here and there dispersed
About the world, long lost or never found.
And why should I be sad, or lorn of hope?
Why ever make man's good distinct from God's?
Or, finding they are one, why dare mistrust?
Who shall succeed if not one pledged like me?
Mine is no mad attempt to build a world
Apart from His, like those who set themselves
To find the nature of the spirit they bore,
And, taught betimes that all their gorgeous dreams

Were only born to vanish in this life,
Refused to fit them to this narrow sphere,
But chose to figure forth another world
And other frames meet for their vast desires,
Still, all a dream! Thus was life scorned; but life
Shall yet be crowned: twine amaranth! I am priest!"
And again:
"In man's self arise
August anticipations, symbols, types
Of a dim splendour ever on before,
In that eternal circle run by life:
For men begin to pass their nature's bound,
And find new hopes and cares which fast supplant
Their proper joys and griefs; and outgrow all
The narrow creeds of right and wrong, which fade
Before the unmeasured thirst for good; while peace
Rises within them ever more and more.
Such men are even now upon the earth,
Serene amid the half-formed creatures round,
Who should be saved by them and joined with them."

In the last three verses is indicated the doctrine of the regenerating power of exalted personalities, so prominent in Browning's poetry, and which is treated in the next paper. There is no 'tabula rasa' doctrine in these passages, nor in any others, in the poet's voluminous works; and of all men of great intellect and learning (it is always a matter of mere insulated intellect), born in England since the days of John Locke, no one, perhaps, has been so entirely untainted with this doctrine as Robert Browning. It is a doctrine which great spiritual vitality (and that he early possessed), reaching out, as it does, beyond all experience, beyond all transformation of sensations, and all conclusions of the discursive understanding, naturally and spontaneously rejects. It simply says, "I know better", and there an end.

The great function of the poet, as poet, is, with Browning, to open out a way whence the imprisoned splendor may escape, not to effect entry for a light supposed to be without; to trace back the effluence to its spring and source within us, where broods radiance vast, to be elicited ray by ray. In 'Fifine at the Fair', published thirty-seven years after 'Paracelsus', is substantially the same doctrine:

"Truth inside, and outside, truth also; and between
Each, falsehood that is change, as truth is permanence.
The individual soul works through the shows of sense,
(Which, ever proving false, still promise to be true)
Up to an outer soul as individual too;
And, through the fleeting, lives to die into the fixed,
And reach at length 'God, man, or both together mixed'."

In his poem entitled 'Popularity', included in his "fifty men and women", the speaker, in the monologue, "draws" his "true poet", whom HE knows, if others do not; who, though he renders, or stands ready to render, to his fellows, the supreme service of opening out a way whence the imprisoned splendor of their souls may escape, is yet locked safe from end to end of this dark world.

Though there may be, in his own time, no "reapers reaping early in among the bearded barley" and "piling sheaves in uplands airy" who hear his song, he holds the FUTURE fast, accepts the COMING AGES' duty, their present for this past. This true, creative poet, whom the speaker calls "God's glow-worm, creative in the sense of revealing, whose inmost centre, where truth abides in fulness, has that freedom of responsiveness to the divine which makes him the revealer of it to men, plays the part in the world of spirit which, in the material world was played by the fisher who, first on the coast of Tyre the old, fished up the purple-yielding murex. Until the precious liquor, filtered by degrees, and refined to proof, is flasked and priced, and salable at last, the world stands aloof. But when it is all ready for the market, the small dealers, "put blue into their line", and outdare each other in azure feats by which they secure great popularity, and, as a result, fare sumptuously; while he who fished the murex up was unrecognized, and fed, perhaps, on porridge.

Popularity.

I.

Stand still, true poet that you are!
I know you; let me try and draw you.

Some night you'll fail us: when afar
You rise, remember one man saw you,
Knew you, and named a star!

II.

My star, God's glow-worm! Why extend
That loving hand of His which leads you,
Yet locks you safe from end to end
Of this dark world, unless He needs you,
Just saves your light to spend?

III.

His clenched hand shall unclose at last,
I know, and let out all the beauty:
My poet holds the future fast,
Accepts the coming ages' duty,
Their present for this past.

IV.

That day, the earth's feast-master's brow
Shall clear, to God the chalice raising;
"Others give best at first, but Thou
Forever set'st our table praising,
Keep'st the good wine till now!"

V.

Meantime, I'll draw you as you stand,
With few or none to watch and wonder:
I'll say a fisher, on the sand
By Tyre the old, with ocean-plunder,
A netful, brought to land.

VI.

Who has not heard how Tyrian shells
Enclosed the blue, that dye of dyes
Whereof one drop worked miracles,
And colored like Astarte's eyes
Raw silk the merchant sells?

VII.

And each by-stander of them all
Could criticise, and quote tradition
How depths of blue sublimed some pall
To get which, pricked a king's ambition;
Worth sceptre, crown, and ball.

VIII.

Yet there's the dye, in that rough mesh,
The sea has only just o'er-whispered!
Live whelks, each lip's beard dripping fresh,
As if they still the water's lisp heard
Through foam the rock-weeds thresh.

IX.

Enough to furnish Solomon
Such hangings for his cedar-house,
That, when gold-robed he took the throne
In that abyss of blue, the Spouse
Might swear his presence shone

X.

Most like the centre-spike of gold
Which burns deep in the blue-bell's womb
What time, with ardors manifold,
The bee goes singing to her groom,
Drunken and overbold.

XI.

Mere conchs! not fit for warp or woof!
Till cunning come to pound and squeeze
And clarify, refine to proof 2
The liquor filtered by degrees,
While the world stands aloof.

XII.

And there's the extract, flasked and fine,

And priced and salable at last!
And Hobbs, Nobbs, Stokes, and Nokes combine
To paint the future from the past,
Put blue into their line.

XIII.

Hobbs hints blue, straight he turtle eats:
Nobbs prints blue, claret crowns his cup:
Nokes outdares Stokes in azure feats,
Both gorge. Who finished the murex up?
What porridge had John Keats?

The spiritual ebb and flow exhibited in English poetry (the highest tide being reached in Tennyson and Browning) which I have endeavored cursorily to present, bear testimony to the fact that human nature WILL assert its wholeness in the civilized man. And there must come a time, in the progress of civilization, when this ebb and flow will be less marked than it has been heretofore, by reason of a better balancing, which will be brought about, of the intellectual and the spiritual. Each will have its due activity. The man of intellectual pursuits will not have a starved spiritual nature; and the man of predominant spiritual functions will not have an intellect weakened into a submissiveness to formulated, stereotyped, and, consequently, lifeless dogmas.

Robert Browning is in himself the completest fulfilment of this equipoise of the intellectual and the spiritual, possessing each in an exalted degree; and his poetry is an emphasized expression of his own personality, and a prophecy of the ultimate results of Christian civilization.

Chapter 5

The Idea of Personality and of Art as an Intermediate Agency of Personality, as Embodied in Browning's Poetry

General Remarks

"Subsists no law of Life outside of Life.
The Christ himself had been no Lawgiver,
Unless he had given the LIFE, too, with the law."

The importance of Robert Browning's poetry, as embodying the profoundest thought, the subtlest and most complex sentiment, and, above all, the most quickening spirituality of the age, has, as yet, notwithstanding the great increase within the last few years of devoted students, received but a niggardly recognition when compared with that received by far inferior contemporary poets.

There are, however, many indications in the poetical criticism of the day that upon it will ere long be pronounced the verdict which is its due. And the founding of a society in England in 1881, "to gather together some at least of the many admirers of Robert Browning, for the study and discussion of his works, and the publication of papers on them, and extracts from works illustrating them" has already contributed much towards paying a long-standing debt.

Mr. Browning's earliest poems, 'Pauline' (he calls it in the preface to the reprint of it in 1868 "a boyish work", though it exhibits the great basal thought of all his subsequent poetry), was published in 1833, since which time he has produced the largest body of poetry produced by any one poet in English literature; and the range of thought and passion which it exhibits is greater than that of any other poet, without a single exception, since the days of Shakespeare. And he is the most like Shakespeare in his deep interest in human nature in all its varieties of good and evil. Though endowed with a powerful, subtle, and restless intellect, he has throughout his voluminous poetry made the strongest protest that has been made in these days against mere intellect.

And his poetry has, therefore, a peculiar value in an age like the present an age exhibiting "a condition of humanity which has thrown itself wholly on its intellect and its genius in physics, and has done marvels in material science and invention, but at the expense of the interior divinity." It is the human heart, that is, the intuitive, the non-discursive side of man, with its hopes and its prophetic aspirations, as opposed to the analytic, the discursive understanding, which is to him a subject of the deepest and most scrutinizing interest. He knows that its deepest depths are "deeper than did ever plummet sound"; but he also knows that it is in these depths that life's greatest secrets must be sought. The philosophies excogitated by the insulated intellect help nothing toward even a glimpse of these secrets. In one of his later poems, that entitled 'House', he has intimated, and forcibly intimated, his sense of the impossibility of penetrating to the Holy of Holies of this wondrous human heart, though assured as he is that all our hopes in regard to the soul's destiny are warmed and cherished by what radiates thence. He quotes, in the last stanza of this poem, from Wordsworth's sonnet on the Sonnet, "With this same key Shakespeare unlocked his heart," and then adds, "DID Shakespeare? If so, the less Shakespeare he!"

Mrs. Browning, in the Fifth Book of her 'Aurora Leigh', has given a full and very forcible expression to the feeling which has caused the highest dramatic genius of the present day to seek refuge in the poem and the novel. "I will write no plays; because the drama, less sublime in this, makes lower appeals, defends more menially, adopts the standard of the public taste to chalk its height on, wears a dog-chain round its regal neck, and learns to carry and fetch the fashions of the day, to please the day;... 'Tis that, honoring to its worth the drama, i would fear to keep it down to the level of the footlights.... The growing drama has outgrown such toys of simulated stature, face, and speech, it also, peradventure, may outgrow the simulation of the painted scene, boards, actors, prompters, gaslight, and costume; and take for a worthier stage, the soul itself, its shifting fancies and celestial lights, with all its grand orchestral silences to keep the pauses of the rhythmic sounds."

Robert Browning's poetry is, in these days, the fullest realization of what is expressed in the concluding lines of this passage: he has taken for a worthier stage, the soul itself, its shifting fancies and celestial lights, more than any other poet of the age. And he has worked with a thought-and-passion capital greater than the combined thought-and-passion capital of the richest of his poetical contemporaries. And he has thought nobly of the soul, and has treated it as, in its essence, above the fixed and law-bound system of things which we call nature; in other words, he has treated it as supernatural. "Mind," he makes the Pope say, in `The Ring and the Book', and his poetry bears testimony to its being his own conviction and doctrine, "Mind is not matter, nor from matter, but above." With every student of Browning, the recognition and acceptance of this must be his starting-point. Even that which impelled the old dog, in his poem entitled `Tray' (`Dramatic Lyrics', First Series), to rescue the beggar child that fell into the river, and then to dive after the child's doll, and bring it up, after a long stay under water, the poet evidently distinguishes from matter, regards as "not matter nor from matter, but above":

"And so, amid the laughter gay,
Trotted my hero off, old Tray,
Till somebody, prerogatived
With reason, reasoned: 'Why he dived,
His brain would show us, I should say.

'John, go and catch or, if needs be,
Purchase that animal for me!
By vivisection, at expense
Of half-an-hour and eighteen pence,
How brain secretes dog's soul, we'll see!"
In his poem entitled 'Halbert and Hob' ('Dramatic Lyrics', First Series), quoting from Shakespeare's 'King Lear',

"Is there a reason in nature for these hard hearts?" the poet adds, "O Lear, That a reason out of nature must turn them soft, seems clear!"

Mind is, with browning, supernatural, but linked with, and restrained, and even enslaved by, the natural. The soul, in its education, that is, in its awakening, becomes more and more independent of the natural, and, as a consequence, more responsive to higher souls and to the divine. All spirit is mutually attractive, and the degree of attractiveness results from the degree of freedom from the obstructions of the material, or the natural.

Loving the truth implies a greater or less degree of that freedom of the spirit which brings it into sympathy with the true. "If ye abide in my word," says christ (and we must understand by "word" his own concrete life, the word made flesh, and living and breathing), "if ye abide in my word" (that is, continue to live my life), "then are ye truly my disciples; and ye shall know the truth, and the truth shall make you free" (john viii. 32).

In regard to the soul's inherent possessions, its microcosmic potentialities, paracelsus is made to say (and this may be taken, too, as the poet's own creed), "truth is within ourselves; it takes no rise from outward things, whate'er you may believe: There is an inmost centre in us all, where truth abides in fulness; and around, wall upon wall, the gross flesh hems it in, this perfect, clear perception which is truth. A baffling and perverting carnal mesh blinds it, and makes all error: And, to know, rather consists in opening out a way whence the imprisoned splendour may escape, than in effecting entry for a light supposed to be without."

All possible thought is implicit in the mind, and waiting

for release waiting to become EXPLICIT. "Seek within yourself," says Goethe, "and you will find everything; and rejoice that, without, there lies a Nature that says yea and amen to all you have discovered in yourself." And Mrs. Browning, in the person of Aurora Leigh, writes: "The cygnet finds the water; but the man is born in ignorance of his element, and feels out blind at first, disorganized by sin in the blood, his spirit-insight dulled and crossed by his sensations. Presently we feel it quicken in the dark sometimes; then mark, be reverent, be obedient, for those dumb motions of imperfect life are oracles of vital Deity attesting the Hereafter. Let who says `The soul's a clean white paper', rather say, a palimpsest, a prophet's holograph defiled, erased, and covered by a monk's, the Apocalypse by a Longus! poring on which obscure text, we may discern perhaps some fair, fine trace of what was written once, some off-stroke of an alpha and omega expressing the old Scripture."

This "fair, fine trace of what was written once", it was the mission of Christ, it is the mission of all great personalities, of all the concrete creations of Genius, to bring out into distinctness and vital glow. It is not, and cannot be, brought out, and this fact is emphasized in the poetry of Browning, it cannot be brought out, through what is born and resides in the brain: it is brought out, either directly or indirectly, by the attracting power of magnetic personalities, the ultimate, absolute personality being the God-man, Christ.

The human soul is regarded in Browning's poetry as a complexly organized, individualized divine force, destined to gravitate towards the Infinite. How is this force, with its numberless checks and counter-checks, its centripetal and centrifugal tendencies, best determined in its necessarily oblique way? How much earthly ballast must it carry, to keep it sufficiently steady, and how little, that it may not be weighed down with materialistic heaviness? How much certainty must it have of its course, and how much uncertainty, that it may shun the "torpor of assurance", and not lose the vigour which comes of a dubious and obstructed road, "which who stands upon is apt to doubt if it's indeed a road."

"Pure faith indeed," says Bishop Blougram, to Gigadibs, the literary man, "you know not what you ask! naked belief in God the Omnipotent, Omniscient, Omnipresent, sears too much the sense of conscious creatures, to be borne. It were the seeing him, no flesh shall dare. Some think, Creation's meant to show him forth: I say, it's meant to hide him all it can, and that's what all the blessed Evil's for. Its use in time is to environ us, our breath, our drop of dew, with shield enough against that sight till we can bear its stress. Under a vertical sun, the exposed brain and lidless eye and disimprisoned heart less certainly would wither up at once, than mind, confronted with the truth of Him. But time and earth case-harden us to live; the feeblest sense is trusted most: the child feels God a moment, ichors o'er the place, plays on and grows to be a man like us. With me, faith means perpetual unbelief kept quiet like the snake 'neath Michael's foot, who stands calm just because he feels it writhe."

There is a remarkable passage to the same effect in 'Paracelsus', in which Paracelsus expatiates on the "just so much of doubt as bade him plant a surer foot upon the sun-road." And in 'Easter Day':

"You must mix some uncertainty
With faith, if you would have faith BE."

And the good Pope in 'The Ring and the Book', alluding to the absence of true Christian soldiership, which is revealed by Pompilia's case, says: "Is it not this ignoble CONFIDENCE, cowardly hardihood, that dulls and damps, makes the old heroism impossible? Unless...what whispers me of times to come? What if it be the mission of that age my death will usher into life, to SHAKE THIS TORPOR OF ASSURANCE FROM OUR CREED, reintroduce the DOUBT discarded, bring the formidable danger back we drove long ago to the distance and the dark?"

True healthy doubt means, in Browning, that the spiritual nature is sufficiently quickened not to submit to the conclusions of the insulated intellect. It WILL reach out beyond them, and assert itself, whatever be the resistance offered by the intellect. Mere doubt, without any resistance from the intuitive, non-discursive side of our nature, is the dry-rot of the soul. The spiritual functions are "smothered in surmise". Faith is not a matter of blind belief, of slavish assent and acceptance, as many no-faith people seem to regard it. It is what Wordsworth calls it, "a passionate intuition", and springs out of quickened and refined sentiment, out of inborn instincts which are as cultivable as are any other elements of our complex nature, and which, too, may be blunted beyond a consciousness of their possession. And when one in this latter state denies the reality of faith, he is not unlike one born blind denying the reality of sight.

A reiterated lesson in Browning's poetry, and one that results from his spiritual theory, is, that the present life is a tabernacle-life, and that it can be truly lived only as a tabernacle-life; for only such a life is compatible with the ever-continued aspiration and endeavor which is a condition ot, and inseparable from, spiritual vitality.

Domizia, in the tragedy of 'Luria', is made to say:
"How inexhaustibly the spirit grows!
One object, she seemed erewhile born to reach
With her whole energies and die content,
So like a wall at the world's edge it stood,
With naught beyond to live for, is that reached?
Already are new undream'd energies
Outgrowing under, and extending farther
To a new object; there's another world!"
The dying John in 'A Death in the Desert', is made to say:
"I say that man was made to grow, not stop;
That help he needed once, and needs no more,
Having grown up but an inch by, is withdrawn:
For he hath new needs, and new helps to these.
This imports solely, man should mount on each
New height in view; the help whereby he mounts,
The ladder-rung his foot has left, may fall,
Since all things suffer change save God the Truth.
Man apprehends him newly at each stage
Whereat earth's ladder drops, its service done;
And nothing shall prove twice what once was proved."

And again:

"Man knows partly but conceives beside,
Creeps ever on from fancies to the fact,
And in this striving, this converting air
Into a solid he may grasp and use,
Finds progress, man's distinctive mark alone,
Not God's, and not the beasts': God is, they are,
Man partly is and wholly hopes to be.
Such progress could no more attend his soul
Were all it struggles after found at first
And guesses changed to knowledge absolute,
Than motion wait his body, were all else
Than it the solid earth on every side,
Where now through space he moves from rest to rest.
Man, therefore, thus conditioned, must expect
He could not, what he knows now, know at first;
What he considers that he knows to-day,
Come but to-morrow, he will find misknown;
Getting increase of knowledge, since he learns
Because he lives, which is to be a man,
Set to instruct himself by his past self:
First, like the brute, obliged by facts to learn,
Next, as man may, obliged by his own mind,
Bent, habit, nature, knowledge turned to law.
God's gift was that man should conceive of truth
And yearn to gain it, catching at mistake,
As midway help till he reach fact indeed.
The statuary ere he mould a shape
Boasts a like gift, the shape's idea, and next
The aspiration to produce the same;
So, taking clay, he calls his shape thereout,
Cries ever, 'Now I have the thing I see':
Yet all the while goes changing what was wrought,
From falsehood like the truth, to truth itself.
How were it had he cried, 'I see no face,
No breast, no feet i' the ineffectual clay'?
Rather commend him that he clapped his hands,
And laughed, 'It is my shape and lives again!'

Enjoyed the falsehood touched it on to truth,
Until yourselves applaud the flesh indeed
In what is still flesh-imitating clay.
Right in you, right in him, such way be man's!
God only makes the live shape at a jet.
Will ye renounce this fact of creatureship?
The pattern on the Mount subsists no more,
Seemed awhile, then returned to nothingness,
But copies, Moses strove to make thereby
Serve still and are replaced as time requires:
By these make newest vessels, reach the type!
If ye demur, this judgment on your head,
Never to reach the ultimate, angels' law,
Indulging every instinct of the soul
There where law, life, joy, impulse are one thing."
Browning has given varied and beautiful expressions to these
ideas throughout his poetry.
The soul must rest in nothing this side of the infinite.
If it does rest in anything, however relatively noble
that thing may be, whether art, or literature, or science,
or theology, even, it declines in vitality it torpifies.
However great a conquest the combatant may achieve in any
of these arenas, "striding away from the huge gratitude,
his club shouldered, lion-fleece round loin and flank", he must
be
"bound on the next new labour, height o'er height ever
surmounting
destiny's decree!"
"Rejoice that man is hurled
From change to change unceasingly,
His soul's wings never furled!"

But this tabernacle-life, which should ever look ahead, has its claims which must not be ignored, and its standards which must not be too much above present conditions. Man must "fit to the finite his infinity" ('Sordello'). Life may be over-spiritual as well as over-worldly. "Let us cry, 'All good things are ours, nor soul helps flesh more, now, than flesh helps soul!'" The figure the poet employs in 'The Ring and the Book' to illustrate the art process, may be as aptly applied to life itself the greatest of all arts. The life-artist must know how to secure the proper degree of malleability in this mixture of flesh and soul. He must mingle gold with gold's alloy, and duly tempering both effect a manageable mass. There may be too little of alloy in earth-life as well as too much too little to work the gold and fashion it, not into a ring, but ring-ward. "On the earth the broken arcs; in the heaven a perfect round" (`Abt Vogler'). "Oh, if we draw a circle premature, heedless of far gain, greedy for quick returns of profit, sure, bad is our bargain" (`A Grammarian's Funeral').

'Rabbi Ben Ezra'.

'An Epistle containing the Strange Medical Experiences of Karshish, the Arab Physician', is one of Browning's most remarkable psychological studies. It may be said to polarize the idea, so often presented in his poetry, that doubt is a condition of the vitality of faith. In this poem, the poet has treated a supposed case of a spiritual knowledge "increased beyond the fleshly faculty heaven opened to a soul while yet on earth, earth forced on a soul's use while seeing heaven", a spiritual state, less desirable and far less favorable to the true fulfilment of the purposes of earth-life, than that expressed in the following lines from 'Easter Day':

"A world of spirit as of sense
Was plain to him, yet not TOO plain,
Which he could traverse, not remain
A GUEST IN: else were permanent
Heaven on earth, which its gleams were meant
To sting with hunger for full light", etc.

The Epistle is a subtle representation of a soul conceived with absolute spiritual standards, while obliged to live in a world where all standards are relative and determined by the circumstances and limitations of its situation.

The spiritual life has been too distinctly revealed for fulfilling aright the purposes of earth-life, purposes which the soul, while in the flesh, must not ignore, since, in the words of Rabbi Ben Ezra, "all good things are ours, nor soul helps flesh more, now, than flesh helps soul." The poem may also be said to represent what is, or should be, the true spirit of the man of science. In spite of what Karshish writes, apologetically, he betrays his real attitude throughout, towards the wonderful spiritual problem involved.

It is, as many of Browning's Monologues are, a double picture one direct, the other reflected, and the reflected one is as distinct as the direct. The composition also bears testimony to Browning's own soul-healthfulness. Though the spiritual bearing of things is the all-in-all, in his poetry, the robustness of his nature, the fulness and splendid equilibrium of his life, protect him against an inarticulate mysticism. Browning is, in the widest and deepest sense of the word, the healthiest of all living poets; and in general constitution the most Shakespearian.

What he makes Shakespeare say, in the Monologue entitled 'At the Mermaid', he could say, with perhaps greater truth, in his own person, than Shakespeare could have said it:

"Have you found your life distasteful?
My life did and does smack sweet.
Was your youth of pleasure wasteful?
Mine I save and hold complete.
Do your joys with age diminish?
When mine fail me, I'll complain.
Must in death your daylight finish?
My sun sets to rise again.
I find earth not gray but rosy,
Heaven not grim but fair of hue.
Do I stoop? I pluck a posy.
Do I stand and stare? All's blue."

It is the spirit expressed in these lines which has made his poetry so entirely CONSTRUCTIVE. With the destructive spirit he has no affinities. The poetry of despair and poets with the dumps he cannot away with.

Perhaps the most comprehensive passage in Browning's poetry, expressive of his ideal of a complete man under the conditions of earth-life, is found in 'Colombe's Birthday', Act IV. Valence says of Prince Berthold:

"He gathers earth's WHOLE GOOD into his arms,

standing, as man, now, stately, strong and wise marching to fortune, not surprised by her: one great aim, like a guiding star above which tasks strength, wisdom, stateliness, to lift his manhood to the height that takes the prize; a prize not near lest overlooking earth, he rashly spring to seize it nor remote, so that he rests upon his path content: but day by day, while shimmering grows shine, and the faint circlet prophesies the orb, he sees so much as, just evolving these, the stateliness, the wisdom, and the strength to due completion, will suffice this life, and lead him at his grandest to the grave."

Browning fully recognizes, to use an expression in his 'Fra Lippo Lippi', fully recognizes "the value and significance of flesh." A healthy and well-toned spiritual life is with him the furthest removed from asceticism. To the passage from his 'Rabbi Ben Ezra' already quoted, "all good things are ours, nor soul helps flesh more, now, than flesh helps soul", should be added what David sings to Saul, in the poem entitled 'Saul'. Was the full physical life ever more beautifully sung?

- "Oh! our manhood's prime vigour! no spirit feels waste,
- Not a muscle is stopped in its playing, nor sinew unbraced.
- Oh, the wild joys of living! the leaping from rock up to rock,
- The strong rending of boughs from the fir-tree, the cool silver shock
- Of the plunge in a pool's living water, the hunt of the bear,
- And the sultriness sho7wing the lion is couched in his lair.
- And the meal, the rich dates yellowed over with gold dust divine,
- And the locust-flesh steeped in the pitcher, the full draught of wine,
- And the sleep in the dried river-channel where bulrushes tell
- That the water was wont to go warbling so softly and well.
- How good is man's life, the mere living! how fit to employ

- All the heart and the soul and the senses for ever in joy!"

Though this is said in the person of the beautiful shepherd-boy, David, whoever has lived any time with Browning, through his poetry, must be assured that it is also an expression of the poet's own experience of the glory of flesh. He has himself been an expression of the fullest physical life: and now, in his five and seventieth year, since the 7th of last May, he preserves both mind and body in a magnificent vigour. If his soul had been lodged in a sickly, rickety body, he could hardly have written these lines from 'Saul'. Nor could he have written 'Caliban upon Setebos', especially the opening lines: "Will sprawl, now that the heat of day is best, flat on his belly in the pit's much mire, with elbows wide, fists clenched to prop his chin. And, while he kicks both feet in the cool slush, and feels about his spine small eft-things course, run in and out each arm, and make him laugh: and while above his head a pompion-plant, coating the cave-top as a brow its eye, creeps down to touch and tickle hair and beard, and now a flower drops with a bee inside, and now a fruit to snap at, catch and crunch, he looks out o'er yon sea which sunbeams cross and recross till they weave a spider-web (meshes of fire, some great fish breaks at times), and talks to his own self, howe'er he please, touching that other, whom his dam called God."

There's a grand passage in 'Balaustion's Adventure: including a transcript from Euripides', descriptive of Herakles as he returns, after his conflict with Death, leading back Alkestis, which shows the poet's sympathy with the physical. The passage is more valuable as revealing that sympathy, from the fact that it's one of his additions to Euripides:

"There stood the strength,
Happy as always; something grave, perhaps;
The great vein-cordage on the fret-worked brow,
Black-swollen, beaded yet with battle-drops
The yellow hair o' the herɔ! his big frame
A-quiver with each muscle sinking back
Into the sleepy smooth it leaped from late.
Under the great guard of one arm, there leant

A shrouded something, live and woman-like,
Propped by the heart-beats 'neath the lion-coat.
When he had finished his survey, it seemed,
The heavings of the heart began subside,
The helping breath returned, and last the smile
Shone out, all Herakles was back again,
As the words followed the saluting hand."

It is not so much the glory of flesh which Euripides represents in Herakles, as the indulgence of appetite, at a time, too, when that indulgence is made to appear the more culpable and gross.

This idea of "the value and significance of flesh", it is important to note, along with the predominant spiritual bearing of Browning's poetry. It articulates everywhere the spiritual, so to speak makes it healthy and robust, and protects it against volatility and from running into mysticism.

The Idea of Personality as Embodied in Browning's Poetry

A cardinal idea in Browning's poetry is the regeneration of men through a personality who brings fresh stuff for them to mould, interpret, and prove right, new feeling fresh from God whose life re-teaches them what life should be, what faith is, loyalty and simpleness, all once revealed, but taught them so long since that they have but mere tradition of the fact, truth copied falteringly from copies faint, the early traits all dropped away. ('Luria'.) The intellect plays a secondary part. Its place is behind the instinctive, spiritual antennae which conduct along their trembling lines, fresh stuff for the intellect to stamp and keep fresh instinct for it to translate into law.

"A people is but the attempt of many to rise to the completer life of one." (`A Soul's Tragedy'.)

Only the man who supplies new feeling fresh from God, quickens and regenerates the race, and sets it on the King's highway from which it has wandered into by-ways not the man of mere intellect, of unkindled soul, that supplies only stark-naked thought. Through the former, "God stooping shows sufficient of His light for those i' the dark to rise by." (`R. and B., Pompilia'.) In him men discern "the dawn of the next nature, the new man whose will they venture in the place of theirs, and whom they trust to find them out new ways to the new heights which yet he only sees." (`Luria'.) It is by reaching towards, and doing fealty to, the greater spirit which attracts and absorbs their own, that, "trace by trace old memories reappear, old truth returns, their slow thought does its work, and all's re-known." (`Luria'.)

"Some existence like a pact
And protest against Chaos,...
... The fullest effluence of the finest mind,
All in degree, no way diverse in kind
From minds above it, minds which, more or less
Lofty or low, move seeking to impress
Themselves on somewhat; but one mind has climbed
Step after step, by just ascent sublimed.
Thought is the soul of act, and, stage by stage,
Is soul from body still to disengage,
As tending to a freedom which rejects
Such help, and incorporeally affects
The world, producing deeds but not by deeds,
Swaying, in others, frames itself exceeds,
Assigning them the simpler tasks it used
To patiently perform till Song produced
Acts, by thoughts only, for the mind: divest
Mind of e'en Thought, and, lo, God's unexpressed
Will dawns above us!" ('Sordello'.)

A dangerous tendency of civilization is that towards crystallization towards hardened, inflexible conventionalisms which "refuse the soul its way".

Such crystallization, such conventionalisms, yield only to the dissolving power of the spiritual warmth of life-full personalities. The quickening, regenerating power of personality is everywhere exhibited in browning's poetry. It is emphasized in 'luria', and in the monologues of the canon caponsacchi and pompilia, in the 'ring and the book'; it shines out, or glints forth, in 'colombe's birthday', in 'saul', in 'sordello', and in all the love poems. I would say, en passant, that love is always treated by browning as a spiritual claim;

while duty may be only a worldly one. See especially the poem entitled 'bifurcation'. In 'balaustion's adventure: Including a transcipt from euripides', the regenerating power of personality may be said to be the leavening idea, which the poet has introduced into the greek play. It is entirely absent in the original. It baptizes, so to speak, the greek play, and converts it into a christian poem. It is the "new truth" of the poet's 'christmas eve'.

After the mourning friends have spoken their words of consolation to the bereaved husband, the last word being, "dead, thy wife living, the love she left", admetos "turned on the comfort, with no tears, this time. He was beginning to be like his wife. I told you of that pressure to the point, word slow pursuing word in monotone, alkestis spoke with; so admetos, now, solemnly bore the burden of the truth. And as the voice of him grew, gathered strength, and groaned on, and persisted to the end, we felt how deep had been descent in grief, and with what change he came up now to light, and left behind such littleness as tears."

And when alkestis was brought back by herakles, "the hero twitched the veil off: And there stood, with such fixed eyes and such slow smile, alkestis' silent self! It was the crowning grace of that great heart to keep back joy: Procrastinate the truth until the wife, who had made proof and found the husband wanting, might essay once more, hear, see, and feel him renovated now able to do, now, all herself had done, risen to the height of her: So, hand in hand, the two might go together, live and die." (Compare with this the restoration of hermione to her husband, in `the winter's tale', act v.)

A good intellect has been characterized as the chorus of divinity. Substitute for "good intellect", an exulted magnetic personality, and the thought is deepened. An exalted magnetic personality is the chorus of divinity, which, in the great drama of humanity, guides and interprets the feelings and sympathies of other souls and thus adjusts their attitudes towards the divine. It is not the highest function of such a personality to teach, but rather to inform, in the earlier and deeper sense of the word. Whatever mere doctrine he may promulgate, is of inferior importance to the spontaneous action of his concrete life, in which the true, the beautiful, and the good, breathe and live. What is born in the brain dies there, it may be; at best, it does not, and cannot of itself, lead up to the full concrete life. It is only through the spontaneou and unconscious fealty which an inferior does to a superior soul (a fealty resulting from the responsiveness of spirit to spirit), that the former is slowly and silently transformed into a more or less approximate image of the latter. The stronger personality leads the weaker on by paths which the weaker knows not, upward he leads him, though his steps be slow and vacillating. Humility, in the Christian sense, means this fealty to the higher. It doesn't mean self-abasement, self-depreciation, as it has been understood to mean, by both the Romish and the Protestant Church. Pride, in the Christian sense, is the closing of the doors of the soul to a great magnetic guest.

Browning beautifully expresses the transmission of personality in his 'Saul'. But according to Browning's idea, personality cannot strictly be said to be transmitted. Personality rather evokes its LIKE from other souls, which are "all in degree, no way diverse in kind." ('Sordello'.)

David has reached an advanced stage in his symbolic song to Saul. He thinks now what next he shall urge "to sustain him where song had restored him? Song filled to the verge his cup with the wine of this life, pressing all that it yields of mere fruitage, the strength and 0the beauty: beyond, on what fields glean a vintage more potent and perfect to brighten the eye and bring blood to the lip, and commend them the cup they put by?" So once more the string of the harp makes response to his spirit, and he sings:

- "In our flesh grows the branch of this life, in our soul it bears fruit.
- Thou hast marked the slow rise of the tree, how its stem trembled first
- Till it passed the kid's lip, the stag's antler; then safely outburst
- The fan-branches all round; and thou mindest when these, too, in turn

- Broke a-bloom and the palm-tree seemed perfect; yet more was to learn,
- E'en the good that comes in with the palm-fruit. Our dates shall we slight,
- When their juice brings a cure for all sorrow? or care for the plight
- Of the palm's self whose slow growth produced them? Not so! stem and branch
- Shall decay, nor be known in their place, while the palm-wine shall staunch
- Every wound of man's spirit in winter. I pour thee such wine.
- Leave the flesh to the fate it was fit for! the spirit be thine!
- By the spirit, when age shall o'ercome thee, thou still shalt enjoy
- More indeed, than at first when, inconscious, the life of a boy.
- Crush that life, and behold its wine running! each deed thou hast done
- Dies, revives, goes to work in the world; until e'en as the sun
- Looking down on the earth, though clouds spoil him, though tempests efface,
- Can find nothing his own deed produced not, must everywhere trace
- The results of his past summer-prime, so, each ray of thy will,
- Every flash of thy passion and prowess, long over, shall thrill
- Thy whole people, the countless, with ardour, till they too give forth
- A like cheer to their sons: Who in turn, fill the south and the north
- With the radiance thy deed was the germ of."

In the concluding lines is set forth what might be characterized as the apostolic succession of a great personality the succession of those "who in turn fill the South and the

North with the radiance his deed was the germ of." What follows in David's song gives expression to the other mode of transmitting a great personality that is, through records that "give unborn generations their due and their part in his being", and also to what those records owe their effectiveness, and are saved from becoming a dead letter.

- "Is Saul dead? In the depth of the vale make his tomb bid arise
- A grey mountain of marble heaped four-square, till, built to the skies,
- Let it mark where the great First King slumbers: whose fame
- would ye know?
- Up above see the rock's naked face, where the record shall go
- In great characters cut by the scribe, Such was Saul, so he did;
- With the sages directing the work, by the populace chid,
- For not half, they'll affirm, is comprised there! Which fault to amend,
- In the grove with his kind grows the cedar, whereon they shall spend
- (See, in tablets 'tis level before them) their praise, and record
- With the gold of the graver, Saul's story, the statesman's great word
- Side by side with the poet's sweet comment. The river's a-wave
- With smooth paper-reeds grazing each other when prophet-winds rave:
- So the pen gives unborn generations their due and their part
- In thy being! Then, first of the mighty, thank God that thou art!"

What is said in this passage is applicable to the record we have of Christ's life upon earth. Christianity has only to a very limited extent been perpetuated through the letter of the New

Testament. It has been perpetuated chiefly through transmissions of personalities, through apostolic succession, in a general sense, and through embodiments of his spirit in art and literature "the stateman's great word", "the poet's sweet comment". Were it not for this transmission of the quickening power of personality, the New Testament would be to a great extent a dead letter. It owes its significance to the quickened spirit which is brought to the reading of it. The personality of Christ could not be, through a plastic sympathy, moulded out of the New Testament records, without the aid of intermediate personalities.

The Messianic idea was not peculiar to the Jewish race the idea of a Person gathering up within himself, in an effective fulness and harmony, the restorative elements of humanity, which have lost their power through dispersion and consequent obscuration. There have been Messiahs of various orders and ranks in every age, great personalities that have realized to a greater or less extent (though there has been but one, the God-Man, who fully realized), the spiritual potentialities in man, that have stood upon the sharpest heights as beacons to their fellows. In the individual the species has, as it were, been gathered up, epitomized, and intensified, and he has thus been a prophecy, and to some extent a fulfilment of human destiny.

"A poet must be earth's ESSENTIAL king", as Sordello asserts, and he is that by virtue of his exerting or shedding the influence of his essential personality. "If caring not to exert the proper essence of his royalty, he, the poet, trifle malapert with accidents instead good things assigned as heralds of a better thing behind" he is "deposed from his kingly throne, and his glory is taken from him". Of himself, Sordello says: "The power he took most pride to test, whereby all forms of life had been professed at pleasure, forms already on the earth, was but a means of power beyond, whose birth should, in its novelty, be kingship's proof. Now, whether he came near or kept aloof the several forms he longed to imitate, not there the kingship lay, he sees too late. Those forms, unalterable first as last, proved him her copier, not the protoplast of nature:

what could come of being free by action to exhibit tree for tree, bird, beast, for beast and bird, or prove earth bore one veritable man or woman more? Means to an end such proofs are: *what the end?"*

The answer given involves the great Browning idea of the quickening power of personality: "Let essence, whatsoe'er it be, extend never contract!"

By "essence" we must understand that which "constitutes man's self, is what Is", as the dying John, in 'A Death in the Desert', expresses it that which backs the active powers and the conscious intellect, "subsisting whether they assist or no".

"Let essence, whatsoe'er it be, extend never contract!" Sordello says. "Already you include the multitude"; that is, you gather up in yourself, in an effective fulness and harmony, what lies scattered and ineffective in the multitude; "then let the mulitude include yourself"; that is, be substantiated, essenced with yourself; "and the result were new: themselves before, the multitude turn YOU" (become yourself). "This were to live and move and have, in them, your being, and secure a diadem you should transmit (because no cycle yearns beyond itself, but on itself returns) when the full sphere in wane, the world o'erlaid long since with you, shall have in turn obeyed some orb still prouder, some displayer, still more potent than the last, of human will, and some new king depose the old."

This is a most important passage to get hold of in studying Browning. It may be said to gather up Browning's philosophy of life in a nutshell.

There's a passage to the same effect in 'Balaustion's Adventure', in regard to the transmission of the poet's essence. The enthusiastic Rhodian girl, Balaustion, after she has told the play of Euripides, years after her adventure, to her four friends, Petale, Phullis, Charope, and Chrusion, says:

"I think I see how... you, I, or any one, might mould a new Admetos, new Alkestis. Ah, that brave bounty of poets, the one royal race that ever was, or will be, in this world! They give no gift that bounds itself, and ends i' the giving and the taking: theirs so breeds i' the heart and soul of the taker, so transmutes the man who only was a man before, that he grows god-like in his turn, can give he also: share the poet's privilege, bring forth new good, new beauty from the old. As though the cup that gave the wine, gave too the god's prolific giver of the grape, that vine, was wont to find out, fawn around his footstep, springing still to bless the dearth, at bidding of a Mainad."

Art as an Intermediate Agency of Personality

If Browning's idea of the quickening, the regeneration, the rectification of personality, through a higher personality, be fully comprehended, his idea of the great function of Art, as an intermediate agency of personality, will become plain. To emphasize the latter idea may be said to be the ultimate purpose of his masterpiece, 'The Ring and the Book'.

The complexity of the circumstances involved in the Roman murder case, adapts it admirably to the poet's purpose namely, to exhibit the swervings of human judgment in spite of itself, and the conditions upon which the rectification of that judgment depends.

This must be taken, however, as only the articulation, the framework, of the great poem. It is richer in materials, of the most varied character, than any other long poem in existence. To notice one feature of the numberless features of the poem, which might be noticed, Browning's deep and subtle insight into the genius of the Romish Church is shown in it more fully than in any other of his poems, though special phases of that genius are distinctly exhibited in numerous poems: a remarkable one being 'The Bishop orders his Tomb at St. Praxed's Church'. It is questionable whether any work of any kind has ever exhibited that genius more fully and distinctly than 'The Ring and the Book' exhibits it. The reader breathes throughout the ecclesiastical atmosphere of the Eternal City.

To return from this digression, the several monologues of which the poem consists, with the exception of those of the Canon Caponsacchi, Pompilia, and the Pope, are each curious and subtle and varied exponents of the workings, without the guidance of instinct at the heart, of the prepossessed, prejudiced intellect, and of the sources of its swerving into error. What is said of the "feel after the vanished truth" in the monologue entitled `Half Rome' the speaker being a jealous husband will serve to characterize, in a general way, "the feel after truth" exhibited in the other monologues: "honest enough, as the way is: all the same, harboring in the arts amiss, by but a hair's-breadth at the shoulder-blade, the arm o' the feeler, dip he ne'er so brave; and so leads waveringly, lets fall wide o' the mark his finger meant to find, and fix truth at the bottom, that deceptive speck."

The poet could hardly have employed a more effective metaphor in which to embody the idea of mental swerving. The several monologues all going over the same ground, are artistically justified in their exhibiting, each of them, a quite distinct form of this swerving. For the ultimate purpose of the poet, it needed to be strongly emphasized. The student of the poem is amazed, long before he gets over all these monologues, at the Protean capabilities of the poet's own intellect. It takes all conceivable attitudes toward the case, and each seems to be a perfectly easy one.

These monologues all lead up to the great moral of the poem, which is explicitly set forth at the end, namely, "that our human speech is naught, our human testimony false, our fame and human estimation, words and wind. Why take the artistic way to prove so much? Because, it is the glory and good of Art, that Art remains the one way possible of speaking truth, to mouths like mine, at least. How look a brother in the face and say, Thy right is wrong, eyes hast thou yet art blind, thine ears are stuffed and stopped, despite their length: and, oh, the foolishness thou countest faith! Say this as silvery as tongue can troll the anger of the man may be endured, the shrug, the disappointed eyes of him are not so bad to bear but here's the plague, that all this trouble comes of telling truth, which truth, by when it reaches him, looks false, seems to be just the thing it would supplant, nor recognizable by whom it left: while falsehood would have done the work of truth. But art, wherein man nowise speaks to men, only to mankind, art may tell a truth obliquely, do the thing shall breed the thought", that is, bring what is implicit within the soul, into the right attitude to become explicit bring about a silent adjustment through sympathy induced by the concrete; in other words, prepare the way for the perception of the truth "do the thing shall breed the thought, nor wrong the thought missing the mediate word"; meaning, that art, so to speak, is the word made flesh, is the truth, and, as art, has nothing directly to do with the explicit. "So may you paint your picture, twice show truth, beyond mere imagery on the wall, so, note by note, bring music from your mind, deeper than ever the andante dived, so write a book shall mean beyond the facts, suffice the eye and save the soul beside."

And what is the inference the poet would have us draw from this passage? It is, that the life and efficacy of art depends on the personality of the artist, which "has informed, transpierced, thridded, and so thrown fast the facts eise free, as right through ring and ring runs the djereed and binds the loose, one bar without a break." And it is really this fusion of the artist's soul, which kindles, quickens, informs those who contemplate, respond to, reproduce sympathetically within themselves the greater spirit which attracts and absorbs their own. The work of art is apocalyptic of the artist's own personality. It cannot be impersonal. As is the temper of his spirit, so is, must be, the temper of his art product. It is hard to believe, almost impossible to believe, that `titus andronicus' could have been written by shakespeare, the external testimony to the authorship, notwithstanding. Even if he had written it as a burlesque of such a play as marlow's `jew of malta', he could not have avoided some revelation of that sense of moral proportion which is omnipresent in his plays. But i can find no shakespeare in `titus andronicus'. Are we not certain what manner of man shakespeare was from his works (notwithstanding that critics are ever asserting their impersonality) far more certain than if his biography had been written by one who knew him all his life, and sustained to him the most intimate relations? We know Shakespeare or he CAN be known, if the requisite conditions are met, better, perhaps, than any other great author that ever lived know, in the deepest sense of the word, in a sense other than that in which we know Dr. Johnson, through Boswell's Biography. The moral proportion which is so signal a characteristic of his Plays could not have been imparted to them by the conscious intellect. It was SHED from his spiritual constitution.

"And long it was not after, when I was confirmed in this opinion, that he who would not be frustrate of his hope to write well hereafter in laudable things, ought himself to be a true poem." Milton's 'Apology for Sinectymnuus'.

By "speaking truth" in art's way, browning means, inducing a right attitude toward, a full and free sympathy with, the true, which is a far more important and effective way of speaking truth than delivering truth `in re'. A work of art, worthy of the name, need not be true to fact, but must be true in its spiritual attitude, and being thus true, it will tend to induce a corresponding attitude in those who do fealty to it. It will have the influence, though in an inferior degree, it may be, of a magnetic personality. Personality is the ultimate source of spiritual quickening and adjustment. Literature and all forms of art are but the intermediate agencies of personalities. The artist cannot be separated from his art. As is the artist so must be his art. The `aura', so to speak, of a great work of art, must come from the artist's own personality. The spiritual worth of shakespeare's `winter's tale' is not at all impaired by the fact that bohemia is made a maritime country, that whitsun pastorals and christian burial, and numerous other features of shakespeare's own age, are introduced into pagan times, that queen hermione speaks of herself as a daughter of the emperor of russia, that her statue is represented as executed by julio romano, an italian painter of the 16th century, that a puritan sings psalms to hornpipes, and, to crown all, that messengers are sent to consult the oracle of apollo, at delphi, which is represented as an island! All this jumble, this gallimaufry, i say, does not impair the spiritual worth of the play. As an art-product, it invites a rectified attitude toward the true and the sweet.

If we look at the letter of the trial scene in 'the merchant of venice', it borders on the absurd; but if we look at its spirit, we see the shakespearian attitude of soul which makes for righteousness, for the righteousness which is inherent in the moral constitution of the universe.

The inmost, secretest life of shakespeare's plays came from the personality, the inmost, secretest life, of the man shakespeare. We might, with the most alert sagacity, note and tabulate and aggregate his myriad phenomenal merits as a dramatic writer, but we might still be very far from that something back of them all, or rather that immanent something, that mystery of personality, that microcosmos, that "inmost centre, where truth abides in fulness", as browning makes paracelsus characterize it, "constituting man's self, is what is", as he makes the dying john characterize it, in `a death in the desert', that "innermost of the inmost, most interior of the interne", as mrs.

Browning characterizes it, "the hidden soul", as dallas characterizes it, which is projected into, and constitutes the soul of, the plays, and which is reached through an unconscious and mystic sympathy on the part of him who habitually communes with and does fealty to them. That personality, that living force, co-operated spontaneously and unconsciously with the conscious powers, in the creative process; and when we enter into a sympathetic communion with the concrete result of that creative process, our own mysterious personalities, being essentially identical with, though less quickened than, shakespeare's, respond, though it may be but feebly, to his. This response is the highest result of the study of shakespeare's works.

It is a significant fact that shakespearian critics and editors, for nearly two centuries, have been a 'genus irritabile', to which genus Shakespeare himself certainly did not belong. The explanation may partly be, that they have been too much occupied with the letter, and have fretted their nerves in angry dispute about readings and interpretations; as theologians have done in their study of the sacred records, instead of endeavoring to reach, through the letter, the personality of which the letter is but a manifestation more or less imperfect. To know a personality is, of course, a spiritual knowledge the result of sympathy, that is, spiritual responsiveness.

Intellectually it is but little more important to know one rather than another personality. The highest worth of all great works of genius is due to the fact that they are apocalyptic of great personalities.

Art says, as the divine person said, whose personality and the personalities fashioned after it, have transformed and moulded the ages, "follow me!" Deep was the meaning wrapt up in this command: It was, do as i do, live as i live, not from an intellectual perception of the principles involved in my life, but through a full sympathy, through the awakening, vitalizing, actuating power of the incarnate word.

Art also says, as did the voice from the wilderness, inadequately translated, "repent ye, for the kingdom of heaven is at hand" rather, be transformed, or, as de quincey puts it, "wheel into a new centre your spiritual system; geocentric has that system been up to this hour that is, having earth and the earthly for its starting-point; henceforward make it heliocentric (that is, with the sun, or the heavenly, for its principle of motion)."

The poetry of browning everywhere says this, and says it more emphatically than that of any other poet in our literature. It says everywhere, that not through knowledge, not through a sharpened intellect, but through repentance, in the deeper sense to which i have just alluded, through conversion, through wheeling into a new centre its spiritual system, the soul attains to saving truth. Salvation with him means that revelation of the soul to itself, that awakening, quickening, actuating, attitude-adjusting, of the soul, which sets it gravitating toward the divine.

Browning's idea of conversion is, perhaps, most distinctly expressed in a passage in the monologue of the canon caponsacchi, in 'the ring and the book', wherein he sets forth the circumstances under which his soul was wheeled into a new centre, after a life of dalliance and elegant folly, and made aware of "the marvellous dower of the life it was gifted and filled with". He has been telling the judges, before whom he has been summoned, the story of the letters forged by guido to entrap him and pompilia, and of his having seen "right through the thing that tried to pass for truth and solid, not an empty lie".

The conclusion and the resolve he comes to, are expressed in the soliloquy which he repeats to the judges, as having uttered at the time: "So, he not only forged the words for her but words for me, made letters he called mine: What i sent, he retained, gave these in place, all by the mistress messenger! As i recognized her, at potency of truth, so she, by the crystalline soul, knew me, never mistook the signs. Enough of this let the wraith go to nothingness again, here is the orb, have only thought for her!" What follows admits us to the very heart of browning's poetry admits us to the great idea which is almost, in these days, strange to say, peculiarly his which no other poet, certainly, of this intellectual, analytic, scientific age, with its "patent, truth-extracting processes", has brought out with the same degree of distinctness the great idea which may be variously characterized as that of soul-kindling, soul-quickening, adjustment of soul-attitude, regeneration, conversion, through personality a kindling, quickening, adjustment, regeneration, conversion in which thought is not even a coefficient. As expressed in sordello,

"Divest mind of e'en thought, and lo, god's unexpressed will dawns above us!" "Thought?" The canon goes on to say, "thought? Nay, sirs, what shall follow was not thought: I have thought sometimes, and thought long and hard. I have stood before, gone round a serious thing, tasked my whole mind to touch it and clasp it close,... God and man, and what duty i owe both, i dare say i have confronted these in thought: But no such faculty helped here. I put forth no thought, powerless, all that night i paced the city: It was the first spring. By the invasion i lay passive to, in rushed new things, the old were rapt away; alike abolished the imprisonment of the outside air, the inside weight o' the world that pulled me down. Death meant, to spurn the ground, soar to the sky, die well and you do that. The very immolation made the bliss; death was the heart of life, and all the harm my folly had crouched to avoid, now proved a veil hiding all gain my wisdom strove to grasp.... Into another state, under new rule I knew myself was passing swift and sure; whereof the initiatory pang approached, felicitous annoy, as bitter-sweet as when the virgin band, the victors chaste, feel at the end the earthy garments drop, and rise with something of a rosy shame into immortal nakedness: so I lay, and let come the proper throe would thrill into the ecstasy and out-throb pain.

I' the gray of the dawn it was I found myself facing the pillared front o' the Pieve mine, my church: it seemed to say for the first time, `But am not I the Bride, the mystic love o' the Lamb, who took thy plighted troth, my priest, to fold thy warm heart on my heart of stone and freeze thee nor unfasten any more? This is a fleshly woman, let the free bestow their life blood, thou art pulseless now!'... Now, when I found out first that life and death are means to an end, that passion uses both, indisputably mistress of the man whose form of worship is self-sacrifice now, from the stone lungs sighed the scrannel voice, `Leave that live passion, come be dead with me!' As if, i' the fabled garden, I had gone on great adventure, plucked in ignorance hedge-fruit, and feasted to satiety, laughing at such high fame for hips and haws, and scorned the achievement: then come all at once o' the prize o' the place, the thing of perfect gold, the apple's self: and, scarce my eye on that, was 'ware as well of the sevenfold dragon's watch. Sirs, i obeyed. Obedience was too strange, this new thing that had been struck into me by the look of the lady, to dare disobey the first authoritative word. 'Twas god's. I had been lifted to the level of her, could take such sounds into my sense. I said, `We two are cognizant o' the Master now; it is she bids me bow the head: how true, I am a priest! I see the function here; I thought the other way self-sacrifice: this is the true, seals up the perfect sum. I pay it, sit down, silently obey.'"

Numerous and varied expressions of the idea of conversion set forth in this passage, occur in Browning's poetry, evidencing his deep sense of this great and indispensable condition of soul-life, of being born anew (or from above, as it should be rendered in the Gospel, a'/nwqen, that is, through the agency of a higher personality), in order to see the kingdom of God evidencing his conviction that "the kingdom of God cometh not with observation: for lo! the kingdom of God is within you." In the poem entitled 'Cristina', the speaker is made to say,

- "Oh, we're sunk enough here, God knows! but not quite so sunk that moments,
- Sure tho' seldom, are denied us, when the spirit's true endowments
- Stand out plainly from its false ones, and apprise it if pursuing
- Or the right way or the wrong way, to its triumph or undoing.
- There are flashes struck from midnights, there are fire-flames noon-days kindle,
- Whereby piled-up honors perish, whereby swollen ambitions dwindle,
- While just this or that poor impulse, which for once had play unstifled,
- Seems the sole work of a life-time that away the rest have Mtrifled."

And again, when the Pope in 'The Ring and the Book' has come to the decision to sign the death-warrant of Guido and his accomplices, he says: "For the main criminal I have no hope except in such a SUDDENNESS OF FATE. I stood at Naples once, a night so dark I could have scarce conjectured there was earth anywhere, sky or sea or world at all: but the night's black was burst through by a blaze thunder struck blow on blow, earth groaned and bore, through her whole length of mountain visible: There lay the city thick and plain with spires, and, like a ghost disshrouded, white the sea. So may the truth be flashed out by one blow, and guido see, one instant, and be saved. Else i avert my face, nor follow him into that sad obscure sequestered state where god unmakes but to remake the soul he else made first in vain; which must not be. Enough, for i may die this very night: And how should i dare die, this man let live? Carry this forthwith to the governor!"

Browning is the most essentially Christian of living poets. Though he rarely speaks 'in propria persona' in his poetry, any one who has gone over it all, can have no doubt as to his own most vital beliefs. What the Beauty-loving Soul in Tennyson's 'Palace of Art' say of herself, cannot be suspected even, of Browning:

"I take possession of man's mind and deed.
I care not what the sects may brawl.
I sit as God holding no form of creed,
But contemplating all."

Religion with him is, indeed, the all-in-all; but not any particular form of it as a finality. This is not a world for finalities of any kind, as he constantly teaches us: it is a world of broken arcs, not of perfect rounds. Formulations of some kind he would, no doubt, admit there must be, as in everything else; but with him all formulations and tabulations of beliefs, especially such as "make square to a finite eye the circle of infinity", are, at the best, only PROVISIONAL, and, at the worst, lead to spiritual standstill, spiritual torpor, "a ghastly smooth life, dead at heart." The essential nature of Christianity is contrary to special prescription, do this or do that, believe this or believe that. Christ gave no recipes.

Christianity is with Browning, and this he sets forth again and again, a LIFE, quickened and motived and nourished by the Personality of Christ. And all that he says of this Personality can be accepted by every Christian, whatever theological view he may entertain of Christ. Christ's teachings he regards but as INCIDENTS of that Personality, and the records we have of his sayings and doings, but a fragment, a somewhat distorted one, it may be, out of which we must, by a mystic and plastic sympathy, aided by the Christ spirit which is immanent in the Christian world, mould the Personality, and do fealty to it. The Christian must endeavor to be able to say, with the dying John, in Browning's `Death in the Desert', "To me that story, ay, that Life and Death of which I wrote `it was' to me, it is."

The poem entitled 'Christmas Eve' contains the fullest and most explicit expression, in Browning, of his idea of the personality of Christ, as being the all-in-all of Christianity.

"The truth in God's breast
Lies trace for trace upon ours impressed:

Though He is so bright and we so dim,
We are made in His image to witness Him:
And were no eye in us to tell,
Instructed by no inner sense,
The light of Heaven from the dark of Hell,
That light would want its evidence,
Though Justice, Good, and Truth, were still
Divine, if, by some demon's will,
Hatred and wrong had been proclaimed
Law through the worlds, and Right misnamed,
No mere exposition of morality
Made or in part or in totality,
Should win you to give it worship, therefore:
And if no better proof you will care for,
Whom do you count the worst man upon earth?
Be sure, he knows, in his conscience, more
Of what Right is, than arrives at birth
In the best man's acts that we bow before:
And thence I conclude that the real God-function
Is to furnish a motive and injunction
For practising what we know already.
And such an injunction and such a motive
As the God in Christ, do you waive, and 'heady,
High-minded', hang your tablet votive
Outside the fane on a finger-post?
Morality to the uttermost,
Supreme in Christ as we all confess,
Why need WE prove would avail no jot
To make Him God, if God he were not?
Where is the point where Himself lays stress?
Does the precept run 'Believe in Good,
In Justice, Truth, now understood
For the first time'? or 'Believe in ME,
Who lived and died, yet essentially
Am Lord of Life'? Whoever can take
The same to his heart and for mere love's sake
Conceive of the love, that man obtains
A new truth; no conviction gains

Of an old one only, made intense
By a fresh appeal to his faded sense."
"Subsists no law of life outside of life."
"The Christ himself had been no Lawgiver,
Unless he had given the LIFE, too, with the law."
Mrs. Browning's 'Aurora Leigh'.

If all Christendom could take this remarkable poem of 'Christmas Eve' to its heart, its tolerance, its Catholic spirit, and, more than all, the fealty it exhibits to the Personality who essentially is Lord of Life, what a revolution it would undergo! and what a mass of dogmatic and polemic theology would become utterly obsolete! The most remarkable thing, perhaps, about the vast body of Christian theology which has been developed during the eighteen centuries which have elapsed since Christ was in the flesh, is, that it is occupied so largely, it might almost be said, exclusively, with what christ and his disciples taught, and with fierce discussions about the manifold meanings which have been ingeniously extorted from the imperfect record of what he taught. British museum libraries of polemics have been written in defence of what christ himself would have been indifferent to, and written with an animosity towards opponents which has been crystallized in a phrase now applied in a general way to any intense hate odium theologicum.

If the significance of Christ's mission, or a large part of it, is to be estimated by his teachings, from those teachings important deductions must be made, as many of them had been delivered long before his time. Browning has something to say on this point, in this same poem of 'Christmas Eve':

"Truth's atmosphere may grow mephitic
When Papist struggles with Dissenter,
Impregnating its pristine clarity,
One, by his daily fare's vulgarity,
Its gust of broken meat and garlic;
One, by his soul's too-much presuming
To turn the frankincense's fuming
An vapors of the candle starlike
Into the cloud her wings she buoys on.

Each that thus sets the pure air seething,
May poison it for healthy breathing
But the Critic leaves no air to poison;
Pumps out by a ruthless ingenuity
Atom by atom, and leaves you vacuity.
Thus much of Christ, does he reject?
And what retain? His intellect?
What is it I must reverence duly?
Poor intellect for worship, truly,
Which tells me simply what was told
(If mere morality, bereft
Of the God in Christ, be all that's left)
Elsewhere by voices manifold;
With this advantage, that the stater
Made nowise the important stumble
Of adding, he, the sage and humble,
Was also one with the Creator."

Browning's poetry is instinct with the essence of Christianity the LIFE of Christ. There is no other poetry, there is no writing of any form, in this age, which so emphasizes the fact (and it's the most consoling of all facts connected with the Christian religion), that the Personality, Jesus Christ, is the impregnable fortress of Christianity. Whatever assaults and inroads may be made upon the original records by goettingen professors, upon the august fabric of the church, with its creeds and dogmas, and formularies, and paraphernalia, this fortress will stand forever, and mankind will forever seek and find refuge in it.

The poem entitled 'cleon' bears the intimation (there's nothing directly expressed thereupon), that christianity is something distinct from, and beyond, whatever the highest civilization of the world, the civilization of greece, attained to before christ. Through him the world obtained "a new truth no conviction gained of an old one merely, made intense by a fresh appeal to the faded sense."

Cleon, the poet, writes to protos in his tyranny (that is, in the greek sense, sovereignty). Cleon must be understood as representing the ripe, composite result, as an individual, of what constituted the glory of greece her poetry, sculpture, architecture, painting, and music, and also her philosophy. He acknowledges the gifts which the king has lavished upon him. By these gifts we are to understand the munificent national patronage accorded to the arts. "The master of thy galley still unlades gift after gift; they block my court at last and pile themselves along its portico royal with sunset, like a thought of thee."

By the slave women that are among the gifts sent to cleon, seems to be indicated the degradation of the spiritual by its subjection to earthly ideals, as were the ideals of greek art. This is more particularly indicated by the one white she-slave, the lyric woman, whom further on in his letter, cleon promises to the king he will make narrate (in lyric song we must suppose) his fortunes, speak his great words, and describe his royal face.

He continues, that in such an act of love, the bestowal of princely gifts upon him whose song gives life its joy, men shall remark the king's recognition of the use of life that his spirit is equal to more than merely to help on life in straight ways, broad enough for vulgar souls, by ruling and the rest. He ascribes to the king, in the building of his tower (and by this must be understood the building up of his own selfhood), a higher motive than work for mere work's sake, that higher motive being, the luring hope of some eventual rest atop of it (the tower), whence, all the tumult of the building hushed, the first of men may look out to the east.

Tennyson uses a similar figure in 'the two voices'. The speaker, who is meditating whether "to be or not to be", says:

"Were this not well, to bide mine hour,
Though watching from a ruined tower
How grows the day of human power."

The ruined tower is his own dilapidated selfhood, whence he takes his outlook upon the world.

By the eventual rest atop of the tower, is indicated the aim of the greek civilization, to reach a calm within the finite, while the soul is constituted and destined to gravitate forever towards the infinite to "force our straitened sphere... Display completely here the mastery another life should learn."

(`Sordello'.) the eventual rest in this world is not the christian ideal. Earth-life, whatever its reach, and whatever its grasp, is to the christian a broken arc, not a perfect round.

Cleon goes on to recount his accomplishments in the arts, and what he has done in philosophy, in reply to the first requirement of protos's letter, protos, as it appears, having heard of, and wonderingly enumerated, the great things cleon has effected; and he has written to know the truth of the report. Cleon replies, that the epos on the king's hundred plates of gold is his, and his the little chaunt so sure to rise from every fishing-bark when, lights at prow, the seamen haul their nets; that the image of the sun-god on the light-house men turn from the sun's self to see, is his; that the poecile, o'erstoried its whole length with painting, is his, too; that he knows the true proportions of a man and woman, not observed before; that he has written three books on the soul, proving absurd all written hitherto, and putting us to ignorance again; that in music he has combined the moods, inventing one; that, in brief, all arts are his, and so known and recognized.

At this he writes the King to marvel not. We of these latter days, he says, being more COMPOSITE, appear not so great as our forerunners who, in their simple way, were greater in a certain single direction, than we; but our composite way is greater. This life of men on earth, this sequence of the soul's achievements here, he finds reason to believe, was intended to be viewed eventually as a great whole, the individual soul being only a factor toward the realization of this great whole toward spelling out, so to speak, Zeus's idea in the race. Those divine men of old, he goes on to say, reached each at one point, the outside verge that rounds our faculty, and where they reached, who could do more than reach? I have not chaunted, he says, verse like Homer's, nor swept string like Terpander, nor carved and painted men like Phidias and his friend; I am not great as they are, point by point; but I have entered into sympathy with these four, running these into one soul, who, separate, ignored each other's arts. The wild flower was the larger I have dashed rose-blood upon its petals, pricked its cup's honey with wine, and driven its seed to fruit, and show a better flower, if not so large. And now he comes to the important questions in the King's letter whether he, the poet, his soul thus in men's hearts, has not attained the very crown and proper end of life whether, now life closeth up, he faces death with success in his right hand, whether he fears death less than he, the King, does himself, the fortunate of men, who assigns the reason for thinking that he does, that he, the poet, leaves much behind, his life stays in the poems men shall sing, the pictures men shall study; while the King's life, complete and whole now in its power and joy, dies altogether with his brain and arm, as HE leaves not behind, as the poet does, works of art embodying the essence of his life which, through those works, will pass into the lives of men of all succeeding times. Cleon replies that if in the morning of philosophy, the King, with the light now in him, could have looked on all earth's tenantry, from worm to bird, ere man appeared, and if Zeus had questioned him whether he would improve on it, do more for visible creatures than was done, he would have answered, "Ay, by making each grow conscious in himself: all's perfect else, life's mechanics can no further go, and all this joy in natural life is put, like fire from off thy fingers into each, so exquisitely perfect is the same. But 'tis pure fire and they mere matter are; it has THEM, not they IT: and so I choose, for man, that a third thing shall stand apart from both, a quality arise within the soul, which, intro-active, made to supervise and feel the force it has, may view itself and so be happy." But it is this quality, Cleon continues, which makes man a failure.

This sense of sense, this spirit consciousness, grew the only life worth calling life, the pleasure-house, watch-tower, and treasure-fortress of the soul, which whole surrounding flats of natural life seemed only fit to yield subsistence to; a tower that crowns a country. But alas! the soul now climbs it just to perish there, for thence we have discovered that there's a world of capability for joy, spread round about us, meant for us, inviting us; and still the soul craves all, and still the flesh replies, "Take no jot more than ere you climbed the tower to look abroad! Nay, so much less, as that fatigue has brought deduction to it." After expatiating on this sad state of man, he arrives at the same conclusion as the King in his letter: "I agree in sum, O King, with thy profound discouragement, who seest the wider but to sigh the more. Most progress is most failure! thou sayest well."

And now he takes up the last point of the King's letter, that he, the King, holds joy not impossible to one with artist-gifts, who leaves behind living works. Looking over the sea, as he writes, he says, "Yon rower with the moulded muscles there, lowering the sail, is nearer it that I." He presents with clearness, and with rigid logic, the DILEMMA of the growing soul; shows the vanity of living in works left behind, and in the memory of posterity, while he, the feeling, thinking, acting man, shall sleep in his urn. The horror of the thought makes him dare imagine at times some future state unlimited in capability for joy, as this is in DESIRE for joy. But no! Zeus had not yet revealed such a state; and alas! he must have done so were it possible!

He concludes, "Live long and happy, and in that thought die, glad for what was! Farewell." And then, as a matter of minor importance, he informs the King, in a postscript, that he cannot tell his messenger aright where to deliver what he bears to one called Paulus. Protos, it must be understood, having heard of the fame of Paul, and being perplexed in the extreme, has written the great apostle to know of his doctrine. But Cleon writes that it is vain to suppose that a mere barbarian Jew, one circumcised, hath access to a secret which is shut from them, and that the King wrongs their philosophy in stooping to inquire of such an one. "Oh, he finds adherents, who does not. Certain slaves who touched on this same isle, preached him and Christ, and, as he gathered from a bystander, their doctrines could be held by no sane man."

There is a quiet beauty about this poem which must insinuate itself into the feelings of every reader. In tone it resembles the 'Epistle of Karshish, the Arab Physician'. The verse of both poems is very beautiful. No one can read these two poems, and 'Bishop Blougram's Apology', and 'The Bishop orders his Tomb at St. Praxed's Church', and not admit that Browning is a master of blank verse in its most difficult form a form far more difficult than that of the epic blank verse of Milton, or the Idyllic blank verse of Tennyson, argumentative and freighted with thought, and, at the same time, almost chatty, as it is, and bearing in its course exquisitely poetical conceptions. The same may be said of much of the verse of 'The Ring and the Book', especially that of the monologues of the Canon Caponsacchi, Pompilia, the Pope, and Count Guido Franceschini. But this by the way.

'Cleon' belongs to a grand group of poems, in which Browning shows himself to be, as I've said, the most essentially Christian of living poets the poet who, more emphatically than any of his contemporaries have done, has enforced the importance, the indispensableness of a new birth, the being born from above as the condition not only of soul vitality and progress, but also of intellectual rectitude. In this group of poems are embodied the profoundest principles of education principles which it behoves the present generation of educators to look well to. The acquisition of knowledge is a good thing, the sharpening of the intellect is a good thing, the cultivation of philosophy is a good thing; but there is something of infinitely more importance than all these it is, the rectification, the adjustment, through that mysterious operation we call sympathy, of the unconscious personality, the hidden soul, which co-operates with the active powers, with the conscious intellect, and, as this unconscious personality is rectified or unrectified, determines the active powers, the conscious intellect, for righteousness or unrighteousness.

The attentive reader of Browning's poetry must soon discover how remarkably homogeneous it is in spirit. There are many authors, and great authors too, the reading of whose collected works gives the impression of their having "tried their hand" at many things. No such impression is derivable from the voluminous poetry of Browning. Wide as is its range, one great and homogeneous spirit pervades and animates it all, from the earliest to the latest. No other living poet gives so decided an assurance of having a BURDEN to deliver. An appropriate general title to his works would be, 'The Burden of Robert Browning to the 19th Century'. His earliest poems show distinctly his ATTITUDE toward things. We see in what direction the poet has set his face what his philosophy of life is, what soul-life means with him, what regeneration means, what edification means in its deepest sense of building up within us the spiritual temple. And if he had left this world after writing no more than those poems of his youth, `Pauline' and `Paracelsus', a very fair `ex-pede-Herculem' estimate might have been made of the possibilities which he has since so grandly realized.

Chapter 6

Mr. Browning's "Obscurity"

It was long the FASHION and that fashion has not yet passed away with skimming readers and perfunctory critics to charge Mr. Browning with being "wilfully obscure, unconscientiously careless, and perversely harsh."

There are readers and readers. One class, constituting, perhaps, not more than one-tenth of one per cent, or a thousandth part of the whole number, "read, mark, learn, and inwardly digest"; the remaining ninety-nine and nine-tenths per cent, through a habit of loose and indiscriminate reading, are unequal to the sustained concentration of mind demanded by the higher poetry, the language of which is characterized by a severe economy of expression a closeness of texture, resulting from the elliptical energy of highly impassioned thought.

Reading is, perhaps, more superficial at the present day than it ever was before. There is an almost irresistible temptation to reverse the "multum legendum esse non multa" of Quintilian, overwhelmed as we are with books, magazines, and newspapers, which no man can number, and of which thousands and tens of thousands of minds endeavor to gobble up all they can; and yet, from want of all digestive and assimilating power, they are pitiably famished and deadened.

Sir John Lubbock has lately been interested in the preparation of a list of the best hundred books, and to that end has solicited the aid of a number of prominent scholars. Prof. Edward Dowden remarks thereupon, in an article on 'The Interpretation of Literature', "It would have been more profitable for us had we been advised how to read any one of the hundred; for what, indeed, does it matter whether we read the best books or the worst, if we lack the power or the instinct or the skill by which to reach the heart of any of them? Books for most readers are, as Montaigne says, 'a languid pleasure'; and so they must be, unless they become living powers, with a summons or a challenge for our spirit, unless we embrace them or wrestle with them."

To return from this digression to the charge against Browning of obscurity. And, first, it should be said that Browning has so much material, such a large thought and passion capital, that we never find him making a little go a great way, by means of EXPRESSION, or rather concealing the little by means of rhetorical tinsel. We can never justly demand of him what the Queen in 'Hamlet' demands of Polonius, "more matter with less art". His thought is wide-reaching and discursive, and the motions of his mind rapid and leaping. The connecting links of his thought have often to be supplied by an analytic reader whose mind is not up to the required tension to spring over the chasm. He shows great faith in his reader and "leaves the mere rude explicit details", as if he thought,

"'tis but brother's speech
We need, speech where an accent's change gives each
The other's soul."
'Sordello'.

A truly original writer like Browning, original, I mean, in his spiritual attitudes, is always more of less difficult to the uninitiated, for the reason that he demands of his reader new standpoints, new habits of thought and feeling; says, virtually, to his reader, Metanoei^te; and until these new standpoints are taken, these new habits of thought and feeling induced, the difficulty, while appearing to the reader at the outset, to be altogether objective, will really be, to a great extent, subjective, that is, will be in himself.

Goethe, in his 'Wahrheit und Dichtung', says: "Wer einem Autor Dunkelheit vorwerfen will, sollte erst sein eigenes Innere besuchen, ob es denn da auch recht hell ist. In der Daemmerung wird eine sehr deutliche Schrift unlesbar."

He who would charge an author with obscurity, should

first look into his own mind, to know whether it is quite clear there. In the dusk a very distinct handwriting becomes illegible.

And George Henry Lewes, in his 'Life of Goethe', well says: "A masterpiece excites no sudden enthusiasm; it must be studied much and long, before it is fully comprehended; we must grow up to it, for it will not descend to us. Its emphasis grows with familiarity. We never become disenchanted; we grow more and more awe-struck at its infinite wealth. We discover no trick, for there is none to discover. Homer, Shakespeare, Raphael, Beethoven, Mozart, never storm the judgment; but once fairly in possession, they retain it with unceasing influence."

And Professor Dowden, in the article from which I have just quoted, says: "Approaching a great writer in this spirit of courageous and affectionate fraternity, we need all our forces and all our craft for the friendly encounter. If we love ease and lethargy, let us turn in good time and fly. The interpretation of literature, like the interpretation of Nature, is no mere record of facts; it is no catalogue of the items which make up a book such catalogues and analyses of contents encumber our histories of literature with some of their dreariest pages. The interpretation of literature exhibits no series of dead items, but rather the life and power of one mind at play upon another mind duly qualified to receive and manifest these.

Hence, one who would interpret the work of a master must summon up all his powers, and must be alive at as many points as possible. He who approaches his author as a whole, bearing upon life as a whole, is himself alive at the greatest possible number of points, will be the best and truest interpreter. For he will grasp what is central, and at the same time will be sensitive to the value of all details, which details he will perceive not isolated, but in connection with one another, and with the central life to which they belong and from which they proceed."

In his poem entitled 'Pacchiarotto, and how he worked in distemper', Mr. Browning turns upon his critics, whom he characterizes as "the privileged fellows, in the drabs, blues, and yellows" (alluding to the covers of the leading British Reviews), and especially upon Alfred Austin, the author of that work of wholesale condemnation, 'The Poetry of the Period', and gives them a sound and well-deserved drubbing. At the close of the onset he says:

"Was it `grammar' wherein you would `coach' me
You, pacing in even that paddock
Of language allotted you ad hoc,
With a clog at your fetlocks, you scorners
Of me free from all its four corners?
Was it 'clearness of words which convey thought?'
Ay, if words never needed enswathe aught
But ignorance, impudence, envy
And malice what word-swathe would then vie
With yours for a clearness crystalline?
But had you to put in one small line
Some thought big and bouncing as noddle
Of goose, born to cackle and waddle
And bite at man's heel as goose-wont is,
Never felt plague its puny os frontis
You'd know, as you hissed, spat and sputtered,
Clear 'quack-quack' is easily uttered!"

In a letter written to Mr. W. G. Kingsland, in 1868, Mr. Browning says: "I can have little doubt that my writing has been in the main too hard for many I should have been pleased to communicate with; but I never designedly tried to puzzle people, as some of my critics have supposed. On the other hand, I never pretended to offer such literature as should be a substitute for a cigar or a game at dominoes to an idle man. So, perhaps, on the whole I get my deserts, and something over not a crowd, but a few I value more."

It was never truer of any author than it is true of Browning, that 'Le style c'est l'homme'; and Browning's style is an expression of the panther-restlessness and panther-spring of his impassioned intellect. The musing spirit of a Wordsworth or a Tennyson he partakes not of. Mr. Richard Holt Hutton's characterization of the poet's style, as a "crowded note-book style", is not a particularly happy one. In the passage, which he cites from Sordello, to illustrate the "crowded note-book style", occurs the following parenthesis:

" (To be by him themselves made act,
Not watch Sordello acting each of them.)"

"What the parenthesis means," he says, "I have not the most distant notion. Mr. Browning might as well have said, 'to be by him her himself herself themselves made act', etc., for any vestige of meaning I attach to this curious mob of pronouns and verbs. It is exactly like the short notes of a speech intended to be interpreted afterwards by one who had heard and understood it himself."

At first glance, this parenthesis is obscure; but the obscurity is not due to its being "exactly like the short notes of a speech", etc. It is due to what the "obscurity" of Mr. Browning's language, as language, is, in nine cases out of ten, due, namely, to the COLLOCATION of the words, not to an excessive economy of words. He often exercises a liberty in the collocation of his words which is beyond what an uninflected language like the English admits of, without more or less obscurity. There are difficult passages in Browning which, if translated into Latin, would present no difficulty at all; for in Latin, the relations of words are more independent of their collocation, being indicated by their inflections.

The meaning of the parenthesis is, and, independently of the context, a second glance takes it in (the wonder is, Mr. Hutton didn't take it in),

"To be themselves made by him [to] act,
Not each of them watch Sordello acting."

There are two or three characteristics of the poet's diction which may be noticed here: The suppression of the relative, both nominative and accusative or dative, is not uncommon; and, until the reader becomes familiar with it, it often gives, especially if the suppression is that of a subject relative, a momentary, but only a momentary, check to the understanding of a passage.

The following examples are from 'The Ring and the Book':

"Checking the song of praise in me, had else

Swelled to the full for God's will done on earth."

I. The Ring and the Book, v. 591.

i.e., which had (would have) else swelled to the full, etc.

"This that I mixed with truth, motions of mine
That quickened, made the inertness malleolable
O' the gold was not mine,"

I. The Ring and the Book, v. 703.

"Harbouring in the centre of its sense
A hidden germ of failure, shy but sure,
Should neutralize that honesty and leave
That feel for truth at fault, as the way is too."

I. The Ring and the Book, v. 851.

"Elaborate display of pipe and wheel
Framed to unchoak, pump up and pour apace
Truth in a flowery foam shall wash the world."

I. The Ring and the Book, v. 1113.

"see in such
A star shall climb apace and culminate,"

III. The Other Half Rome, v. 846.

"Guido, by his folly, forced from them
The untoward avowal of the trick o' the birth,
Would otherwise be safe and secret now."

IV. Tertium Quid, v. 1599.

"so I
Lay, and let come the proper throe would thrill
Into the ecstasy and outthrob pain."

VI. Giuseppe Caponsacchi, v. 972.

"blind?
Ay, as a man would be inside the sun,
Delirious with the plentitude of light
Should interfuse him to the finger-ends"

X. The Pope, 1564.

"You have the sunrise now, joins truth to truth."

X. The Pope, 1763.

"One makes fools look foolisher fifty-fold
By putting in their place the wise like you,

To take the full force of an argument
Would buffet their stolidity in vain."

XI. Guido, 858.

Here the infinitive "To take" might be understood, at first look, as the subject of "Would buffet"; but it depends on "putting", etc., and the subject relative "that" is suppressed: "an argument [that] would buffet their stolidity in vain."

"Will you hear truth can do no harm nor good?"

XI. Guido, 1915.

"I who, with outlet for escape to heaven,
Would tarry if such flight allowed my foe
To raise his head, relieved of that firm foot
Had pinned him to the fiery pavement else!"

XI. Guido, 2099.

i.e.,

"that firm foot [that] had (would have) pinned."

..."ponder, ere ye pass,
Each incident of this strange human play
Privily acted on a theatre,
Was deemed secure from every gaze but God's,"

XII. The Book and the Ring, v. 546.

"As ye become spectators of this scene
A soul made weak by its pathetic want
Of just the first apprenticeship to sin,
Would thenceforth make the sinning soul secure
From all foes save itself, that's truliest foe,"

XII. The Book and the Ring, v. 559.

i.e., "sin, [that] would."

"Was he proud, a true scion of the stock
Which bore the blazon, shall make bright my page"

XII. The Book and the Ring, v. 821.

The use of the infinitive without the prepositive "to", is frequently extended beyond present usage, especially in 'Sordello' and 'The Ring and the Book'. The following are examples:

"W1ho fails, through deeds howe'er diverse, RE-TRACK
My purpose still, my task?"

Sordello, p. 168.

"failed Adelaide SEE then
Who was the natural chief, the man of men?"
Sordello, p. 175.

*"but when
'Twas time expostulate, attempt withdraw
Taurello from his child,"...*
Sordello, p. 180.

Here are two infinitives, with the prepositive omitted, "expostulate" and "attempt", both dependent on the noun "time", and another, "withdraw", without the prepositive, dependent on "attempt": "but when 'twas time [to] expostulate, [to] attempt [to] withdraw", etc.

*"For thus he ventured, to the verge,
Push a vain mummery."...*
Sordello, p.190.

i.e., for thus he ventured [to] push to the verge a vain mummery.

*"as yet
He had inconsciously contrived FORGET
I' the whole, to dwell o' the points"...*
Sordello, p. 190.

"Grown bestial, dreaming how BECOME divine."
Sordello, p. 191.

"And the whole music it was framed AFFORD,"
Sordello, p. 203.

*"Was such a lighting-up of faith, in life,
Only allowed initiate, set man's step
In the true way by help of the great glow?"*
R. and B. X. The Pope, v. 1815.

i.e. only allowed [to] initiate, [to] set man's step, etc.

*"If I might read instead of print my speech,
Ay, and enliven speech with many a flower
Refuses obstinately blow in print."*
R. and B. IX. Johannes-Baptista Bottinius, v. 4.

Here the subject relative of "refuses" is omitted, and the verb followed by an infinitive without the prepositive: "many a flower [that] refuses obstinately to blow in print." Instead of the modern analytic form, the simple form of the past subjunctive derived from the Anglo-Saxon inflectional form, and identical with that of the past indicative, is frequently employed, the context only showing that it is the subjunctive. (See Abbott's 'Shakespearian Grammar', 361 et seq.)

- "Would we some prize might hold
- To match those manifold
- Possessions of the brute, gain most; as we did best!"
- Rabbi Ben Ezra, St. xi.
- i.e., as we should do best.
- "Thus were abolished Spring and Autumn both,"
- I. The Ring and the Book, 1358.
- i.e., would be abolished.
- "His peevishness had promptly put aside
- Such honor and refused the proffered boon,"...
- II. Half Rome (R. and B.), 369.
- i.e., would have promptly put aside.
- " (What daily pittance pleased the plunderer dole.)"
- X. The Pope (R. and B.), 561.
- i.e., as the context shows, [it] might please the plunderer [to] dole.

"succession to the inheritance
Which bolder crime had lost you:"
IV. Tertium Quid (R. and B.), 1104.
i.e., would have lost you.

But the verbs "be" and "have" are chiefly so used, and not often beyond what present usage allows. Tennyson uses "saw" = `viderem', in the following passage:

"But since I did not see the Holy Thing,
I sware a vow to follow it till I saw."
Sir Percivale in 'The Holy Grail'.

The use of the dative, or indirect object, without "to" or "for". Such datives are very frequent, and scarcely need illustration. The poet has simply carried the use of them beyond the present general usage of the language. But there's a noticeable one in the Pope's Monologue, in 'The Ring and the Book', vv. 1464-1466: The Archbishop of Arezzo, to whom poor Pompilia has applied, in her distress, for protection against her brutal husband, thinks it politic not to take her part, but send her back to him and enjoin obedience and submission. The Pope, in his Monologue, represents the crafty Archbishop as saying, when Pompilia cries, "Protect me from the wolf!"

"No, thy Guido is rough, heady, strong,
Dangerous to disquiet: let him bide!
He needs some bone to mumble, help amuse
The darkness of his den with: so, the fawn
Which limps up bleeding to my foot and lies,
Come to me daughter! thus I throw him back!"

i.e., thus I throw back [to] him the fawn which limps up bleeding to my foot and lies. The parenthesis, "Come to me, daughter", being interposed, and which is introduced as preparatory to his purpose, adds to the difficulty of the construction.

There are, after all, but comparatively few instances in Browning's poetry, where these features of his diction can be fairly condemned. They often impart a crispness to the expressions in which they occur.

The contriving spirit of the poet's language often results in great complexity of construction. Complexity of construction may be a fault, and it may not. It may be justified by the complexity of the thought which it bears along. "Clear quack-quack is easily uttered." But where an author's thought is nimble, far-reaching, elliptical through its energy, and discursive, the expression of it must be more or less complex or involved; he will employ subordinate clauses, and parentheses, through which to express the outstanding, restricting, and toning relations of his thought, that is, if he is a master of perspective, and ranks his grouped thoughts according to their relative importance.

The poet's apostrophe to his wife in the spirit-world, which closes the long prologue to 'The Ring and the Book' (vv. 1391-1416), and in which he invokes her aid and benediction, in the work he has undertaken, presents a greater complexity of construction than is to be met with anywhere else in his works; and of this passage it may be said, as it may be said of any other having a complex construction, supposing this to be the only difficulty, that it's hard rather than obscure, and demands close reading. But, notwithstanding its complex structure and the freight of thought conveyed, the passage has a remarkable LIGHTSOMENESS of movement, and is a fine specimen of blank verse. The unobtrusive, but distinctly felt, alliteration which runs through it, contributes something toward this lightsomeness. The first two verses have a Tennysonian ring:

"O lyric Love, half-angel and half-bird
And all a wonder and a wild desire,
Boldest of hearts that ever braved the sun,
Took sanctuary within the holier blue,
And sang a kindred soul out to his face,
Yet human at the red-ripe of the heart
When the first summons from the darkling earth
Reached thee amid thy chambers, blanched their blue,
And bared them of the glory to drop down,
To toil for man, to suffer or to die,
This is the same voice: can thy soul know change?
Hail then, and hearken from the realms of help!
Never may I commence my song, my due
To God who best taught song by gift of thee,
Except with bent head and beseeching hand
That still, despite the distance and the dark,
What was, again may be; some interchange
Of grace, some splendour once thy very thought,
Some benediction anciently thy smile:
Never conclude, but raising hand and head
Thither where eyes, that cannot reach, yet yearn
For all hope, all sustainment, all reward,
Their utmost up and on, so blessing back
In those thy realms of help, that heaven thy home,
Some whiteness which, I judge, thy face makes proud,
Some wanness where, I think, thy foot may fall!"

In the last three verses of 'The Ring and the Book' the poet again addresses his "Lyric Love" to express the wish that the Ring, which he has rounded out of the rough ore of the Roman murder case, might but lie "in guardianship" outside hers, "Thy rare gold ring of verse (the poet praised) Linking our England to his Italy." The reference is to the inscription on Casa Guidi, Via Maggiore, 9. Florence:

Qui scrisse e mori
Elisabetta barrett browning
Che in cuore di donna conciliava
Scienza di dotto e spirito di poeta
E fece del suo verso aureo anello
Fra italia e inghilterra
Pone questo memoria
Firenze grata
1861.

See elaborate analysis of this invocation, by dr. F. J. Furnivall, read at the forty-eighth meeting of the browning society, february 25, 1887, being no. 39 of the society's papers.

But, after all, the difficulties in browning which result from the construction of the language, be that what it may, are not the main difficulties, as has been too generally supposed. The main difficulties are quite independent of the construction of the language.

Many readers, especially those who take an intellectual attitude toward all things, in the heavens above and in the earth beneath, suppose that they are prepared to understand almost anything which is understandable if it is only put right. This is a most egregious mistake, especially in respect to the subtle and complex spiritual experiences which the more deeply subjective poetry embodies. What de quincey says in his paper on kant, of the comprehension of the higher philosophical truths, can, with still better reason, be said of the responsiveness to the higher spiritual truths: "No complex or very important truth was ever yet transferred in full development from one mind to another: Truth of that character is not a piece of furniture to be shifted; it is a seed which must be sown, and pass through the several stages of growth. No doctrine of importance can be transferred in a matured shape into any man's understanding from without: It must arise by an act of genesis within the understanding itself." 'Letters to a young man'. Letter v.

And so it may be said in regard to the responsiveness to

the higher spiritual truths i don't say comprehension of the higher spiritual truths (that word pertains rather to an intellectual grasp), but responsiveness to the higher spiritual truths. Spiritual truths must be spiritually responded to; they are not and cannot be intellectually comprehended. The condition of such responsiveness it may require a long while to fulfil. New attitudes of the soul, a meta/noia, may be demanded, before such responsiveness is possible. And what some people may regard in the higher poetry as obscure, by reason of the mode of its presentation on the part of the poet, may be only relatively so that is, the obscurity may be wholly due to the wrong attitudes, or the no attitudes, of their own souls, and to the limitations of their spiritual experiences. In that case "the patient must minister to himself".

While on the subject of "obscurity", i must notice a difficulty which the reader at first experiences in his study of browning's poetry a difficulty resulting from the poet's favorite art-form, the dramatic or psychologic monologue. The largest portion of his voluminous poetry is in this form. Some speaker is made to reveal his character, and, sometimes, by reflection, or directly, the character of some one else to set forth some subtle and complex soul-mood, some supreme, all-determining movement or experience of a life; or, it may be, to ratiocinate subtly on some curious question of theology, morals, philosophy, or art. Now it is in strictly preserving the monologue character that obscurity often results. A monologue often begins with a startling abruptness, and the reader must read along some distance before he gathers what the beginning means. Take the monologue of Fra Lippo Lippi for example. The situation is necessarily left more or less unexplained. The poet says nothing `in propria persona', and no reply is made to the speaker by the person or persons addressed. Sometimes a look, a gesture, or a remark, must be supposed on the part of the one addressed, which occasions a responsive remark. Sometimes the speaker IMPUTES a question; and the reader is sometimes obliged to stop and consider whether a question is imputed by the speaker to the one he is addressing, or is a direct question of his own. This is often the case throughout

'The Ring and the Book'. But to the initiated, these features of the monologue present little or no difficulty, and they conduce to great compactness of composition a closeness of texture which the reader comes in time to enjoy, and to prefer to a more loosely woven diction.

The dramatic monologue differs from a soliloquy in this: while there is but one speaker, the presence of a silent second person is supposed, to whom the arguments of the speaker are addressed. Perhaps such a situation may be termed a novelty of invention in our Poet. It is obvious that the dramatic monologue gains over the soliloquy in that it allows the artist greater room in which to work out his conception of character. We cannot gaze long at a solitary figure on a canvas, however powerfully treated, without feeling some need of relief. In the same way a soliloquy (comp.

The great soliloquies of Shakespeare) cannot be protracted to any great length without wearying the listener. The thoughts of a man in self-communion are apt to run in a certain circle, and to assume a monotony. The introduction of a second person acting powerfully upon the speaker throughout, draws the latter forth into a more complete and varied expression of his mind. The silent person in the background, who may be all the time master of the situation, supplies a powerful stimulus to the imagination of the reader. Rev. Prof. E. Johnson's "Paper on 'Bishop Blougram's Apology'" ('Browning Soc. Papers', Pt. III., p. 279).

The monologue entitled 'My Last Duchess. Ferrara' is a good example of the constitution of this art-form. It is one of the most perfect in artistic treatment, and exhibits all the features I have just noticed. Originally, this monologue and that now entitled 'Count Gismond. Aix in Provence', had the common title, 'Italy and France', the former being No. I. Italy; the latter, No. II. France. The poet, no doubt, afterward thought that the Duke of the one monologue, and the Count of the other, could not justly be presented as representatives, respectively, of Italy and France. In giving the monologues new titles, 'My Last Duchess' and 'Count Gismond', he added to the one, 'Ferrara', and to the other, 'Aix in Provence', thus locally restricting the order of character which they severally represent.

In 'My Last Duchess', the speaker is a soulless VIRTUOSO a natural product of a proud, arrogant, and exclusive aristocracy, on the one hand, and on the other, of an old and effete city, like Ferrara, where art, rather than ministering to soul-life and true manliness of character, has become an end to itself is valued for its own sake.

The Duke is showing, with the weak pride of the mere virtuoso, a portrait of his last Duchess, to some one who has been sent to negotiate another marriage. We see that he is having an entertainment or reception of some kind in his palace, and that he has withdrawn from the company with the envoy to the picture-gallery on an upper floor. He has pulled aside the curtain from before the portrait, and in remarking on the expression which the artist, Fra Pandolf, has given to the face, he is made to reveal a fiendish jealousy on his part, occasioned by the sweetness and joyousness of his late Duchess, who, he thought, should show interest in nothing but his own fossilized self. "She had," he says, "a heart how shall I say? too soon made glad, too easily impressed; she liked whate'er she looked on, and her looks went everywhere. Sir, 'twas all one! My favour at her breast, the dropping of the daylight in the West, the bough of cherries some officious fool broke in the orchard for her, the white mule she rode with round the terrace all and each would draw from her alike the approving speech, or blush, at least. She thanked men, good! but thanked somehow I know not how as if she ranked my gift of a nine-hundred-years-old name with anybody's gift."

Her fresh interest in things, and the sweet smile she had for all, due to a generous soul-life, proved fatal to the lovely Duchess: "Oh sir, she smiled, no doubt, whene'er I passed her; but who passed without much the same smile? This grew; I gave commands; then all smiles stopped together."

He succeeded, and he seems to be proud of it, in shutting off all her life-currents, pure, and fresh, and sparkling, as they were, and we must suppose that she than sank slowly and uncomplainingly away. What a deep pathos there is in "then all smiles stopped together"! "I gave commands" certainly must not be understood to mean commands for her death, as it is understood by the writer of the articles in `The Saint Paul's Magazine' for December, 1870, and January, 1871.

See Preface: Note to the Third Edition.

The contemptible meanness and selfishness of jealousy were never exhibited with greater power, than they are exhibited in this short monologue a power largely due to the artistic treatment. The jealousy of Leontes, in 'The Winter's Tale', of Shakespeare, is nobility itself, in comparison with the Duke's. How distinctly, while indirectly, the sweet Duchess is, with a few masterly touches, placed before us! The poet shows his artistic skill especially in his indirect, reflected portraitures. This short composition, comprising as it does but fifty-six lines, is, of itself, sufficient to prove the poet a consummate artist. Tennyson's TECHNIQUE is quite perfect, almost "faultily faultless", indeed; but in no one of his compositions has he shown an equal degree of art-power, in the highest sense of the word.

'My Last Duchess'

"That's my last Duchess painted on the wall,
Looking as if she were alive. I call
That piece a wonder, now: Fra Pandolf's hands
Worked busily a day, and there she stands.
Will't please you sit and look at her? I said,
'Fra Pandolf' by design: for never read
Strangers like you that pictured countenance,
The depth and passion of its earnest glance,
But to myself they turned (since none puts by
The curtain I have drawn for you, but I)
And seemed as they would ask me, if they durst,
How such a glance came there; so, not the first
Are you to turn and ask thus. Sir, 'twas not
Her husband's presence only, called that spot
Of joy into the Duchess' cheek: perhaps
Fra Pandolf chanced to say 'Her mantle laps
Over my lady's wrist too much', or 'Paint
Must never hope to reproduce the faint

Half-flush that dies along her throat': such stuff
Was courtesy, she thought, and cause enough
For calling up that spot of joy. She had
A heart how shall I say? too soon made glad,
Too easily impressed; she liked whate'er
She looked on, and her looks went everywhere.
Sir, 'twas all one! My favour at her breast,
The dropping of the daylight in the West,
The bough of cherries some officious fool
Broke in the orchard for her, the white mule
She rode with round the terrace all and each
Would draw from her alike the approving speech,
Or blush, at least. She thanked men, good! but thanked
Somehow I know not how as if she ranked
My gift of a nine-hundred-years-old name
With anybody's gift. Who'd stoop to blame
This sort of trifling? Even had you skill
In speech (which I have not) to make your will
Quite clear to such an one, and say, 'Just this
Or that in you disgusts me; here you miss,
Or there exceed the mark' and if she let
Herself be lessoned so, nor plainly set
Her wits to yours, forsooth, and made excuse,
E'en then would be some stooping; and I choose
Never to stoop. Oh sir, she smiled, no doubt,
Whene'er I passed her; but who passed without
Much the same smile? This grew; I gave commands;
Then all smiles stopped together. There she stands
As if alive. Will't please you rise? We'll meet
The company below, then. I repeat,
The Count your master's known munificence
Is ample warrant that no just pretence
Of mine for dowry will be disallowed;
Though his fair daughter's self, as I avowed
At starting, is my object. Nay, we'll go
Together down, sir. Notice Neptune, though,
Taming a sea-horse, thought a rarity,
Which Claus of Innsbruck cast in bronze for me!

Claus of Innsbruck and also Fra Pandolf (v. 3) are imaginary artists. The last ten verses illustrate well the poet's skilful management of his difficult art-form. After the envoy has had his look at the portrait, the Duke, thinking it time to return to his guests, says "Will't please you rise? We'll meet the company below, then." His next speech, which indicates what he has been talking about, during the envoy's study of the picture, must be understood as uttered while they are moving toward the stairway. The next, "Nay, we'll go together down, sir", shows that they have reached the head of the stairway, and that the envoy has politely motioned the Duke to lead the way down. This is implied in the "Nay". The last speech indicates that on the stairway is a window which affords an outlook into the courtyard, where he calls the attention of the envoy to a Neptune, taming a sea-horse, cast in bronze for him by Claus of Innsbruck. The pride of the virtuoso is also implied in the word, "though".

It should be noticed, also, that the Duke values his wife's picture wholly as a picture, not as the "counterfeit presentment" and reminder of a sweet and lovely woman, who might have blessed his life, if he had been capable of being blessed. It is to him a picture by a great artist, and he values it only as such. He says, parenthetically, "since none puts by the curtain I have drawn for you, but I." It's too precious a work of art to be entrusted to anybody else.

Chapter 7

Browning's Verse

It seems to be admitted, even by many of the poet's most devoted students, that his verse is, in its general character, harsh and rugged. To judge it fairly, one must free his mind of many merely conventional canons in regard to verse. Pure music is absolute. The music of verse moves, or should move, under the conditions of the thought which articulates it. It should serve as a chorus to the thought, expressing a mystic sympathy with it. Verse may be very musical, and yet more or less mechanical; that is, it may CLOTHE thought and sentiment, but not be a part of it, not EMBODY it. Unrippled verse, which many readers demand, MUST be more or less mechanical. Such verse flows according to its own sweet will, independently of the thought-articulation. But the thought-articulation may be so flimsy that it's well enough for the verse so to flow.

The careful student of Browning's language-shaping must discover the requisite susceptibility to vitality of form being supposed that his verse is remarkably organic: often, indeed, more organic, even when it appears to be clumsy, than the "faultily faultless" verse of Tennyson. The poet who has written 'In a Gondola', 'By the Fireside', 'Meeting at Night', 'Parting at Morning', 'Gold Hair', 'May and Death', 'Love among the Ruins', 'Home Thoughts from Abroad', 'Home Thoughts from the Sea', the Incantation in 'The Flight of the Duchess' (some of which are both song and picture), and many, many more that might be named, certainly has the very highest faculty of word and verse music, of music, too, that is entirely new in English Poetry; and it can be shown that he always exercises that faculty whenever there's a real artistic occasion for it, not otherwise. Verse-music is never with him a mere literary indulgence. The grotesquerie of rhythm and rhyme which some of his poems exhibit, is as organic as any other feature of his language-shaping, and shows the rarest command of language. He has been charged with having "failed to reach continuous levels of musical phrasing". It's a charge which every one who appreciates Browning's verse in its higher forms (and its higher forms are not those which are addressed especially to the physical ear) will be very ready to admit.

In the general tenor of his poetry, he is ABOVE the Singer, he is the Seer and Revealer, who sees great truths beyond the bounds of the territory of general knowledge, instead of working over truths within that territory; and no seer of modern times has had his eyes more clearly purged with euphrasy and rue. Poetry is with him, in the language of Mr. E. Paxton Hood ('Eclectic and Congregational Rev.', Dec., 1868), "no jingle of words, or pretty amusement for harpsichord or piano, but rather a divine trigonometry, a process of celestial triangulation, a taking observations of celestial places and spheres, an attempt to estimate our world, its place, its life amidst the boundless immeasurable sweeps of space and time; or if describing, then describing the animating stories of the giants, how they fought and fell, or conquered...a great all-inclusive strength of song, which is as a battle march to warriors, or as the refreshment of brooks and dates to the spent and toiling soldiers on their way, is more than the pretty idyll, whose sweet and plaintive story pleases the idle hour or idle ear."

The Rev. Prof. E. Johnson, in the section entitled 'Poets of the Ear and of the Eye', of his valuable paper on 'Conscience and Art in Browning' ('Browning Soc. Papers', Part III., pp. 345-380), has ably shown that "the economy of music is a necessity of Browning's Art" that music, instead of ever being an end to itself, is with him a means to a much higher end. He says: "All poetry may be classified according to its form or its contents. Formal classification is easy, but of little use. When we have distinguished compositions as dramatic, lyrical, or characterized a poet in like manner, we have done little. What we want to ascertain is the peculiar quality of the imaginative stuff with which he plastically works, and to appreciate its worth. This is always a great task, but one particularly necessary in the case of Browning, because the stuff in which he has wrought is so novel in the poet's hands. Psychology itself is comparatively a new and modern study, as a distinct science; but a psychological poet, who has made it his business to clothe psychic abstractions 'in sights and sounds', is entirely a novel appearance in literature.

"Now that phrase 'clothing in sights and sounds' may yield us the clue to the classification we are seeking. The function of artists, that is, musicians, poets in the narrower sense, and painters, is to clothe Truth in sights and sounds for the hearing and seeing of us all. Their call to do this lies in their finer and fuller aesthetic faculty. The sense of hearing and that of seeing stand in polar opposition, and thus a natural scale offers itself by which we may rank and arrange our artists. At the one end of the scale is the acoustic artist, i.e., the musician. At the other end of the scale is the optic artist, the painter and sculptor. Between these, and comprising both these activities in his own, is the poet, who is both acoustic and optic artist.

He translates the sounds of the world, both external and internal, the tumult of storms, the murmurs of waves, the SUSURRUS of the woodland, the tinkling of brooks, the throbbing of human hearts, the cries of all living creatures; all those groans of pain, stammers of desire, shrieks of despair, yawns even of languor, which are ever breaking out of the heart of things; and beside all this, the hearsay, commonplace, proverbial lore of the world. He turns these into melodies which shall be caught up by those who listen. In short, he converts by his alchemy the common stuff of pain and of joy into music. But he is optic as well as acoustic; that is, he calls up at the same time by his art a procession of images which march or dance across the theatre of the listener's fancy. Now the question of classification on this scheme comes to this, Does the particular poet who invites our attention deal more with the aesthesis of the ear or with that of the eye? Does he more fill our ear with sweet tunes or our fancy with shapes and colours? Does he compel us to listen and shut our eyes, or to open our eyes wide and dispense with all but the faintest musical accompaniment? What sense, in short, does he mainly address himself to? Goethe said that he was a `seeing' man; W. von Humboldt, the great linguist, that he was a `listening' man. The influence of Milton's blindness on his poetry was noticed by Lessing. The short-sightedness of Wieland has also been detected in his poetry.

"If we apply these tests to Browning, there can be, I think, no doubt as to the answer. He is, in common with all poets, both musician and painter, but much more the latter than the former. He is never for a moment the slave of his ear, if I may so express it. We know that he has, on the contrary, the mastery of music. But music helps and supports his imagination, never controls it. Music is to Browning an inarticulate revelation of the truth of the supersensual world, the `earnest of a heaven'. He is no voluptuary in music. Music is simply the means by which the soul wings its way into the azure of spiritual theory and contemplation. Take only `Saul' and `Abt Vogler' in illustration. `Saul' is a magnificent interpretation of the old theme, a favorite with the mystics, that evil spirits are driven out by music.

But in this interpretation it is not the mere tones, the thrumming on the harp, it is the religious movement of the intelligence, it is the truth of Divine love throbbing in every chord, which constitutes the spell. And so in `Abt Vogler'; the abbot's instrument is only the means whereby he strikes out the light of faith and hope within him. Not to dwell upon this point, I would only say that it seems clear that Browning has the finest acoustic gifts, and could, if he had chosen, have scattered musical bons-bons through every page. But he has printed no `versus inopes rerum, nugaeque canorae' (Hor. ad Pis.). He has had higher objects in view, and has dispensed better stuff than that which lingers in the ear, and tends to suppress rather than support the higher activity of thought.

"When for a moment he shuts his eyes, and falls purely into the listening or `musing' mood, he becomes the instrument of a rich deep music, breaking out of the heart of the unseen world, as in the Dirge of unfaithful Poets in `Paracelsus', or the Gypsy's Incantation in the `Flight of the Duchess', or the Meditation at the crisis of Sordello's temptation.

"When the keen inquisitive intelligence is in its full waking activity there grows `more of the words' and thought, and `less of the music', to invert a phrase of the poet's. The melody ceases, the rhythm is broken, as in all intense, earnest conversation. At times only the tinkle of the pairing rhymes, of which Browning has made a most witty use, reminds that we are called to partake a mood in which commonplace associations are melting into the ideal. I believe the economy of music is a necessity of Browning's art; and it would be only fair, if those who attack him on this ground would consider how far thought of such quality as his admits of being chanted, or otherwise musically accompanied.

In plain words the problem is, how far the pleasures of sound and of sense can be united in poetry; and it will be found in every case that a poet sacrifices something either to the one or to the other. Browning has said something in his arch way on this point. In effect, he remarks, Italian prose can render a simple thought more sweetly to the ear than either Greek or English verse. It seems clear from many other of his critical remarks that he considers the demand for music in preference to thought in poetry, as the symptom of a false taste.

"Browning's poetry is to be gazed at, rather than listened to and recited, for the most part. It is infinitely easier to listen for an hour to spiritual music than to fix one's whole attention for a few minutes on a spiritual picture. In the latter act of mind we find a rich musical accompaniment distracting, while a slight musical accompaniment is probably helpful. And perhaps we may characterize Browning's poetry as a series of spiritual pictures with a faint musical accompaniment.

"For illustration by extreme contrast, Milton may be compared with Browning. Milton was a great hearsay poet, Browning repeats no hearsay. In reading Milton, the difficulty is to keep up the mental tension where there is so little thought, strictly speaking. With Browning the highest tension is exacted.

"He is pre-eminently the looker, the seer, the `maker-see'; the reporter, the painter of the scenery and events of the soul. And if the sense of vision is our noblest, and we instinctively express the acts of intelligence in terms drawn from physical vision, the poet who leans most towards the `SEER of Power and Love in the absolute, Beauty and Goodness in the concrete', takes the higher rank. This is no matter for bigotry of taste. Singers and seers, musicians and reporters, and reproducers of every degree, who have something to tell us or to show us of the `world as God has made it, where all is beauty', we have need of all. But of singers there are many, of seers there are few, that is all."

In the most difficult form of verse, namely, blank verse, Browning has shown himself a great master, and has written some of the very best in the literature. And great as is the extent of his blank verse, the 'Ring and the Book' alone containing 21,116 verses, it never entirely lapses into prose.

One grand merit of blank verse is in the SWEEP of it; another, in its pause-melody, which can be secured only by a skilful recurrence of an unbroken measure; without this, variety of pause ceases to be variety, and results in a metrical chaos; a third is in its lightsomeness of movement, its go, when well-freighted with thought. All these merits are found united in much of Browning's blank verse, especially in that of 'The Ring and the Book'. As an example of this, take the following passage from the monologue of the Canon Caponsacchi. It gives expression to his vision of Count Guido's spiritual down-sliding; "in the lowest deep a lower deep still threatening to devour him, opens wide":

"And thus I see him slowly and surely edged
Off all the table-land whence life upsprings
Aspiring to be immortality,
As the snake, hatched on hill-top by mischance,
Despite his wriggling, slips, slides, slidders down
Hill-side, lies low and prostrate on the smooth
Level of the outer place, lapsed in the vale:

So I lose Guido in the loneliness,
Silence, and dusk, till at the doleful end,
At the horizontal line, creation's verge,
From what just is to absolute nothingness
Lo, what is this he meets, strains onward still?
What other man, deep further in the fate,
Who, turning at the prize of a foot-fall
To flatter him and promise fellowship,
Discovers in the act a frightful face
Judas, made monstrous by much solitude!
The two are at one now! Let them love their love
That bites and claws like hate, or hate their hate
That mops and mows and makes as it were love!
There, let them each tear each in devil's-fun,
Or fondle this the other while malice aches
Both teach, both learn detestability!
Kiss him the kiss, Iscariot! Pay that back,
That smatch o' the slaver blistering on your lip
By the better trick, the insult he spared Christ
Lure him the lure o' the letters, Aretine!
Lick him o'er slimy-smooth with jelly-filth
O' the verse-and-prose pollution in love's guise!
The cockatrice is with the basilisk!
There let him grapple, denizens o' the dark,
Foes or friends, but indissolubly bound,
In their one spot out of the ken of God
Or care of man for ever and ever more!"

Browning has distinctly indicated the standard by which he estimates art-work, in the closing paragraph of his Essay 'On the Poet objective and subjective; on the latter's aim; on Shelley as man and poet'.

"I would rather," he says, "consider Shelley's poetry as a sublime fragmentary essay towards a presentment of the correspondency of the universe to Deity, of the natural to the spiritual, and of the actual to the ideal, than I would isolate and separately appraise the worth of many detachable portions which might be acknowledged as utterly perfect in a lower moral point of view, under the mere conditions of art. It would be easy to take my stand on successful instances of objectivity in Shelley: there is the unrivalled 'Cenci'; there is the 'Julian and Maddalo' too; there is the magnificent 'Ode to Naples': why not regard, it may be said, the less organized matter as the radiant elemental foam and solution, out of which would have been evolved, eventually, creations as perfect even as those? But I prefer to look for the highest attainment, not simply the high, and, seeing it, I hold by it. There is surely enough of the work 'Shelley' to be known enduringly among men, and, I believe, to be accepted of God, as human work may; and around the imperfect proportions of such, the most elaborated productions of ordinary art must arrange themselves as inferior illustrations."

The italics are mine. I would say, but without admitting imperfect art on the part of Browning, for I regard him as one of the greatest of literary artists, that HE must be estimated by the standard presented in this passage, by the "presentment", everywhere in his poetry, "of the correspondency of the universe to Deity, of the natural to the spiritual, and of the actual to the ideal."

The same standard is presented in 'Andrea del Sarto', in 'Old Pictures in Florence', and in other of his poems.

Chapter 8

Complete Text of the Poems

"Heap cassia, sandal-buds and stripes"

Heap cassia, sandal-buds and stripes
Of labdanum, and aloe-balls,
with dull nard an Indian wipes
From out her hair: such balsam falls Down sea-side mountain pedestals,
From tree-tops where tired winds are fain, Spent with the vast and howling main, To treasure half their island-gain. And strew faint sweetness from some old.
Egyptian's fine worm-eaten shroud Which breaks to dust when once unrolled;
Or shredded perfume, like a cloud From closet long to quiet vowed,
With mothed and dropping arras hung, Mouldering her lute and books among, As when a queen, long dead, was young.

A Grammarian's Funeral Shortly After the Revival of Learning in Europe

Let us begin and carry up this corpse,
Singing together.
Leave we the common crofts, the vulgar thorpes
Each in its tether
Sleeping safe on the bosom of the plain,
Cared-for till cock-crow:
Look out if yonder be not day again
Rimming the rock-row!

That's the appropriate country; there, man's thought,
Rarer, intenser,
Self-gathered for an outbreak, as it ought,
Chafes in the censer.
Leave we the unlettered plain its herd and crop;
Seek we sepulture
On a tall mountain, citied to the top,
Crowded with culture!
All the peaks soar, but one the rest excels;
Clouds overcome it;
No! yonder sparkle is the citadel's
Circling its summit.
Thither our path lies; wind we up the heights:
Wait ye the warning
Our low life was the level's and the night's;
He's for the morning.
Step to a tune, square chests, erect each head,
'Ware the beholders!
This is our master, famous calm and dead,
Borne on our shoulders.
Sleep, crop and herd! sleep, darkling thorpe and croft,
Safe from the weather!
He, whom we convoy to his grave aloft,
Singing together,
He was a man born with thy face and throat,
Lyric Apollo!
Long he lived nameless: how should spring take note
Winter would follow
Till lo, the little touch, and youth was gone!
Cramped and diminished,
Moaned he, "New measures, other feet anon!
"My dance is finished"
No, that's the world's way: (keep the mountain-side,
Make for the city!)
He knew the signal, and stepped on with pride
Over men's pity;
Left play for work, and grappled with the world
Bent on escaping:

"What's in the scroll," quoth he, "thou keepest furled
"Show me their shaping,
"Theirs who most studied man, the bard and sage,—
"Give!"So, he gowned him,
Straight got by heart that hook to its last page:
Learned, we found him.
Yea, but we found him bald too, eyes like lead,
Accents uncertain:
"Time to taste life," another would have said,
"Up with the curtain!"
This man said rather, "Actual life comes next
"Patience a moment!
"Grant I have mastered learning's crabbed text,
"Still there's the comment.
"Let me know all! Prate not of most or least,
"Painful or easy!
"Even to the crumbs I'd fain eat up the feast,
"Ay, nor feel queasy."
Oh, such a life as he resolved to live,
When he had learned it,
When he had gathered all books had to give!
Sooner, he spurned it.
Image the whole, then execute the parts—
Fancy the fabric
Quite, ere you build, ere steel strike fire from quartz,
Ere mortar dab brick!

(Here's the town-gate reached: there's the market-place
Gaping before us.)

Yea, this in him was the peculiar grace
(Hearten our chorus!)
That before living he'd learn how to live—
No end to learning:
Earn the means firstGod surely will contrive
Use for our earning.
Others mistrust and say, "But time escapes:
"Live now or never!"
He said, "What's time Leave Now for dogs and apes!

"Man has Forever."
Back to his book then: deeper drooped his head
Calculus racked him:
Leaden before, his eyes grew dross of lead:
Tussis_ attacked him.
"Now, master, take a little rest!"not he!
(Caution redoubled,
Step two abreast, the way winds narrowly!)
Not a whit troubled
Back to his studies, fresher than at first,
Fierce as a dragon
He (soul-hydroptic with a sacred thirst)
Sucked at the flagon.
Oh, if we draw a circle premature,
Heedless of far gain,
Greedy for quick returns of profit, sure
Bad is our bargain!
Was it not great did not he throw on God,
(He loves the burthen)—
God's task to make the heavenly period
Perfect the earthen
Did not he magnify the mind, show clear
Just what it all meant
He would not discount life, as fools do here,
Paid by instalment.
He ventured neck or nothingheaven's success
Found, or earth's failure:
"Wilt thou trust death or not" He answered "Yes:
"Hence with life's pale lure!"
That low man seeks a little thing to do,
Sees it and does it:
This high man, with a great thing to pursue,
Dies ere he knows it.
That low man goes on adding nine to one,
His hundred's soon hit:
This high man, aiming at a million,
Misses an unit.
That, has the world hereshould he need the next,

Let the world mind him!
This, throws himself on God, and unperplexed
Seeking shall find him.
So, with the throttling hands of death at strife,
Ground he at grammar;
Still, thro' the rattle, parts of speech were rife:
While he could stammer
He settled _Hoti's_ businesslet it be!—
Properly based _Oun_—
Gave us the doctrine of the enclitic _De_,
Dead from the waist down.
Well, here's the platform, here's the proper place:
Hail to your purlieus,
All ye highfliers of the feathered race,
Swallows and curlews!
Here's the top-peak; the multitude below
Live, for they can, there:
This man decided not to Live but Know—
Bury this man there
Herehere's his place, where meteors shoot, clouds form,
Lightnings are loosened,
Stars come and go! Let joy break with the storm,
Peace let the dew send!
Lofty designs must close in like effects
Loftily lying,
Leave himstill loftier than the world suspects,
Living and dying.
A Grammarian's Funeral Shortly after the Revival of Learnin Let us begin and carry up this corpse,
Singing together.
Leave we the common crofts, the vulgar thorpes
Each in its tether
Sleeping safe on the bosom of the plain,
Cared-for till cock-crow:
Look out if yonder be not day again
Rimming the rock-row!
That's the appropriate country; there, man's thought,
Rarer, intenser,

Self-gathered for an outbreak, as it ought,
Chafes in the censer.
Leave we the unlettered plain its herd and crop;
Seek we sepulture
On a tall mountain, citied to the top,
Crowded with culture!
All the peaks soar, but one the rest excels;
Clouds overcome it;
No! yonder sparkle is the citadel's
Circling its summit.
Thither our path lies; wind we up the heights:
Wait ye the warning
Our low life was the level's and the night's;
He's for the morning.
Step to a tune, square chests, erect each head,
'Ware the beholders!
This is our master, famous, calm and dead,
Borne on our shoulders.
Sleep, crop and herd! sleep, darkling thorpe and croft,
Safe from the weather!
He, whom we convoy to his grave aloft,
Singing together,
He was a man born with thy face and throat,
Lyric Apollo!
Long he lived nameless: how should spring take note
Winter would follow
Till lo, the little touch, and youth was gone!
Cramped and diminished,
Moaned he, "New measures, other feet anon!
My dance is finished"
No, that's the world's way: (keep the mountain-side,
Make for the city!)
He knew the signal, and stepped on with pride
Over men's pity;
Left play for work, and grappled with the world
Bent on escaping:
"What's in the scroll," quoth he, "thou keepest furled
"Show me their shaping,

"Theirs who most studied man, the bard and sage,—
"Give!"So, he gowned him,
Straight got by heart that hook to its last page:
Learned, we found him.
Yea, but we found him bald too, eyes like lead,
Accents uncertain:
"Time to taste life," another would have said,
"Up with the curtain!"
This man said rather, "Actual life comes next
"Patience a moment!
"Grant I have mastered learning's crabbed text,
"Still there's the comment.
"Let me know all! Prate not of most or least,
"Painful or easy!
"Even to the crumbs I'd fain eat up the feast,
"Ay, nor feel queasy."
Oh, such a life as he resolved to live,
When he had learned it,
When he had gathered all books had to give!
Sooner, he spurned it.
Image the whole, then execute the parts—
Fancy the fabric
Quite, ere you build, ere steel strike fire from quartz,
Ere mortar dab brick!
(Here's the town-gate reached: there's the market-place
Gaping before us.)
Yea, this in him was the peculiar grace
(Hearten our chorus!)
That before living he'd learn how to live—
No end to learning:
Earn the means firstGod surely will contrive
Use for our earning.
Others mistrust and say, "But time escapes:
"Live now or never!"
He said, "What's time Leave Now for dogs and apes!
"Man has Forever."
Back to his book then: deeper drooped his head
Calculus racked him:

Leaden before, his eyes grew dross of lead:
Tussis attacked him.
"Now, master, take a little rest!"not he!
(Caution redoubled,
Step two abreast, the way winds narrowly!)
Not a whit troubled
Back to his studies, fresher than at first,
Fierce as a dragon
He (soul-hydroptic with a sacred thirst)
Sucked at the flagon.
Oh, if we draw a circle premature,
Heedless of far gain,
Greedy for quick returns of profit, sure
Bad is our bargain!
Was it not great did not he throw on God,
(He loves the burthen)—
God's task to make the heavenly period
Perfect the earthen
Did not he magnify the mind, show clear
Just what it all meant
He would not discount life, as fools do here,
Paid by instalment.
He ventured neck or nothingheaven's success
Found, or earth's failure:
"Wilt thou trust death or not" He answered "Yes:
"Hence with life's pale lure!"
That low man seeks a little thing to do,
Sees it and does it:
This high man, with a great thing to pursue,
Dies ere he knows it.
That low man goes on adding nine to one,
His hundred's soon hit:
This high man, aiming at a million,
Misses an unit.
That, has the world hereshould he need the next,
Let the world mind him!
This, throws himself on God, and unperplexed
Seeking shall find him.

So, with the throttling hands of death at strife,
Ground he at grammar;
Still, thro' the rattle, parts of speech were rife:
While he could stammer
He settled _Hoti's_ businesslet it be!—
Properly based _Oun_—
Gave us the doctrine of the enclitic _De_,
Dead from the waist down.
Well, here's the platform, here's the proper place:
Hail to your purlieus,
All ye highfliers of the feathered race,
Swallows and curlews!
Here's the top-peak; the multitude below
Live, for they can, there:
This man decided not to Live but Know-
Bury this man there
Here—here's his place, where meteors shoot, clouds form,
Lightnings are loosened,
Stars come and go! Let joy break with the storm,
Peace let the dew send!
Lofty designs must close in like effects:
Loftily lying,
Leave him—still loftier than the world suspects,
Living and dying.

A Light Woman

I.

Far as our story approaches the end,
Which do you pity the most of us three—My friend,
Or the mistress of my friend
With her wanton eyes, or me

II.

Friend was already too good to lose,
And seemed in the way of improvement yet, When
She crossed his path with her hunting-noose
And over him drew her net.

III.

I saw him tangled in her toils,
A shame, said I, if she adds just him To her nine-
And-ninety other spoils,
The hundredth for a whim!

IV.

Before my friend be wholly hers,
How easy to prove to him, I said, An eagle's the
Game her pride prefers,
Though she snaps at a wren instead!

V.

I gave her eyes my own eyes to take,
My hand sought hers as in earnest need, And round
She turned for my noble sake,
And gave me herself indeed.

VI.

Eagle am I, with my fame in the world,
The wren is he, with his maiden face. You look away
And your lip is curled
Patience, a moment's space!

VII.

For see, my friend goes shaling and white;
He eyes me as the basilisk:
I have turned, it appears, his day to night,
Eclipsing his sun's disk.

VIII.

And I did it, he thinks, as a very thief:
"Though I love herthat, he comprehends—
"One should master one's passions, (love, in chief)
"And be loyal to one's friends!"

IX.

She,she lies in my hand as tame
As a pear late basking over a wall; Just a

Touch to try and off it came;
'Tis mine,can I let it fall

X.

No mind to eat it, that's the worst!
Were it thrown in the road, would the
Case assist 'Twas quenching a dozen blue-flies' thirst
When I gave its stalk a twist.

XI.

I,what I seem to my friend, you see:
What I soon shall seem to his love, you guess:
What I seem to myself, do you ask of me
No hero, I confess.

XII.

'Tis an awkward thing to play with souls,
And matter enough to save one's own:
Yet think of my friend, and the burning coals
He played with for bits of stone!

XIII.

Likes to show the truth for the truth;
That the woman was light is very true:
But suppose she says,Never mind that youth!
What wrong have I done to you

XIV.

Well, any how, here the story stays,
So far at least as I understand;
And, Robert Browning, you writer of plays,
Here's a subject made to your hand!

A Lovers' Quarrel

I.

Oh, what a dawn of day!

How the March sun feels like May!
All is blue again
After last night's rain,
And the South dries the hawthorn-spray.
Only, my Love's away!
I'd as lief that the blue were grey,

II.

Which rillets swell, Must be dancing down the dell,
With a foaming head
On the beryl bed
Paven smooth as a hermit's cell;
Each with a tale to tell,
Could my Love but attend as well.

III.

Dearest, three months ago!
When we lived blocked-up with snow,—
When the wind would edge
In and in his wedge,
In, as far as the point could go—
Not to our ingle, though,
Where we loved each the other so!

IV.

With so little cause! We devised games out of straws.
We would try and trace
One another's face
In the ash, as an artist draws;
Free on each other's flaws,
How we chattered like two church daws!

V.

In the `Times''a scold At the Emperor deep and cold;
He has taken a bride
To his gruesome side,
That's as fair as himself is bold: There they
Sit ermine-stoled, And she powders her hair with gold.

VI.

Fancy the Pampas' sheen! Miles and
miles of gold and green
Where the sunflowers blow In a solid glow,
Andto break now and then the screen—
Black neck and eyeballs keen,
Up a wild horse leaps between!

VII.

Try, will our table turn
Lay your hands there light, and yearn
Till the yearning slips
Thro' the finger-tips
In a fire which a few discern,
And a very few feel burn,
And the rest, they may live and learn!

VIII.

we would up and pace, For a change, about the place,
Each with arm o'er neck: 'Tis our quarter-deck,
are seamen in woeful case.
Help in the ocean-space! Or, if no help, we'll embrace.

IX.

See, how she looks now, dressed
In a sledging-cap and vest! '
Tis a huge fur cloak—Like a reindeer's yoke
The lappet along the breast:
Sleeves for her arms to rest,
Or to hang, as my Love likes best.

X.

Me to flirt a fan As the Spanish ladies can,
Or I tint your lip
With a burnt stick's tip
you turn into such a man!
Just the two spots that span
Half the bill of the young male swan.

XI.

Dearest, three months ago When the mesmerizer Snow
With his hand's first sweep Put the earth to sleep:
'Twas a time when the heart could show
Allhow was earth to know,
'Neath the mute hand's to-and-fro

XII.

Three months ago When we loved each other so,
Lived and loved the same Till an evening came
When a shaft from the devil's bow
Pierced to our ingle-glow,
And the friends were friend and foe!

XIII.

From the heart beneath—'Twas a bubble born of breath,
Neither sneer nor vaunt, Nor reproach nor taunt.
See a word, how it severeth!
Oh, power of life and death
In the tongue, as the Preacher saith!

XIV.

And will you cast For a word, quite off at last
Me, your own, your You,—Since, as truth is true,
I was You all the happy past—
Me do you leave aghast
With the memories We amassed

XV.

If you knew the light That your soul casts in my sight,
How I look to you
For the pure and true
And the beauteous and the right,—
Bear with a moment's spite
When a mere mote threats the white!

XVI.

What of a hasty word
Is the fleshly heart not stirred

By a worm's pin-prick
Where its roots are quick
See the eye, by a fly's foot blurred—
Ear, when a straw is heard
Scratch the brain's coat of curd!

XVII.

Be the world or fair More or less, how can I care
'Tis the world the same For my praise or blame,
And endurance is easy there.
Wrong in the one thing rare—Oh, it is hard to bear!

XVIII.

'S the spring back or close,
When the almond-blossom blows:
We shall have the word
In a minor third
There is none but the cuckoo knows:
Heaps of the guelder-rose!
I must bear with it, I suppose.

XIX.

But November come, Were the noisy birds struck dumb
At the warning slash
Of his driver's-lash—
I would laugh like the valiant Thumb
Facing the castle glum
And the giant's fee-faw-fum!

XX.

Were the world well stripped
Of the gear wherein equipped
We can stand apart,
Heart dispense with heart
The sun, with the flowers unnipped,—
Oh, the world's hangings ripped,
We were both in a bare-walled crypt!

XXI.

In the crypt would cry "But one freezes here! and why
"When a heart, as chill,
"At my own would thrill
"Back to life, and its fires out-fly
"Heart, shall we live or die
"The rest... . settle by-and-by!"

XXII.

She'd efface the score, And forgive me as before.
It is twelve o'clock: I shall hear her knock
The worst of a storm's uproar,
I shall pull her through the door,
I shall have her for evermore!

A Pretty Woman

I.

That fawn-skin-dappled hair of hers,
And the blue eye
Dear and dewy,
And that infantine fresh air of hers!

II.

To think men cannot take you, Sweet,
And enfold you,
Ay, and hold you,
And so keep you what they make you, Sweet!

III

You like us for a glance, you know—
For a word's sake
Or a sword's sake,
All's the same, whate'er the chance, you know.

IV.

And in turn we make you ours, we say—
You and youth too,

Eyes and mouth too,
All the face composed of flowers, we say.

V.

All's our own, to make the most of, Sweet—
Sing and say for,
Watch and pray for,
Keep a secret or go boast of, Sweet!

VI.

But for loving, why, you would not, Sweet,
Though we prayed you,
Paid you, brayed you
in a mortarfor you could not, Sweet!

VII.

So, we leave the sweet face fondly there:
Be its beauty
Its sole duty!
Let all hope of grace beyond, lie there!

VIII.

And while the face lies quiet there,
Who shall wonder That I ponder
A conclusion I will try it there.

IX.

As,why must one, for the love foregone,
Scout mere liking
Thunder-striking
Earth,the heaven, we looked above for, gone!

X.

Why, with beauty, needs there money be,

Love with liking
Crush the fly-king
In his gauze, because no honey-bee

XI.

May not liking be so simple-sweet,
If love grew there
'Twould undo there
All that breaks the cheek to dimples sweet

XII.

Is the creature too imperfect,
Would you mend it
And so end it
Since not all addition perfects aye!

XIII.

Or is it of its kind, perhaps,
Just perfection—
Whence, rejection
Of a grace not to its mind, perhaps

XIV.

Shall we burn up, tread that face at once
Into tinder,
And so hinder
Sparks from kindling all the place at once

XV.

Or else kiss away one's soul on her
Your love-fancies!
A sick man sees
Truer, when his hot eyes roll on her!

XVI.

Thus the craftsman thinks to grace the rose,—
Plucks a mould-flower
For his gold flower,
Uses fine things that efface the rose:

XVII.

Rosy rubies make its cup more rose,

Precious metals
Ape the petals,—
Last, some old king locks it up, morose!

XVIII.

Then how grace a rose I know a way!
Leave it, rather.
Must you gather
Smell, kiss, wear itat last, throw away!

A Serenade At The Villa

I.

was I, you heard last night,

When there rose no moon at all,

Nor, to pierce the strained and tight

Tent of heaven, a planet small:
Life was dead and so was light.

II.

Twinkle from the fly,
Not a glimmer from the worm;
When the crickets stopped their cry,
When the owls forbore a term,
You heard music; that was I.

III.

Earth turned in her sleep with pain,
Sultrily suspired for proof:
At heaven and out again,
Lightning!where it broke the roof,
Bloodlike, some few drops of rain.

IV.

What they could my words expressed,
O my love, my all, my one!

helped the verses best,
And when singing's best was done,
To my lute I left the rest.

V.

Wore night; the East was gray,
White the broad-faced hemlock-flowers:
There would be another day;
Ere its first of heavy hours Found me,
I had passed away.

VI.

Became of all the hopes,
Words and song and lute as well Say,
This struck you"When life gropes
"Feebly for the path where fell "
Light last on the evening slopes,

VII.

"One friend in that path shall be,
"To secure my step from wrong;
"One to count night day for me,
"Patient through the watches long,
"Serving most with none to see."

VIII.

sayas something bodes—
"So, the worst has yet a worse! "When life halts 'neath double loads,
"Better the taskmaster's curse "Than such music on the roads!

IX.

"When no moon succeeds the sun,
"Nor can pierce the midnight's tent "Any star, the smallest one,
"While some drops, where lightning rent, "Show the final storm begun—

X.

"When the fire-fly hides its spot,
"When the garden-voices fail "In the darkness thick and hot,—
"Shall another voice avail,
"That shape be where these are not

XI.

"Has some plague a longer lease,
"Proffering its help uncouth "Can't one even die in peace
"As one shuts one's eyes on youth, "Is that face the last one sees"

XII.

How dark your villa was,
Windows fast and obdurate! How the garden grudged me grass
Where I stoodthe iron gate Ground its teeth to let me pass!

A Toccata Of Galuppi's

I.

Oh Galuppi, Baldassaro, this is very sad to find!
Can hardly misconceive you; it would prove me deaf and blind; But although I take your meaning, 'tis with such a heavy mind!

II.

You come with all your music, and here's all the good it brings. What, they lived once thus at Venice where the merchants were the kings, Where Saint Mark's is, where the Doges used to wed the sea with rings

III.

Ay, because the sea's the street there; and 'tis arched by... what you call... Shylock's bridge with houses on it, where they kept the carnival: I was never out of Englandit's as if I saw it all.

IV.

Young people take their pleasure when the sea was warm in May Balls and masks begun at midnight, burning ever to mid-day, When they made up fresh adventures for the morrow, do you say

V.

A lady such a lady, cheeks so round and lips so red,—On her neck the small face buoyant, like a bell-flower on its bed, O'er the breast's superb abundance where a man might base his head

VI.

And it was graceful of themthey'd break talk off and afford She, to bite her mask's black velvethe, to finger on his sword, While you sat and played Toccatas, stately at the clavichord

VII.

Those lesser thirds so plaintive, sixths diminished, sigh on sigh, Told them something Those suspensions, those solutions"Must we die" Those commiserating sevenths"Life might last! we can but try!"

VIII.

"Were you happy""Yes.""And are you still as happy""Yes. And you" "Then, more kisses!""Did _I_ stop them, when a million seemed so few" Hark, the dominant's persistence till it must be answered to!

IX.

So, an octave struck the answer. Oh, they praised you, I dare say!

"Brave Galuppi! that was music! good alike at grave and gay! "I can always leave off talking when I hear a master play!"

X.

They left you for their pleasure: till in due time, one by

one, Some with lives that came to nothing, some with deeds as well undone, Death stepped tacitly and took them where they never see the sun.

XI.

When I sit down to reason, think to take my stand nor swerve, While I triumph o'er a secret wrung from nature's close reserve, In you come with your cold music till I creep thro' every nerve.

XII.

, you, like a ghostly cricket, creaking where a house was burned: "Dust and ashes, dead and done with, Venice spent what Venice earned. "The soul, doubtless, is immortalwhere a soul can be discerned.

XIII.

"Yours for instance: you know physics, something of geology, "Mathematics are your pastime; souls shall rise in their degree; "Butterflies may dread extinction,you'll not die, it cannot be!

XIV.

"As for Venice and her people, merely born to bloom and drop, "Here on earth they bore their fruitage, mirth and folly were the crop: "What of soul was left, I wonder, when the kissing had to stop

XV.

"Dust and ashes!" So you creak it, and I want the heart to scold. Dear dead women, with such hair, toowhat's become of all the gold Used to hang and brush their bosoms I feel chilly and grown old.. An overturea touch piece.

I.

A Woman's Last Word I.
Let's contend no more, Love,
Strive nor weep:

All be as before, Love,
Only sleep!

II.

What so wild as words are
I and thou
In debate, as birds are,
Hawk on bough!

III.

See the creature stalking
While we speak!
Hush and hide the talking,
Cheek on cheek!

IV.

What so false as truth is,
False to thee
Where the serpent's tooth is
Shun the tree—

V.

Where the apple reddens
Never pry—
Lest we lose our Edens,
Eve and I.

VI.

Be a god and hold me
With a charm!
Be a man and fold me
With thine arm!

VII.

Teach me, only teach, Love
As I ought
I will speak thy speech, Love,
Think thy thought—

VIII.

Meet, if thou require it,
Both demands,
Laying flesh and spirit
In thy hands.

IX.

That shall be to-morrow
Not to-night:
I must bury sorrow
Out of sight:

X.

Must a little weep, Love,
(Foolish me!)

After

Take the cloak from his face, and at first
Let the corpse do its worst!
He lies in his rights of a man!
Death has done all death can.
And, absorbed in the new life he leads,
He recks not, he heeds
Nor his wrong nor my vengeance; both strike
On his senses alike,
And are lost in the solemn and strange
Surprise of the change.
What avails death to erase
His offence, my disgrace I would
We were boys as of old
In the field, by the fold:
His outrage, God's patience, man's scorn
Were so easily borne!
I stand here now, he lies in his place:
Cover the face!

Aix In Provence

God who savest man, save most of men Count Gismond

who saved me! Count Gauthier, when he chose his post, Chose time and place and company To suit it; when he struck at length My honour, 'twas with all his strength.

II.

Doubtlessly ere he could draw
All points to one, he must have schemed! That miserable morning saw Few half so happy as I seemed, While being dressed in queen's array To give our tourney prize away.

III.

Thought they loved me, did me grace
To please themselves; 'twas all their deed; God makes, or fair or foul, our face;
If showing mine so caused to bleed My cousins' hearts, they should have dropped A word, and straight the play had stopped.

IV.

Too, so beauteous! Each a queen
By virtue of her brow and breast; Not needing to be crowned, I mean,
As I do. E'en when I was dressed, Had either of them spoke, instead Of glancing sideways with still head!

V.

No: they let me laugh, and sing
My birthday song quite through, adjust The last rose in my garland, fling
A last look on the mirror, trust My arms to each an arm of theirs, And so descend the castle-stairs—

VI.

Come out on the morning-troop
Of merry friends who kissed my cheek, And called me queen, and made me stoop
Under the canopy(a streak
That pierced it, of the outside sun, Powdered with gold its gloom's soft dun)—

VII.

They could let me take my state
And foolish throne amid applause of
all come there to celebrate
My queen's-dayOh I think the cause Of much was, they forgot no crowd Makes up for parents in their shroud!

VIII.

That be, all eyes were bent
Upon me, when my cousins cast Theirs down; 'twas time I should present
The victor's crown, but... there, 'twill last No long time... the old mist again Blinds me as then it did. How vain!

IX.

Gismond's at the gate, in talk
With his two boys: I can proceed. Well, at that moment, who should stalk
Forth boldlyto my face, indeed—But Gauthier, and he thundered "Stay!" And all stayed. "Bring no crowns, I say!

X.

"Bring torches! Wind the penance-sheet
"About her! Let her shun the chaste, "Or lay herself before their feet!
"Shall she whose body I embraced "A night long, queen it in the day "For honour's sake no crowns, I say!"

XI.

What I answered As I live,
I never fancied such a thing As answer possible to give.
What says the body when they spring Some monstrous torture-engine's whole Strength on it No more says the soul.

XII.

Out strode Gismond; then I knew
That I was saved. I never met His face before, but, at first view,

I felt quite sure that God had set Himself to Satan; who would spend
A minute's mistrust on the end

XIII.

Strode to Gauthier, in his throat
Gave him the lie, then struck his mouth With one back-handed blow that wrote
In blood men's verdict there. North, South, East, West, I looked. The lie was dead, And damned, and truth stood up instead.

XIV.

Glads me most, that I enjoyed
The heart of the joy, with my content In watching Gismond unalloyed
By any doubt of the event: God took that on himI was bid
Watch Gismond for my part: I did.

XV.

I not watch him while he let
His armourer just brace his greaves, Rivet his hauberk, on the fret
The while! His foot... my memory leaves No least stamp out, nor how anon He pulled his ringing gauntlets on.

XVI.

E'en before the trumpet's sound
Was finished, prone lay the false knight, Prone as his lie, upon the ground:
Gismond flew at him, used no sleight O' the sword, but open-breasted drove, Cleaving till out the truth he clove.

XVII.

Done, he dragged him to my feet
And said "Here die, but end thy breath "In full confession, lest thou fleet
"From my first, to God's second death! "Say, hast thou

lied" And, "I have lied "To God and her," he said, and died.

XVIII.

Gismond, kneeling to me, asked
What safe my heart holds, though no word Could I repeat now, if I tasked
My powers forever, to a third Dear even as you are. Pass the rest Until I sank upon his breast.

XIX.

My head his arm he flung
Against the world; and scarce I felt His sword (that dripped by me and swung)
A little shifted in its belt:
he began to say the while How South our home lay many a mile.

XX.

'Mid the shouting multitude
We two walked forth to never more Return. My cousins have pursued
Their life, untroubled as before I vexed them. Gauthier's dwelling-place God lighten! May his soul find grace!

XXI.

Our elder boy has got the clear
Great brow; tho' when his brother's black Full eye slows scorn, it... Gismond here And have you brought my tercel back I just was telling Adela
How many birds it struck since May. A male of the peregrine falcon.

By The Fire-Side

I.

Well I know what I mean to do
When the long dark autumn-evenings come:
And where, my soul, is thy pleasant hue

With the music of all thy voices,
Dumb In life's November too!

II.

Shall be found by the fire, suppose,
O'er a great wise book as beseemeth age,
While the shutters flap as the cross-wind blows
And I turn the page, and I turn the page,
Not verse now, only prose!

III.

The young ones whisper, finger on lip,
"There he is at it, deep in Greek:
"Now then, or never, out we slip
"To cut from the hazels by the creek
"A mainmast for our ship!"

IV.

Shall be at it indeed, my friends:
Greek puts already on either side
Such a branch-work forth as soon extends
To a vista opening far and wide,
And I pass out where it ends.

V.

Outside-frame, like your hazel-trees:
But the inside-archway widens fast,
And a rarer sort succeeds to these,
And we slope to Italy at last
And youth, by green degrees.

VI.

Follow wherever I am led,
Knowing so well the leader's hand:
Oh woman-country, wooed not wed,
Loved all the more by earth's male-lands,
Laid to their hearts instead!

VII.

Look at the ruined chapel again
Half-way up in the Alpine gorge!
Is that a tower, I point you plain,
Or is it a mill, or an iron-forge
Breaks solitude in vain

VIII.

Turn, and we stand in the heart of things:
The woods are round us, heaped and dim;
From slab to slab how it slips and springs,
The thread of water single and slim,
Through the ravage some torrent brings!

IX.

It feed the little lake below
That speck of white just on its marge
Is Pella; see, in the evening-glow,
How sharp the silver spear-heads charge
When Alp meets heaven in snow!

X.

Our other side is the straight-up rock;
And a path is kept 'twixt the gorge and it
By boulder-stones where lichens mock
The marks on a moth, and small ferns fit
Their teeth to the polished block.

XI.

The sense of the yellow mountain-flowers,
And thorny balls, each three in one,
The chestnuts throw on our path in showers!
For the drop of the woodland fruit's begun,
These early November hours,

XII.

Crimson the creeper's leaf across

Like a splash of blood, intense, abrupt,
O'er a shield else gold from rim to boss,
And lay it for show on the fairy-cupped
Elf-needled mat of moss,

XIII.

The rose-flesh mushrooms, undivulged
Last eveningnay, in to-day's first dew
Yon sudden coral nipple bulged,
Where a freaked fawn-coloured flaky crew
Of toadstools peep indulged.

XIV.

Yonder, at foot of the fronting ridge
That takes the turn to a range beyond,
Is the chapel reached by the one-arched bridge
Where the water is stopped in a stagnant pond
Danced over by the midge.

XV.

The chapel and bridge are of stone alike,
Blackish-grey and mostly wet;
hemp-stalks steep in the narrow dyke.
See here again, how the lichens fret
And the roots of the ivy strike!

XVI.

Poor little place, where its one priest comes
On a festa-day, if he comes at all,
The dozen folk from their scattered homes,
Gathered within that precinct small
By the dozen ways one roams—

XVII.

Drop from the charcoal-burners' huts,
Or climb from the hemp-dressers' low shed,
Leave the grange where the woodman stores his nuts,
Or the wattled cote where the fowlers spread
Their gear on the rock's bare juts.

XVIII.

Has some pretension too, this front,
With its bit of fresco half-moon-wise
Set over the porch, Art's early wont:
'Tis John in the Desert, I surmise,
But has borne the weather's brunt—

XIX.

Not from the fault of the builder, though,
For a pent-house properly projects
three carved beams make a certain show,
Datinggood thought of our architect's—
Five, six, nine, he lets you know.

XX.

And all day long a bird sings there,
And a stray sheep drinks at the pond at times;
The place is silent and aware;
It has had its scenes, its joys and crimes,
But that is its own affair.

XXI.

My perfect wife, my Leonor,
Oh heart, my own, oh eyes, mine too,
Whom else could I dare look backward for,
With whom beside should I dare pursue
The path grey heads abhor

XXII.

It leads to a crag's sheer edge with them;
Youth, flowcry all the way, there stops—
Not they; age threatens and they contemn,
Till they reach the gulf wherein youth drops,
One inch from life's safe hem!

XXIII.

Me, youth led... I will speak now,
No longer watch you as you sit

Reading by fire-light, that great brow
And the spirit-small hand propping it,
Mutely, my heart knows how—

XXIV.

If I think but deep enough,
You are wont to answer, prompt as rhyme;
And you, too, find without rebuff
Response your soul seeks many a time
Piercing its fine flesh-stuff.

XXV.

Own, confirm me! If I tread
This path back, is it not in pride
To think how little I dreamed it led
To an age so blest that, by its side,
Youth seems the waste instead

XXVI.

Own, see where the years conduct!
At first, 'twas something our two souls
Should mix as mists do; each is sucked
In each now: on, the new stream rolls,
Whatever rocks obstruct.

XXVII.

When our one soul understands
The great Word which makes all things new,
When earth breaks up and heaven expands,
How will the change strike me and you
In the house not made with hands

XXVIII.

I must feel your brain prompt mine,
Your heart anticipate my heart,
You must be just before, in fine,
See and make me see, for your part,
New depths of the divine!

XXIX.

Who could have expected this
When we two drew together first
Just for the obvious human bliss,
To satisfy life's daily thirst
With a thing men seldom miss

XXX.

Back with me to the first of all,
Let us lean and love it over again,
Let us now forget and now recall,
Break the rosary in a pearly rain,
And gather what we let fall!

XXXI.

Did I saythat a small bird sings
All day long, save when a brown pair
Of hawks from the wood float with wide wings
Strained to a bell: 'gainst noon-day glare
You count the streaks and rings.

XXXII.

At afternoon or almost eve
'Tis better; then the silence grows
To that degree, you half believe
It must get rid of what it knows,
Its bosom does so heave.

XXXIII.

Hither we walked then, side by side,
Arm in arm and cheek to cheek,
And still I questioned or replied,
While my heart, convulsed to really speak,
Lay choking in its pride.

XXXIV.

The crumbling bridge we cross,
And pity and praise the chapel sweet,

And care about the fresco's loss,
And wish for our souls a like retreat,
And wonder at the moss.

XXXV.

And kneel on the settle under,
Look through the window's grated square:
Nothing to see! For fear of plunder,
The cross is down and the altar bare,
As if thieves don't fear thunder.

XXXVI.

Stoop and look in through the grate,
See the little porch and rustic door,
Read duly the dead builder's date;
Then cross the bridge that we crossed before,
Take the path againbut wait!

XXXVII.

Moment, one and infinite!
The water slips o'er stock and stone;
The West is ender, hardly bright:
How grey at once is the evening grown—
One star, its chrysolite!

XXXVIII.

Two stood there with never a third,
But each by each, as each knew well:
The sights we saw and the sounds we heard,
The lights and the shades made up a spell
Till the trouble grew and stirred.

XXXIX.

The little more, and how much it is!
And the little less, and what worlds away!
How a sound shall quicken content to bliss,
Or a breath suspend the blood's best play,
And life be a proof of this!

XL.

She willed it, still had stood the screen
So slight, so sure, 'twixt my love and her:
I could fix her face with a guard between,
And find her soul as when friends confer,
Friendslovers that might have been.

XLI.

For my heart had a touch of the woodland-time,
Wanting to sleep now over its best.
The whole tree in the summer-prime,
But bring to the Iast leaf no such test!
"Hold the last fast!" runs the rhyme.

XLII.

A chance to make your little much,
To gain a lover and lose a friend,
Venture the tree and a myriad such,
When nothing you mar but the year can mend:
But a last leaffear to touch!

XLIII.

Should it unfasten itself and fall
Eddying down till it find your face
At some slight windbest chance of all!
Be your heart henceforth its dwelling-place
You trembled to forestall!

XLIV.

How well, those dark grey eyes,
That hair so dark and dear, how worth
That a man should strive and agonize,
And taste a veriest hell on earth
For the hope of such a prize!

XIIV.

Might have turned and tried a man,
Set him a space to weary and wear,

And prove which suited more your plan,
His best of hope or his worst despair,
Yet end as he began.

XLVI.

But you spared me this, like the heart you are,
And filled my empty heart at a word.
If two lives join, there is oft a scar,
They are one and one, with a shadowy third;
One near one is too far.

XLVII.

Moment after, and hands unseen
Were hanging the night around us fast
But we knew that a bar was broken between
Life and life: we were mixed at last
In spite of the mortal screen.

XLVIII.

Forests had done it; there they stood;
We caught for a moment the powers at play:
They had mingled us so, for once and good,
Their work was donewe might go or stay,
They relapsed to their ancient mood.

XLIX.

The world is made for each of us!
How all we perceive and know in it
Tends to some moment's product thus,
When a soul declares itselfto wit,
By its fruit, the thing it does

L.

Hate that fruit or love that fruit,
It forwards the general deed of man,
And each of the Many helps to recruit
The life of the race by a general plan;
Each living his own, to boot.

LI.

I am named and known by that moment's feat;
There took my station and degree;
grew my own small life complete,
As nature obtained her best of me—
One born to love you, sweet!

LII.

And to watch you sink by the fire-side now
Back again, as you mutely sit
by fire-light, that great brow
And the spirit-small hand propping it,
Yonder, my heart knows how!

LIII.

Earth has gained by one man the more,
And the gain of earth must be heaven's gain too;
And the whole is well worth thinking o'er
When autumn comes: which I mean to do
One day, as I said before.

MARCHING ALONG.

I.

Kentish Sir Byng stood for his King,
Bidding the crop-headed Parliament swing:
And, pressing a troop unable to stoop
See the rogues flourish and honest folk droop,
Marched them along, fifty-score strong,
Great-hearted gentlemen, singing this song.

II.

God for King Charles! Pym and such carles
To the Devil that prompts 'em their
Treasonous parles! Cavaliers, up!
Lips from the cup,
Hands from the pasty, nor bite take nor sup Till you're—

CHORUS.Marching along, fifty-score strong,
Great-hearted gentlemen, singing this song.

III.

Hampden to hell, and his obsequies'
knell Serve Hazelrig, Fiennes, and young
Harry as well! England, good cheer! Rupert is near!
And loyalists, keep we not here CHORUS.
Marching along, fifty-score strong,
Great-hearted gentlemen, singing this song

IV.

God for King Charles! Pym and his snarls
To the Devil that pricks on such pestilent carles!
Hold by the right, you double your might;
So, onward to Nottingham, fresh for the fight,
CHORUS.March we along, fifty-score strong,
Great-hearted gentlemen, singing this song!

II. GIVE A ROUSE

I.

King Charles, and who'll do him right now
King Charles, and who's ripe for fight now
Give a rouse: here's, in hell's despite now,
King Charles!

II.

Who gave me the goods that went since
Who raised me the house that sank once
Who helped me to gold I spent since
Who found me in wine you drank once
CHORUS.King Charles, and who'll do him right now
King Charles, and who's ripe for fight now
Give a rouse: here's, in hell's despite now, King Charles!

III.

To whom used my boy George quaff else,

By the old fool's side that begot him
For whom did he cheer and laugh else,
While Noll's damned troopers shot him
CHORUS.King Charles, and who'll do him right now
King Charles, and who's ripe for fight now
Give a rouse: here's, in hell's despite now, King Charles!

III. BOOT AND SADDLE

I.

Saddle, to horse, and away!
Rescue my castle before the hot day
Brightens to blue from its silvery grey,
CHORUS.Boot, saddle, to horse, and away!

II.

Past the suburbs, asleep as you'd say;
Many's the friend there, will listen and pray
"God's luck to gallants that strike up the lay—
CHORUS."Boot, saddle, to horse, and away!"

III.

Forty miles off, like a roebuck at bay,
Flouts Castle Brancepeth the Roundheads' array:
Who laughs, "Good fellows ere this, by my fay,
CHORUS."Boot, saddle, to horse, and away!"

IV.

Who My wife Gertrude; that, honest and gay,
Laughs when you talk of surrendering,
"Nay! "I've better counsellors; what counsel they
CHORUS."Boot, saddle, to horse, and away!"
Cavalier Tunes: Boot and Saddle
Boot, saddle, to horse and away!
Rescue my Castle, before the hot day
Brightens to blue from its silvery gray, (Chorus)
Boot, saddle, to horse, and away!
Ride past the suburbs, asleep as you'd say;

Many's the friend there, will listen and pray
"God's luck to gallants that strike up the lay-(Chorus)
Boot, saddle, to horse, and away!"
Forty miles off, like a roebuck at bay,
Flouts Castle Brancepeth the Roundheads' array:
Who laughs, "Good fellows ere this, by my fay, (Chorus)
Boot, saddle, to horse, and away!"
Who My wife Gertrude; that, honest and gay,
Laughs when you talk of surrendering,
"Nay! I've better counsellors; what counsel they
(Chorus)
Boot, saddle, to horse, and away!"
Cavalier Tunes: Give a Rouse King
Charles, and who'll do him right now
King Charles, and who's ripe for fight now
Give a rouse: here's, in Hell's despite now,
King Charles!
Who gave me the goods that went since
Who raised me the house that sank once
Who helped me to gold I spent since
Who found me in wine you drank once
(Chorus)
King Charles, and who'll do him right now
King Charles, and who's ripe for fight now
Give a rouse: here's, in Hell's despite now,
King Charles!
To whom used my boy George quaff else,
By the old fool's side that begot him
For whom did he cheer and laugh else,
While Noll's damned troopers shot him
(Chorus)
King Charles, and who'll do him right now
King Charles, and who's ripe for fight now
Give a rouse: here's, in Hell's despite now,
King Charles! Cavalier Tunes: Marching
Along Kentish Sir Byng stood for his King,
Bidding the crop-headed Parliament swing:
And, pressing a troop unable to stoop

See the rogues flourish and honest folk droop,
Marched them along, fifty score strong,
Great-hearted gentlemen, singing this song.
God for King Charles! Pym and such carles
To the Devil that prompts 'em their treasonous parles!
Cavaliers, up! Lips from the cup,
Hands from the pasty, nor bite take nor sup
Till you're-
(Chorus)
Marching along, fifty-score strong,
Great-hearted gentlemen, singing this song.
Hampden to hell, and his obsequies' knell.
Serve Hazelrig, Fiennes, and young Harry as well!
England, good cheer! Rupert is near!
Kentish and loyalists, keep we not here
(Chorus)
Marching along, fifty-score strong,
Great-hearted gentlemen, singing this song
Then, God for King Charles! Pym and his snarls
To the Devil that pricks on such pestilent carles!
Hold by the right, you double your might;
So, onward to Nottingham, fresh for the fight,
(Chorus)
March we along, fifty-score strong,
Great-hearted gentlemen, singing this song!
Childe Roland To The Dark Tower Came

I.

First thought was, he lied in every word,
That hoary cripple, with malicious eye
Askance to watch the working of his lic
On mine, and mouth scarce able to afford
Suppression of the glee, that pursed and scored
Its edge, at one more victim gained thereby.

II.

Else should he be set for, with his staff
What, save to waylay with his lies, ensnare

All travellers who might find him posted there,
And ask the road I guessed what skull-like laugh
Would break, what crutch 'gin write my epitaph
For pastime in the dusty thoroughfare,

III.

At his counsel I should turn aside
Into that ominous tract which, all agree,
Hides the Dark Tower. Yet acquiescingly
I did turn as he pointed: neither pride
Nor hope rekindling at the end descried,
So much as gladness that some end might be.

IV.

For, what with my whole world-wide wandering,
What with my search drawn out thro' years,
My hope Dwindled into a ghost not fit to cope
That obstreperous joy success would bring,
I hardly tried now to rebuke the spring
My heart made, finding failure in its scope.

V.

When a sick man very near to death
Seems dead indeed, and feels begin and end
The tears and takes the farewell of each friend,
And hears one bid the other go, draw breath
Freelier outside, ("since all is o'er," he saith,
"And the blow fallen no grieving can amend;")

VI.

Some discuss if near the other graves
Be room enough for this, and when a day
Suits best for carrying the corpse away,
With care about the banners, scarves and staves:
And still the man hears all, and only craves
He may not shame such tender love and stay.

VII.

I had so long suffered in this quest,

Heard failure prophesied so oft, been writ
So many times among "The Band"to wit,
The knights who to the Dark
Tower's search addressed Their stepsthat just
to fail as they, seemed best,
And all the doubt was nowshould I be fit

VIII.

Quiet as despair, I turned from him,
That hateful cripple, out of his highway
Into the path he pointed. All the day
Had been a dreary one at best, and dim
Was settling to its close, yet shot one grim
Red leer to see the plain catch its estray.

IX.

Mark! no sooner was I fairly found
Pledged to the plain, after a pace or two,
Than, pausing to throw backward a last view
O'er the safe road, 'twas gone; grey plain all round:
Nothing but plain to the horizon's bound.
I might go on; nought else remained to do.

X.

So, on I went. I think I never saw
Such starved ignoble nature; nothing throve:
For flowersas well expect a cedar grove!
But cockle, spurge, according to their law
Might propagate their kind, with none to awe,
You'd think; a burr had been a treasure-trove.

XI.

No! penury, inertness and grimace,
In some strange sort, were the land's portion.
"See "Or shut your eyes," said nature peevishly,
"It nothing skills: I cannot help my case:
Tis the Last judgment's fire must cure this place,
"Calcine its clods and set my prisoners free."

XII.

If there pushed any ragged thistle-stalk
Above its mates, the head was chopped; the bents
Were jealous else. What made those holes and rents
In the dock's harsh swarth leaves, bruised as to baulk
All hope of greenness'tis a brute must walk
Pashing their life out, with a brute's intents.

XIII.

For the grass, it grew as scant as hair
In leprosy; thin dry blades pricked the mud
Which underneath looked kneaded up with blood.
One stiff blind horse, his every bone a-stare,
Stood stupefied, however he came there:
Thrust out past service from the devil's stud!

XIV.

He might be dead for aught I know,
With that red gaunt and colloped neck a-strain,
And shut eyes underneath the rusty mane;
Seldom went such grotesqueness with such woe;
I never saw a brute I hated so;
He must be wicked to deserve such pain.

XV.

Shut my eyes and turned them on my heart.
As a man calls for wine before he fights,
I asked one draught of earlier, happier sights,
Ere fitly I could hope to play my part.
Think first, fight afterwardsthe soldier's art:
One taste of the old time sets all to rights.

XVI.

It! I fancied Cuthbert's reddening face
Beneath its garniture of curly gold,
Dear fellow, till I almost felt him fold
An arm in mine to fix me to the place,

That way he used. Alas, one night's disgrace!
Out went my heart's new fire and left it cold.

XVII.

Then, the soul of honourthere he stands
Frank as ten years ago when knighted first.
What honest man should dare (he said) he durst.
Goodbut the scene shiftsfaugh! what
Hangman hands Pin to his breast a parchment
His own bands Read it.
Poor traitor, spit upon and curst!

XVIII.

Better this present than a past like that;
Back therefore to my darkening path again!
No sound, no sight as far as eye could strain.
Will the night send a howlet or a bat
I asked: when something on the dismal flat
Came to arrest my thoughts and change their train.

XIX.

Sudden little river crossed my path
As unexpected as a serpent comes.
No sluggish tide congenial to the glooms;
This, as it frothed by, might have been a bath
For the fiend's glowing hoofto see the wrath
Of its black eddy bespate with flakes and spumes.

XX.

Petty yet so spiteful! All along,
Low scrubby alders kneeled down over it;
Drenched willows flung them headlong in a fit
Of route despair, a suicidal throng:
The river which had done them all the wrong,
Whate'er that was, rolled by, deterred no whit.

XXI.

While I forded,good saints, how I feared

To set my foot upon a dead man's cheek,
Each step, or feel the spear I thrust to seek
For hollows, tangled in his hair or beard!
It may have been a water-rat I speared,
But, ugh! it sounded like a baby's shriek.

XXII.

Was I when I reached the other bank.
Now for a better country. Vain presage!
Who were the strugglers, what war did they wage,
Whose savage trample thus could pad the dank
Soil to a plash Toads in a poisoned tank,
Or wild cats in a red-hot iron cage—

XXIII.

Fight must so have seemed in that fell cirque.
What penned them there, with all the plain to choose
No foot-print leading to that horrid mews,
None out of it. Mad brewage set to work
Their brains, no doubt, like galley-slaves the Turk
Pits for his pastime, Christians against Jews.

XXIV.

And more than thata furlong onwhy, there!
What bad use was that engine for, that wheel,
Or brake, not wheelthat harrow fit to reel
Men's bodies out like silk with all the air
Of Tophet's tool, on earth left unaware,
Or brought to sharpen its rusty teeth of steel.

XXV.

Came a bit of stubbed ground, once a wood,
Next a marsh, it would seem, and now mere earth
Desperate and done with; (so a fool finds mirth,
Makes a thing and then mars it, till his mood
Changes and off he goes!) within a rood—
Bog, clay and rubble, sand and stark black dearth.

XXVI.

Blotches rankling, coloured gay and grim,
Now patches where some leanness of the soil's
Broke into moss or substances like boils;
Then came some palsied oak, a cleft in him
Like a distorted mouth that splits its rim
Gaping at death, and dies while it recoils.

XXVII.

Just as far as ever from the end!
Nought in the distance but the evening, nought
To point my footstep further! At the thought,
Great black bird, Apollyon's bosom-friend,
Sailed past, nor beat his wide wing dragon-penned
That brushed my capperchance the guide I sought.

XXVIII.

Looking up, aware I somehow grew,
'Spite of the dusk, the plain had given place
All round to mountainswith such name to grace
Mere ugly heights and heaps now stolen in view.
How thus they had surprised me,solve it, you!
How to get from them was no clearer case.

XXIX.

Half I seemed to recognize some trick
Of mischief happened to me, God knows when—
In a bad dream perhaps. Here ended, then,
Progress this way. When, in the very nick
Of giving up, one time more, came a click
As when a trap shutsyou're inside the den!

XXX.

It came on me all at once,
This was the place! those two hills on the right,
Crouched like two bulls locked horn in horn in fight;
While to the left, a tall scalped mountain... Dunce,

Dotard, a-dozing at the very nonce,
After a life spent training for the sight!

XXXI.

In the midst lay but the Tower itself
The round squat turret, blind as the fool's heart,
Built of brown stone, without a counter-part
In the whole world. The tempest's mocking elf
Points to the shipman thus the unseen shelf
He strikes on, only when the timbers start.

XXXII.

See because of night perhapswhy, day
Came back again for that! before it left,
The dying sunset kindled through a cleft:
The hills, like giants at a hunting, lay,
Chin upon hand, to see the game at bay,—
"Now stab and end the creatureto the heft!"

XXXIII.

Hear when noise was everywhere! it tolled
Increasing like a bell. Names in my ears
Of all the lost adventurers my peers,—
How such a one was strong, and such was bold,
And such was fortunate, yet, each of old
Lost, lost! one moment knelled the woe of years.

XXXIV.

There they stood, ranged along the hill-sides, met
To view the last of me, a living frame
For one more picture! in a sheet of flame I saw them and I knew them all. And yet Dauntless the slug-horn to my lips I set,
And blew. "_Childe Roland to the Dark Tower came._"

Cleon

"As certain also of your own poets have said"-

(Acts.)

LOVE.

The year's done with (_Love me for ever!_)
All March begun with,
April's endeavour; wreaths that bound me
June needs must sever; Now snows fall round me,
Quenching June's fever—
(_Love me for ever!_) Englishman In Italy,
The PIANO DI SORRENTO Fort<u'>,
Fort<u'>, my beloved one,
Sit here by my side,
On my knees put up both little feet!
I was sure, if I tried,
I could make you laugh spite of Scirocco.
Now, open your eyes,
Let me keep you amused till he vanish
In black from the skies,
With telling my memories over
As you tell your beads;
All the Plain saw me gather, I garland
The flowers or the weeds.
Time for rain! for your long hot dry Autumn
Had net-worked with brown
The white skin of each grape on the bunches,
Marked like a quail's crown,
Those creatures you make such account of,
Whose heads,speckled white
Over brown like a great spider's back,
As I told you last night,—
Your mother bites off for her supper.
Red-ripe as could be,
Pomegranates were chapping and splitting
In halves on the tree:
And betwixt the loose walls of great flint-stone,
Or in the thick dust
On the path, or straight out of the rock-side,
Wherever could thrust
Some burnt sprig of bold hardy rock-flower

Its yellow face up,
For the prize were great butterflies fighting,
Some five for one cup.
So, I guessed, ere I got up this morning,
What change was in store,
By the quick rustle-down of the quail-nets
Which woke me before
I could open my shutter, made fast
With a bough and a stone,
And look thro' the twisted dead vine-twigs,
Sole lattice that's known.
Quick and sharp rang the rings down the net-poles,
While, busy beneath,
Your priest and his brother tugged at them,
The rain in their teeth.
And out upon all the flat house-roofs
Where split figs lay drying,
The girls took the frails under cover:
Nor use seemed in trying
To get out the boats and go fishing,
For, under the cliff,
Fierce the black water frothed o'er the blind-rock.
No seeing our skiff
Arrive about noon from Amalfi,
Our fisher arrive
And pitch down his basket before us,
All trembling alive
With pink and grey jellies, your sea-fruit;
You touch the strange lumps,
And mouths gape there, eyes open, all manner
Of horns and of humps,
Which only the fisher looks grave at,
While round him like imps
Cling screaming the children as naked
And brown as his shrimps;
Himself too as bare to the middle
You see round his neck
The string and its brass coin suspended,

That saves him from wreck.
But to-day not a bout reached Salerno,
So back, to a man,
Came our friends, with whose help in the vineyards
Grape-harvest began.
In the vat, halfway up in our house-side,
Like blood the juice spins,
While your brother all bare-legged is dancing
Till breathless he grins
Dead-beaten in effort on effort
To keep the grapes under,
Since still when he seems all but master,
In pours the fresh plunder
From girls who keep coming and going
With basket on shoulder,
And eyes shut against the rain's driving;
Your girls that are older,—
For under the hedges of aloe,
And where, on its bed
Of the orchard's black mould, the love-apple
Lies pulpy and red,
All the young ones are kneeling and filling
Their laps with the snails
Tempted out by this first rainy weather,—
Your best of regales,
As to-night will be proved to my sorrow,
When, supping in state,
We shall feast our grape-gleaners (two dozen,
Three over one plate)
With lasagne so tempting to swallow
In slippery ropes,
And gourds fried in great purple slices,
That colour of popes.
Meantime, see the grape bunch they've brought you:
The rain-water slips
O'er the heavy blue bloom on each globe
Which the wasp to your lips
Still follows with fretful persistence:

Nay, taste, while awake,
This half of a curd-white smooth cheese-ball
That peels, flake by flake,
Like an onion, each smoother and whiter;
Next, sip this weak wine
From the thin green glass flask, with its stopper,
A leaf of the vine;
And end with the prickly-pear's red flesh
That leaves thro' its juice
The stony black seeds on your pearl-teeth.
Scirocco is loose!
Hark, the quick, whistling pelt of the olives
Which, thick in one's track,
Tempt the stranger to pick up and bite them,
Tho' not yet half black!
How the old twisted olive trunks shudder,
The medlars let fall
Their hard fruit, and the brittle great fig-trees
Snap off, figs and all,
For here comes the whole of the tempest!
No refuge, but creep
Back again to my side and my shoulder,
And listen or sleep.
O how will your country show next week,
When all the vine-boughs
Have been stripped of their foliage to pasture
The mules and the cows
Last eve, I rode over the mountains;
Your brother, my guide,
Soon left me, to feast on the myrtles
That offered, each side,
Their fruit-balls, black, glossy and luscious,—
Or strip from the sorbs
A treasure, or, rosy and wondrous,
Those hairy gold orbs!
But my mule picked his sure sobre path out,
Just stopping to neigh
When he recognized down in the valley

His mates on their way
With the faggots and barrels of water;
And soon we emerged
From the plain, where the woods could scarce follow;
And still as we urged
Our way, the woods wondered, and left us,
As up still we trudged
Though the wild path grew wilder each instant,
And place was e'en grudged
'Mid the rock-chasms and piles of loose stones
Like the loose broken teeth
Of some monster which climbed there to die
From the ocean beneath—
Place was grudged to the silver-grey fume-weed
That clung to the path,
And dark rosemary ever a-dying
That, 'spite the wind's wrath,
So loves the salt rock's face to seaward,
And lentisks as staunch
To the stone where they root and bear berries,
And... what shows a branch
Coral-coloured, transparent, with circlets
Of pale seagreen leaves;
Over all trod my mule with the caution
Of gleaners o'er sheaves,
Still, foot after foot like a lady,
Till, round after round,
He climbed to the top of Calvano,
And God's own profound
Was above me, and round me the mountains,
And under, the sea,
And within me my heart to bear witness
What was and shall be.
Oh, heaven and the terrible crystal!
No rampart excludes
Your eye from the life to be lived
In the blue solitudes.
Oh, those mountains, their infinite movement!

Still moving with you;
For, ever some new head and breast of them
Thrusts into view
To observe the intruder; you see it
If quickly you turn
And before they escape you surprise them.
They grudge you should learn
How the soft plains they look on, lean over
And love (they pretend)
Cower beneath them, the flat sea-pine crouches,
The wild fruit-trees bend,
E'en the myrtle-leaves curl, shrink and shut:
All is silent and grave:
'Tis a sensual and timorous beauty,
How fair! but a slave.
So, I turned to the sea; and there slumbered
As greenly as ever
Those isles of the siren, your Galli;
No ages can sever
The Three, nor enable their sister
To join them,halfway
On the voyage, she looked at Ulysses—
No farther to-day,
Tho' the small one, just launched in the wave,
Watches breast-high and steady
From under the rock, her bold sister
Swum halfway already.
Fort<u'>, shall we sail there together
And see from the sides
Quite new rocks show their faces, new haunts
Where the siren abides
Shall we sail round and round them, close over
The rocks, tho' unseen,
That ruffle the grey glassy water
To glorious green
Then scramble from splinter to splinter,
Reach land and explore,
On the largest, the strange square black turret

With never a door,
Just a loop to admit the quick lizards;
Then, stand there and hear
The birds' quiet singing, that tells us
What life is, so clear
The secret they sang to Ulysses
When, ages ago,
He heard and he knew this life's secret
I hear and I know.
Ah, see! The sun breaks o'er Calvano;
He strikes the great gloom
And flutters it o'er the mount's summit
In airy gold fume.
All is over. Look out, see the gipsy,
Our tinker and smith,
Has arrived, set up bellows and forge,
And down-squatted forthwith
To his hammering, under the wall there;
One eye keeps aloof
The urchins that itch to be putting
His jews'-harps to proof,
While the other, thro' locks of curled wire,
Is watching how sleek
Shines the hog, come to share in the windfall
Chew, abbot's own cheek!
All is over. Wake up and come out now,
And down let us go,
And see the fine things got in order
At church for the show
Of the Sacrament, set forth this evening.
To-morrow's the Feast
Of the Rosary's Virgin, by no means
Of Virgins the least,
As you'll hear in the off-hand discourse
Which (all nature, no art)
The Dominican brother, these three weeks,
Was getting by heart.
Not a pillar nor post but is dizened

With red and blue papers;
All the roof waves with ribbons, each altar
A-blaze with long tapers;
But the great masterpiece is the scaffold
Rigged glorious to hold
All the fiddlers and fifers and drummers
And trumpeters bold,
Afraid of Bellini nor Auber,
Who, when the priest's hoarse,
Will strike us up something that's brisk
For the feast's second course.
And then will the flaxen-wigged Image
Be carried in pomp
Thro' the plain, while in gallant procession
The priests mean to stomp.
All round the glad church lie old bottles
With gunpowder stopped,
Which will be, when the Image re-enters,
Religiously popped;
And at night from the crest of Calvano
Great bonfires will hang,
On the plain will the trumpets join chorus,
And more poppers bang.
At all events, cometo the garden
As far as the wall;
See me tap with a hoe on the plaster
Till out there shall fall
scorpion with wide angry nippers!
"Such trifles!" you say Fort<u'>, in my
England at home,
Men meet gravely to-day
And debate, if abolishing Corn-laws
Be righteous and wise
If 'twere proper, Scirocco should vanish
In black from the skies!
The mastic tree (resinous).
Epilogue

I.

Evelyn Hope is dead! Sit and watch by her side an hour. That is her book-shelf, this her bed; She plucked that piece of geranium-flower, Beginning to die too, in the glass; Little has yet been changed, I think: The shutters are shut, no light may pass Save two long rays thro' the hinge's chink.

II.

years old, when she died! Perhaps she had scarcely heard my name; It was not her time to love; beside, Her life had many a hope and aim, Duties enough and little cares, And now was quiet, now astir, Till God's hand beckoned unawares,—And the sweet white brow is all of her.

III.

It too late then, Evelyn Hope What, your soul was pure and true, The good stars met in your horoscope, Made you of spirit, fire and dew—And, just because I was thrice as old And our paths in the world diverged so wide, Each was nought to each, must I be told We were fellow mortals, nought beside

IV.

No, indeed! for God above Is great to grant, as mighty to make, And creates the love to reward the love: I claim you still, for my own love's sake! Delayed it may be for more lives yet, Through worlds I shall traverse, not a few: Much is to learn, much to forget Ere the time be come for taking you.

V.

The time will come,at last it will, When, Evelyn Hope, what meant (I shall say) In the lower earth, in the years long still, That body and soul so pure and gay Why your hair was amber, I shall divine, And your mouth of your own geranium's red—And what you would do with me, in fine, In the new life come in the old one's stead.

VI.

I have lived (I shall say) so much since then, Given up myself so many times, me the gains of various men, Ransacked the ages, spoiled the climes; Yet one thing, one, in my soul's full scope, Either I missed or itself missed me: And I want and find you, Evelyn Hope! What is the issue let us see!

VII.

I loved you, Evelyn, all the while. My heart seemed full as it could hold was place and to spare for the frank young smile, And the red young mouth, and the hair's young gold. So, hush,I will give you this leaf to keep: See, I shut it inside the sweet cold hand! There, that is our secret: go to sleep! You will wake, and remember, and understand.

I. THE FLOWER'S NAME 'S

The garden she walked across,
Arm in my arm, such a short while since:
Hark, now I push its wicket, the moss
Hinders the hinges and makes them wince!
She must ave reached this shrub ere she turned,
As back with that murmur the wicket swung;
For she laid the poor snail, my chance foot spurned,
To feed and forget it the leaves among.

II.

Down this side ofthe gravel-walk
She went while her rope's edge brushed the box:
And here she paused in her gracious talk
To point me a moth on the milk-white phlox.
Roses, ranged in valiant row,
I will never think that she passed you by!
She loves you noble roses, I know;
But yonder, see, where the rock-plants lie!

III.

Flower she stopped at, finger on lip,

Stooped over, in doubt, as settling its claim;
Till she gave me, with pride to make no slip,
Its soft meandering Spanish name:
What a name! Was it love or praise
Speech half-asleep or song half-awake
I must learn Spanish, one of these days,
Only for that slow sweet name's sake.

IV.

If I live and do well,
I may bring her, one of these days,
To fix you fast with as fine a spell,
Fit you each with his Spanish phrase;
But do not detain me now; for she lingers
There, like sunshine over the ground,
And ever I see her soft white fingers
Searching after the bud she found.

V.

You Spaniard, look that you grow not,
Stay as you are and be loved for ever!
Bud, if I kiss you 'tis that you blow not:
Mind, the shut pink mouth opens never!
For while it pouts, her fingers wrestle,
Twinkling the audacious leaves between,
Till round they turn and down they nestle—
Is not the dear mark still to be seen

VI.

I find her not, beauties vanish;
Whither I follow ber, beauties flee;
Is there no method to tell her in Spanish
June's twice June since she breathed it with me
Come, bud, show me the least of her traces,
Treasure my lady's lightest footfall!
Ah, you may flout and turn up your faces—
Roses, you are not so fair after all!

II. SIBRANDUS SCHAFNABURGENSIS

Plague take all your pedants, say I!
He who wrote what I hold in my hand,
Centuries back was so good as to die,
Leaving this rubbish to cumber the land;
This, that was a book in its time,
Printed on paper and bound in leather,
Last month in the white of a matin-prime
Just when the birds sang all together.

II.

The garden I brought it to read,
And under the arbute and laurustine
Read it, so help me grace in my need,
From title-page to closing line.
Chapter on chapter did I count,
As a curious traveller counts Stonehenge;
Added up the mortal amount;
And then proceeded to my revenge.

III.

A plum-tree with a crevice
An owl would build in, were he but sage;
For a lap of moss, like a fine pont-levis
In a castle of the Middle Age,
to a lip of gum, pure amber;
When he'd be private, there might he spend
Hours alone in his lady's chamber:
Into this crevice I dropped our friend.

IV.

Splash, went he, as under he ducked,
At the bottom, I knew, rain-drippings stagnate:
Next, a handful of blossoms I plucked
To bury him with, my bookshelf's magnate;
Then I went in-doors, brought out a loaf,

Half a cheese, and a bottle of Chablis;
Lay on the grass and forgot the oaf
Over a jolly chapter of Rabelais.

V.

This morning, betwixt the moss
And gum that locked our friend in limbo,
A spider had spun his web across,
And sat in the midst with arms akimbo:
So, I took pity, for learning's sake,
And, _de profundis, accentibus ltis,
Cantate!_ quoth I, as I got a rake;
And up I fished his delectable treatise.

VI.

You have it, dry in the sun,
With all the binding all of a blister,
And great blue spots where the ink has run,
And reddish streaks that wink and glister
O'er the page so beautifully yellow:
Oh, well have the droppings played their tricks!
Did he guess how toadstools grow, this fellow
Here's one stuck in his chapter six!

VII.

Did he like it when the live creatures
Tickled and toused and browsed him all over,
And worm, slug, eft, with serious features,
Came in, each one, for his right of trover
When the water-beetle with great blind deaf face
Made of her eggs the stately deposit,
the newt borrowed just so much of the preface
As tiled in the top of his black wife's closet

VIII.

That life and fun and romping,

All that frisking and twisting and coupling,
While slowly our poor friend's leaves were swamping
And clasps were cracking and covers suppling!
As if you bad carried sour John Knox
To the play-house at Paris, Vienna or Munich,
Fastened him into a front-row box,
And danced off the ballet with trousers and tunic.

IX.

Come, old martyr! What, torment enough is it
Back to my room shall you take your sweet self.
Good-bye, mother-beetle; husband-eft, _sufficit!_
See the snug niche I have made on my shelf!
A.'s book shall prop you up, B.'s shall cover you,
Here's C. to be grave with, or D. to be gay,
And with E. on each side, and F. right over you,
Dry-rot at ease till the Judgment-day!

SHE SPEAKS.

I.

To-morrow, if a harp-string, say, Is used to tie the jasmine back That overfloods my room with sweets, Contrive your Zorzi somehow meets My Zanze! If the ribbon's black, The Three are watching: keep away!

II.

In A Year
Never any more,
While I live,
Need I hope to see his face
As before.
Once his love grown chill,
Mine may strive:
Bitterly we re-embrace,
Single still.

II.

Was it something said,
Something done,
Vexed him was it touch of hand,
Turn of head
Strange! that very way
Love begun:
I as little understand
Love's decay.

III.

When I sewed or drew,
I recall
How he looked as if I sung,
Sweetly too.
If I spoke a word,
First of all
Up his cheek the colour sprang,
Then he heard.

IV.

Sitting by my side,
At my feet,
So he breathed but air I breathed,
Satisfied!
I, too, at love's brim
Touched the sweet:
I would die if death bequeathed
Sweet to him.

V.

"Speak, I love thee best!"
He exclaimed:
"Let thy love my own foretell!"
I confessed:
"Clasp my heart on thine
"Now unblamed,

"Since upon thy soul as well
"Hangeth mine!"

VI.

Was it wrong to own,
Being truth
Why should all the giving prove
His alone
I had wealth and ease,
Beauty, youth:
Since my lover gave me love,
I gave these.

VII.

That was all I meant,
To be just,
And the passion I had raised,
To content.
Since he chose to change
Gold for dust,
If I gave him what he praised
Was it strange

VIII.

Would he loved me yet,
On and on,
While I found some way undreamed
Paid my debt!
Gave more life and more,
Till, all gone,
He should smile "She never seemed
"Mine before.

IX.

"What, she felt the while,
"Must I think
"Love's so different with us men!" He should smile:
"Dying for my sake—"White and pink!
"Can't we touch these bubbles then "But they break"

X.

Dear, the pang is brief,
Do thy part,
Have thy pleasure! How perplexed
Grows belief!
Well, this cold clay clod
Was man's heart:
Crumble it, and what comes next
Is it God

INCIDENT OF THE FRENCH CAMP

I.

You know, we French stormed Ratisbon:
A mile or so away,
On a little mound, Napoleon
Stood on our storming-day;
Neck out-thrust, you fancy how,
Legs wide, arms locked behind,
As if to balance the prone brow
Oppressive with its mind.

II.

As perhaps he mused "My plans
"That soar, to earth may fall, "
Let once my army-leader Lannes
"Waver at yonder wall,"—
Out 'twixt the battery-smokes there flew
A rider, bound on bound
Full-galloping; nor bridle drew
Until he reached the mound.

III.

Then off there flung in smiling joy,
And held himself erect
By just his horse's mane, a boy:
You hardly could suspect—
(So tight he kept his lips compressed,

Scarce any blood came through)
You looked twice ere you saw his breast
Was all but shot in two.

IV.

"Well," cried he, "Emperor, by God's grace
"We've got you Ratisbon!
"The Marshal's in the market-place,
"And you'll be there anon
"To see your flag-bird flap his vans
"Where I, to heart's desire,
"Perched him!" The chief's eye flashed; his plans
Soared up again like fire.

V.

The chief's eye flashed; but presently
Softened itself, as sheathes
A film the mother-eagle's eye
When her bruised eaglet breathes;
"You're wounded!" "Nay," the soldier's pride
Touched to the quick, he said:
"I'm killed, Sire!" And his chief beside
Smiling the boy fell dead.

LOST LEADER, THE

I.

For a handful of silver he left us,
Just for a riband to stick in his coat—
Found the one gift of which fortune bereft us,
Lost all the others she lets us devote;
They, with the gold to give, doled him out silver,
So much was theirs who so little allowed:
How all our copper had gone for his service!
Ragswere they purple, his heart had been proud!
We that had loved him so, followed him, honoured him,
Lived in his mild and magnificent eye,
Learned his great language, caught his clear accents,

Made him our pattern to live and to die!
Shakespeare was of us, Milton was for us,
Burns, Shelley, were with us,they watch from
Their graves! He alone breaks from the van and
The free-men, He alone sinks to the
Rear and the slaves!

II.

Shall march prospering,not thro' his presence;
Songs may inspirit us,not from his lyre;
Deeds will be done,while he boasts his quiescence,
Still bidding crouch whom the rest bade aspire:
Blot out his name, then, record one lost soul more,
One task more declined, one more foot-path untrod,
One more devils'-triumph and sorrow for angels,
One wrong more to man, one more insult to God!
Life's night begins: let him never come back to us!
There would be doubt, hesitation and pain,
Forced praise on our partthe glimmer of twilight,
Never glad confident morning again!
Fight on well, for we taught himstrike gallantly,
Menace our heart ere we master his own;
Then let him receive the new knowledge and wait us,
Pardoned in heaven, the first by the throne!
Lost Mistress, The

I.

All's over, then: does truth sound bitter
As one at first believes
Hark, 'tis the sparrows' good-night twitter
About your cottage eaves!

II.

And the leaf-buds on the vine are woolly,
I noticed that, to-day;
day more bursts them open fully
You know the red turns grey.

III.

To-morrow we meet the same then, dearest
May I take your hand in mine
Mere friends are we,well, friends the merest
Keep much that I resign:

IV.

Each glance of the eye so bright and black,
Though I keep with heart's endeavour,—
Your voice, when you wish the snowdrops back,
Though it stay in my soul for ever!—

V.

Yet I will but say what mere friends say,
Or only a thought stronger;
I will hold your hand but as long as all may,
Or so very little longer!
Love Among The Ruins

I.

Where the quiet-coloured end of evening smiles,
Miles and miles
On the solitary pastures where our sheep
Half-asleep
Tinkle homeward thro' the twilight, stray or stop
As they crop—
Was the site once of a city great and gay,
(So they say)
Of our country's very capital, its prince
Ages since
Held his court in, gathered councils, wielding far
Peace or war.

II.

Now,the country does not even boast a tree,
As you see,
To distinguish slopes of verdure, certain rills

From the hills
Intersect and give a name to, (else they run
Into one)
Where the domed and daring palace shot its spires
Up like fires
O'er the hundred-gated circuit of a wall
Bounding all,
Made of marble, men might march on nor be pressed,
Twelve abreast.

III.

And such plenty and perfection, see, of grass
Never was!
Such a carpet as, this summer-time, o'erspreads
And embeds
Every vestige of the city, guessed alone,
Stock or stone—
Where a multitude of men breathed joy and woe
Long ago;
Lust of glory pricked their hearts up, dread of shame
Struck them tame;
And that glory and that shame alike, the gold
Bought and sold.

IV.

Now,the single little turret that remains
On the plains,
By the caper overrooted, by the gourd
Overscored,
While the patching houseleek's head of blossom winks
Through the chinks—
Marks the basement whence a tower in ancient time
Sprang sublime,
And a burning ring, all round, the chariots traced
As they raced,
And the monarch and his minions and his dames
Viewed the games.

V.

And I know, while thus the quiet-coloured eve
Smiles to leave
To their folding, all our many-tinkling fleece
In such peace,
And the slopes and rills in undistinguished grey
Melt away—
That a girl with eager eyes and yellow hair
Waits me there
In the turret whence the charioteers caught soul
For the goal,
When the king looked, where she looks now, breathless, dumb
Till I come.

VI.

But he looked upon the city, every side,
Far and wide,
All the mountains topped with temples, all the glades'
Colonnades,
All the causeys, bridges, aqueducts,and then,
All the men!
When I do come, she will speak not, she will stand,
Either hand
On my shoulder, give her eyes the first embrace
Of my face,
Ere we rush, ere we extinguish sight and speech
Each on each.

VII.

In one year they sent a million fighters forth
South and North,
And they built their gods a brazen pillar high
As the sky,
Yet reserved a thousand chariots in full force—
Gold, of course.
Oh heart! oh blood that freezes, blood that burns!

Earth's returns
For whole centuries of folly, noise and sin!
Shut them in,
With their triumphs and their glories and the rest!
Love is best.

MEMORABILIA

I.

Did you once see Shelley plain,
And did he stop and speak to you
And did you speak to him again
How strange it seems and new!

II.

You were living before that,
And also you are living after; And the memory
I started at—
My starting moves your laughter.

III.

Crossed a moor, with a name of its own
And a certain use in the world no doubt,
Yet a hand's-breadth of it shines alone
'Mid the blank miles round about:

IV.

There I picked up on the heather
And there I put inside my breast
A moulted feather, an eagle-feather!
Well, I forget the rest.

Mesmerism

I.

All I believed is true!
    I am able yet
All I want, to get

A method as strange as new:
Dare I trust the same to you

II.

At night, when doors are shut,
And the wood-worm picks,
And the death-watch ticks,
And the bar has a flag of smut,
And a cat's in the water-butt—

III.

And the socket floats and flares,
And the house-beams groan,
And a foot unknown
Surmised on the garret-stairs,
And the locks slip unawares—

IV.

And the spider, to serve his ends,
By a sudden thread,
Arms and legs outspread,
On the table's midst descends,
Comes to find, God knows what friends!—

V.

Since eve drew in, I say,
I have sat and brought (So to speak) my thought
To bear on the woman away,
Till I felt my hair turn grey—

VI.

Till I seemed to have and hold,
In the vacancy
'Twixt the wall and me,
The hair-plait's chestnut gold
To the foot in its muslin fold—

VII.

Have and hold, then and there,

Her, from head to foot,
Breathing and mute, Passive and yet aware,
In the grasp of my steady stare—

VIII.

Hold and have, there and then,
All her body and soul
That completes my whole,
All that women add to men,
In the clutch of my steady ken—

IX.

Having and holding, till
I imprint her fast
On the void at last
The sun does whom he will By the calotypist's skill—

X.

Then,if my heart's strength serve,
And through all and each
Of the veils I reach
her soul and never swerve, Knitting an iron nerve—

XI.

Command her soul to advance
And inform the shape
Which has made escape
And before my countenance
Answers me glance for glance—

XII.

Still with a gesture fit
Of my hands that best Do my soul's behest,
Pointing the power from it,
While myself do steadfast sit—

XIII.

Steadfast and still the same

On my object bent,
While the hands give vent
To my ardour and my aim
And break into very flame—

XIV.

Then I reach, I must believe,
Not her soul in vain,
For to me again
Reaches, and past retrieve
Is wound in the toils I weave;

XV.

And must follow as I require,
As befits a thrall,
Bringing flesh and all,
Essence and earth-attire,
To the source of the tractile fire:

XVI.

Till the house called hers, not mine,
With a growing weight
Seems to suffocate
She break not its leaden line
And escape from its close confine.

XVII.

Out of doors into the night!
On to the maze
Of the wild wood-ways,
Not turning to left nor right
From the pathway, blind with sight—

XVIII.

Thro' rain and wind
O'er the broken shrubs, '
Twixt the stems and stubs,
With a still, composed, strong mind,

Nor a care for the world behind—

XIX.

Swifter and still more swift,
As the crowding peace Doth to joy increase
The wide blind eyes uplift Thro'
The darkness and the drift!

XX.

While Ito the shape, I too
Feel my soul dilate
Nor a whit abate,
Relax not a gesture due,
As I see my belief come true.

XXI.

For, there! have I drawn or no
Life to that lip
Do my fingers dip
In a flame which again they throw
On the cheek that breaks a-glow

XXII.

Ha! was the hair so first
What, unfilleted,
Made alive, and spread
Through the void with a rich outburst,
Chestnut gold-interspersed

XXIII.

Like the doors of a casket-shrine,
See, on either side,
Her two arms divide
Till the heart betwixt makes sign,
Take me, for I am thine

XXIV.

"Nownow"the door is heard!

Hark, the stairs! and near—Nearerand here—
"Now!" and at call the third
She enters without a word.

XXV.

On doth she march and on
To the fancied shape; It is, past escape,
Now: the dream is done
And the shadow and she are one.

XXVI.

I will pray. Do Thou
That ownest the soul,
Yet wilt grant control
To another, nor disallow
For a time, restrain me now!

XXVII.

Admonish me while I may,
Not to squander guilt,
Since require Thou wilt
At my hand its price one day
What the price is, who can say

Old Pictures In Florence

I.

Morn when first it thunders in March,
The eel in the pond gives a leap, they say:
As I leaned and looked over the aloed arch
Of the villa-gate this warm March day,
No flash snapped, no dumb thunder rolled
In the valley beneath where,
white and wide And washed by the morning water-gold,
Florence lay out on the mountain-side.

II.

And bridge and street and square

Lay mine, as much at my beck and call,
Through the live translucent bath of air,
As the sights in a magic crystal ball.
And of all I saw nd of all I praised,
The most to praise and the best to see
Was the startling bell-tower Giotto raised:
But why did it more than startle me

III.

How, with that soul of yours,
Could you play me false who loved you so
Some slights if a certain heart endures
Yet it feels, I would have your fellows know!
I' faith, I perceive not why I should care
To break a silence that suits them best,
But the thing grows somewhat hard to bear
When I find a Giotto join the rest.

IV.

The arch where olives overhead
Print the blue sky with twig and leaf,
(That sharp-curled leaf which they never shed)
'Twixt the aloes, I used to lean in chief,
And mark through the winter afternoons,
By a gift God grants me now and then,
In the mild decline of those suns like moons,
Who walked in Florence, besides her men.

V.

Might chirp and chaffer, come and go
For pleasure or profit, her men alive—
My business was hardly with them, I trow,
But with empty cells of the human hive;
With the chapter-room, the cloister-porch,
The church's apsis, aisle or nave,
Its crypt, one fingers along with a torch,
Its face set full for the sun to shave.

VI.

A fresco peels and drops,
    Wherever an outline weakens and wanes
Till the latest life in the painting stops,
    Stands One whom each fainter pulse-tick pains:
One, wishful each scrap should clutch the brick,
    Each tinge not wholly escape the plaster,
A lion who dies of an ass's kick,
    The wronged great soul of an ancient Master.

VII.

Oh, this world and the wrong it does
    They are safe in heaven with their backs to it,
The Michaels and Rafaels, you hum and buzz
    Round the works of, you of the little wit!
Do their eyes contract to the earth's old scope,
    Now that they see God face to face,
And have all attained to be poets, I hope
    'Tis their holiday now, in any case.

VIII.

They reck of your praise and you!
    But the wronged great soulscan they be quit
Of a world where their work is all to do,
    Where you style them, you of the little wit,
Old Master This and Early the Other,
    Not dreaming that Old and New are fellows:
A younger succeeds to an elder brother,
    Da Vincis derive in good time from Dellos.

IX.

Here where your praise might yield returns,
    And a handsome word or two give help,
Here, after your kind, the mastiff girns
    And the puppy pack of poodles yelp.
What, not a word for Stefano there,
    Of brow once prominent and starry,

Called Nature's Ape and the world's despair
For his peerless painting (See Vasari.)

X.

Stands the Master. Study, my friends,
What a man's work comes to! So he plans it,
Performs it, perfects it, makes amends
For the toiling and moiling, and then, _sic transit!_
Happier the thrifty blind-folk labour,
With upturned eye while the hand is busy,
Not sidling a glance at the coin of their neighbour!
'Tis looking downward that makes one dizzy.

XI.

"If you knew their work you would deal your dole."
May I take upon me to instruct you
Greek Art ran and reached the goal,
Thus much had the world to boast _in fructu_—
The Truth of Man, as by God first spoken,
Which the actual generations garble,
Was re-uttered, and Soul (which Limbs betoken)
And Limbs (Soul informs) made new in marble.

XII.

You saw yourself as you wished you were,
As you might have been, as you cannot be;
Earth here, rebuked by Olympus there:
And grew content in your poor degree
With your little power, by those statues' godhead,
And your little scope, by their eyes' full sway,
And your little grace, by their grace embodied,
And your little date, by their forms that stay.

XIII.

Would fain be kinglier, say, than I am
Even so, you will not sit like Theseus.
You would prove a model The Son of Priam
Has yet the advantage in arms' and knees' use.

You're wrothcan you slay your snake like Apollo
You're grievedstill Niobe's the grander!
You livethere's the Racers' frieze to follow:
You diethere's the dying Alexander.

XIV.

Testing your weakness by their strength,
Your meagre charms by their rounded beauty,
Measured by Art in your breadth and length,
You learnedto submit is a mortal's duty.
When I say "you" 'tis the common soul,
The collective, I mean: the race of
Man That receives life in parts to live in a whole,
And grow here according to God's clear plan.

XV.

Growth came when, looking your last on them all,
You turned your eyes inwardly one fine day
And cried with a startWhat if we so small
Be greater and grander the while than they
Are they perfect of lineament, perfect of stature
In both, of such lower types are we
because of our wider nature;
For time, theirsours, for eternity.

XVI.

Day's brief passion limits their range;
It seethes with the morrow for us and more.
They are perfecthow else they shall never change:
We are faultywhy not we have time in store.
The Artificer's hand is not arrested
With us; we are rough-hewn, nowise polished:
They stand for our copy, and, once invested
With all they can teach, we shall see them abolished.

XVII.

'Tis a life-long toil till our lump be leaven—
The better! What's come to perfection perishes.

Things learned on earth, we shall practise in heaven:
  Works done least rapidly, Art most cherishes.
Thyself shalt afford the example, Giotto!
  Thy one work, not to decrease or diminish,
Done at a stroke, was just (was it not) "O!"
  Thy great Campanile is still to finish.

XVIII.

It true that we are now, and shall be hereafter,
  But what and where depend on life's minute
Hails heavenly cheer or infernal laughter
  Our first step out of the gulf or in it Shall Man,
Such step within his endeavour,
  Man's face, have no more play and action
Than joy which is crystallized for ever,
  Or grief, an eternal petrifaction

XIX.

Which I conclude, that the early painters,
  To cries of "Greek Art and what more wish you"—
Replied, "To become now self-acquainters,
  "And paint man man, whatever the issue!
"Make new hopes shine through the flesh they fray,
  "New fears aggrandize the rags and tatters:
"To bring the invisible full into play!
  "Let the visible go to the dogswhat matters"

XX.

These, I exhort you, their guerdon and glory
  For daring so much, before they well did it.
The first of the new, in our race's story,
  Beats the last of the old; 'tis no idle quiddit.
The worthies began a revolution,
  Which if on earth you intend to acknowledge,
Why, honour them now! (ends my allocution)
  Nor confer your degree when the folk leave college.

XXI.

A fancy some lean to and others hate—
    That, when this life is ended, begins
New work for the soul in another state,
    Where it strives and gets weary, loses and wins:
Where the strong and the weak, this world's congeries,
    Repeat in large what they practised in small,
Through life after life in unlimited series;
    Only the scale's to be changed, that's all.

XXII.

Yet I hardly know. When a soul has seen
    By the means of Evil that Good is best,
Through earth and its noise, what is heaven's serene,—
    When our faith in the same has stood the test—
Why, the child grown man, you burn the rod,
    The uses of labour are surely done;
There remaineth a rest for the people of God:
    And I have had troubles enough, for one.

XXIII.

At any rate I have loved the season
    Of Art's spring-birth so dim and dewy;
My sculptor is Nicolo the Pisan,
    My painterwho but Cimabue
Nor ever was man of them all indeed,
    From these to Ghiberti and Ghirlandaio,
Could say that he missed my critic-meed.
    So, now to my special grievanceheigh ho!

XXIV.

Ghosts still stand, as I said before,
    Watching each fresco flaked and rasped,
Blocked up, knocked out, or whitewashed o'er:
    No getting again what the church has grasped!
The works on the wall must take their chance;
    "Works never conceded to England's thick clime!"

(I hope they prefer their inheritance
Of a bucketful of Italian quick-lime.)

XXV.

When they go at length, with such a shaking
Of heads o'er the old delusion, sadly
Master his way through the black streets taking,
Where many a lost work breathes though badly—
Why don't they bethink them of who has merited
Why not reveal, while their pictures dree
Such doom, how a captive might be out-ferreted
Why is it they never remember me

XXVI.

That I expect the great Bigordi,
Nor Sandro to hear me, chivalric, bellicose;
Nor the wronged Lippino; and not a word I
Say of a scrap of Fr Angelico's:
Are you too fine, Taddeo Gaddi,
To grant me a taste of your intonaco,
Some Jerome that seeks the heaven with a sad eye
Not a churlish saint, Lorenzo Monaco

XXVII.

Could not the ghost with the close red cap,
My Pollajolo, the twice a craftsman,
Save me a sample, give me the hap
Of a muscular Christ that shows the draughtsman
No Virgin by him the somewhat petty,
Of finical touch and tempera crumbly—
Could not Alesso Baldovinetti
Contribute so much, I ask him humbly

XXVIII.

Margheritone of Arezzo,
With the grave-clothes garb and swaddling barret
(Why purse up mouth and beak in a pet so,
You bald old saturnine poll-clawed parrot)

Not a poor glimmering Crucifixion,
    Where in the foreground kneels the donor
If such remain, as is my conviction,
    The hoarding it does you but little honour.

XXIX.

They pass; for them the panels may thrill,
    The tempera grow alive and tinglish;
Their pictures are left to the mercies still
    Of dealers and stealers, Jews and the English,
Who, seeing mere money's worth in their prize,
    Will sell it to somebody calm as
Zeno At naked High Art, and in ecstasies
    Before some clay-cold vile Carlino!

XXX.

No matter for these! But Giotto, you,
    Have you allowed, as the town-tongues babble it,—
Oh, never! it shall not be counted true—
    That a certain precious little tablet
Which Buonarroti eyed like a lover,—
    Was buried so long in oblivion's womb And,
left for another than I to discover,
    Turns up at last! and to whomto whom

XXXI.

That have haunted the dim San Spirito,
    (Or was it rather the Ognissanti)
Patient on altar-step planting a weary toe!
    Nay, I shall have it yet! _Detur amanti!_
My Koh-i-noor-or (if that's a platitude)
    Jewel of Giamschid, the Persian Sofi's eye
So, in anticipative gratitude,
What if I take up my hope and prophesy

XXXII.

The hour grows ripe, and a certain dotard
    Is pitched, no parcel that needs invoicing,

To the worse side of the Mont Saint Gothard,
We shall begin by way of rejoicing;
Of that shooting the sky (blank cartridge),
Nor a civic guard, all plumes and lacquer,
Hunting Radetzky's soul like a partridge
Over Morello with squib and cracker.

XXXIII.

This time we'll shoot better game and bag 'em hot—
No mere display at the stone of Dante,
A kind of sobre Witanagemot
(Ex: "Casa Guidi," _quod videas ante_)
Shall ponder, once Freedom restored to Florence,
How Art may return that departed with her.
Go, hated house, go each trace of the Loraine's,
And bring us the days of Orgagna hither!

XXXIV.

How we shall prologize, how we shall perorate,
Utter fit things upon art and history,
Truth at blood-heat and falsehood at zero rate,
Make of the want of the age no mystery;
Contrast the fructuous and sterile eras,
Showmonarchy ever its uncouth cub licks
Out of the bear's shape into Chimra's,
While Pure Art's birth is still the republic's.

XXXV.

One shall propose in a speech (curt Tuscan,
Expurgate and sobre, with scarcely an "_issimo,_")
To end now our half-told tale of Cambuscan,
And turn the bell-tower's _alt_ to _altissimo_:
And fine as the beak of a young beccaccia
The Campanile, the Duomo's fit ally,
Soar up in gold full fifty braccia,
Completing Florence, as Florence Italy.

XXXVI.

I be alive that morning the scaffold
Is broken away, and the long-pent fire,
Like the golden hope of the world, unbaffled
Springs from its sleep, and up goes the spire
While "God and the People" plain for its motto,
Thence the new tricolour flaps at the sky
At least to foresee that glory of Giotto
And Florence together, the first am I!
A sculptor, died.
Died. Designed the bronze gates of the
Baptistry at Florence. A painter, died.

The son of Fr Lippo Lippi. Wronged, because some of his pictures have been attributed to others. Died. One of Giotto's pupils and assistants. Rough cast. Painter, sculptor, and goldsmith. Distempermixture of water and egg yolk. Sculptor and architect, died All Saints. A Florentine painter, died. Tartar king.

A woodcock

THE AN OLD STORY.

I.

Was roses, roses, all the way,
With myrtle mixed in my path like mad:
The house-roofs seemed to heave and sway,
The church-spires flamed, such flags they had,
A year ago on this very day.

II.

Air broke into a mist with bells,
The old walls rocked with the crowd and cries.
Had I said, "Good folk, mere noise repels—
But give me your sun from yonder skies!"
They had answered, "And afterward, what else"

III.

It was I who leaped at the sun
To give it my loving friends to keep!

Nought man could do, have I left undone:
  And you see my harvest, what I reap
This very day, now a year is run.

IV.

Nobody on the house-tops now—
  Just a palsied few at the windows set;
For the best of the sight is, all allow,
  At the Shambles' Gateor, better yet,
By the very scaffold's foot, I trow.

V.

Go in the rain, and, more than needs,
  A rope cuts both my wrists behind;
And I think, by the feel, my forehead bleeds,
  For they fling, whoever has a mind,
Stones at me for my year's misdeeds.

VI.

Thus I entered, and thus I go!
  In triumphs, people have dropped down dead.
"Paid by the world, what dost thou owe
  "Me"God might question; now instead,
'Tis God shall repay: I am safer so.

Pied Piper Of Hamelin, The A CHILD'S STORY.

I.

Town's in Brunswick, By famous Hanover city; The river Weser, deep and wide, Washes its wall on the southern side; A pleasanter spot you never spied; But, when begins my ditty, Almost five hundred years ago, To see the townsfolk suffer so From vermin, was a pity.

II.

Rats! fought the dogs and killed the cats, And bit the babies in the cradles, And ate the cheeses out of the vats, And licked the soup from the cooks' own ladles, Split open the kegs of salted sprats, Made nests inside men's Sunday hats, And even spoiled the women's chats By drowning their speaking With shrieking and squeaking In fifty different sharps and flats.

III.

At last the people in a body
To the Town Hall came flocking:
"'Tis clear," cried they, "our Mayor's a noddy;
"And as for our Corporationshocking. "To think we buy gowns lined with ermine "For dolts that can't or won't determine "What's best to rid us of our vermin! "You hope, because you're old and obese, "To find in the furry civic robe ease "Rouse up, sirs! Give your brains a racking "To find the remedy we're lacking, "Or, sure.as fate, we'll send you packing!" At this the Mayor and Corporation Quaked with a mighty consternation.

IV.

Hour they sat in council, At length the Mayor broke silence: "For a guilder I'd my ermine gown sell, "I wish I were a mile hence! "It's easy to bid one rack one's brain—"I'm sure my poor head aches again, "I've scratched it so, and all in vain. "Oh for a trap, a trap, a trap!" Just as he said this, what should hap At the chamber door but a gentle tap "Bless us," cried the Mayor, "what's that" (With the Corporation as he sat, Looking little though wondrous fat; Nor brighter was his eye, nor moister Than a too-long-opened oyster, when at noon his paunch grew mutinous For a plate of turtle green and glutinous) "Only a scraping of shoes on the mat "Anything like the sound of a rat "Makes my heart go pit-a-pat!"

V.

"Come in!"the Mayor cried, looking bigger: And in did come the strangest figure! His queer long coat from heel to head Was half of yellow and half of red, And he himself was tall and thin, With sharp blue eyes, each like a pin, And light loose hair, yet swarthy skin, No tuft on cheek nor beard on chin, But lips where smiles went out and in; There was no guessing his kith and kin: And nobody could enough admire The tall man and his quaint attire. Quoth one: "It's as my great-grandsire, "Starting up at the Trump of Doom's tone, "Had walked this way from his painted tombstone!"

VI.

He advanced to the council-table, "Please your honours," said he, "I'm able, "By means of a secret charm, to draw "All creatures living beneath the sun, "That creep or swim or fly or run, "After me so as you never saw! "And I chiefly use my charm "On creatures that do people harm, "The mole and toad and newt and viper; "And people call me the Pied Piper." (And here they noticed round his neck A scarf of red and yellow stripe, To match with his coat of the self-same cheque; And at the scarf's end hung a pipe; And his fingers, they noticed, were ever straying As if impatient to be playing Upon this pipe, as low it dangled Over his vesture so old-fangled.) "Yet," said he, "poor piper as I am, "In Tartary I freed the Cham, "Last June, from his huge swarms of gnats; "I eased in Asia the Nizam "Of a monstrous brood of vampyre-bats: "And as for what your brain bewilders, "If I can rid your town of rats "Will you give me a thousand guilders" "One fifty thousand!"was the exclamation Of the astonished Mayor and Corporation.

VII.

The street the Piper stept, Smiling first a little smile, As if he knew what magic slept In his quiet pipe the while; Then, like a musical adept, blow the pipe his lips he wrinkled, And green and blue his sharp eyes twinkled, Like a candle-flame where salt is sprinkled; And ere three shrill notes the pipe uttered, You heard as if an army muttered; And the muttering grew to a grumbling; And the grumbling grew to a mighty rumbling; And out of the houses the rats came tumbling.

Great rats, small rats, lean rats, brawny rats, Brown rats, black rats, grey rats, tawny rats, Grave old plodders, gay young friskers, Fathers, mothers, uncles, cousins, Cocking tails and pricking whiskers, Families by tens and dozens, Brothers, sisters, husbands, wives—Followed the Piper for their lives.

From street to street he piped advancing, And step for step they followed dancing, Until they came to the river Weser, Wherein all plunged and perished! Save one who, stout as Julius C<ae>sar, Swam across and lived to carry (As he, the manuscript he cherished) To Rat-land home his commentary: Which was, "At the first shrill notes of the pipe, "I heard a sound as of scraping tripe, "And putting apples, wondrous ripe, "Into a cider-press's gripe: "And a moving away of pickle-tub-boards, "And a leaving ajar of conserve-cupboards, "And a drawing the corks of train-oil-flasks, "And a breaking the hoops of butter-casks: "And it seemed as if a voice "(Sweeter far than b<y'> harp or b<y'> psaltery "Is breathed) called out, 'Oh rats, rejoice! " 'The world is grown to one vast drysaltery! " 'So munch on, crunch on, take your nuncheon, " 'Breakfast, supper, dinner, luncheon!' "And just as a bulky sugar-puncheon, "All ready staved, like a great sun shone "Glorious scarce an inch before me, "Just as methought it said, 'Come, bore me!' "I found the Weser rolling o'er me."

VIII.

Should have heard the Hamelin people ringing the bells till they rocked the steeple. "Go," cried the Mayor, "and get long poles, "Poke out the nests and block up the holes! "Consult with carpenters and builders, "And leave in our town not even a trace "Of the rats!"when suddenly, up the face Of the Piper perked in the market-place, With a, "First, if you please, my thousand guilders!"

IX.

A thousand guilders! The Mayor looked blue; So did the Corporation too. For council dinners made rare havoc With Claret, Moselle, Vin-de-Grave, Hock; And half the money would replenish Their cellar's biggest butt with Rhenish. To pay this sum to a wandering fellow With a gipsy coat of red and yellow! "Beside," quoth the Mayor with a knowing wink, "Our business was done at the river's brink; "We saw with our eyes the vermin sink, "And what's dead can't come to life, I think. "So, friend, we're not the folks to shrink "From the duty of giving you something for drink, "And a matter of money to put in your poke; "But as for the guilders, what we spoke "Of them, as you very well know, was in joke. "Beside, our losses have made us thrifty. "A thousand guilders! Come, take fifty!"

X.

The Piper's face fell, and he cried "No trifling! I can't wait, beside! "I've promised to visit by dinnertime "Bagdat, and accept the prime "Of the Head-Cook's pottage, all he's rich in, "For having left, in the Caliph's kitchen, "Of a nest of scorpions no survivor: "With him I proved no bargain-driver, "With you, don't think I'll bate a stiver! "And folks who put me in a passion "May find me pipe after another fashion."

XI.

"How" cried the Mayor, "d'ye think I brook "Being worse treated than a Cook "Insulted by a lazy ribald "With idle pipe and vesture piebald "You threaten us, fellow Do your worst, "Blow your pipe there till you burst!"

XII.

Once more he stept into the street And to his lips again Laid his long pipe of smooth straight cane; And ere he blew three notes (such sweet Soft notes as yet musician's cunning Never gave the enraptured air) There was a rustling that seemed like a bustling Of merry crowds justling at pitching and hustling, Small feet were pattering, wooden shoes clattering, Little hands clapping and little tongues chattering, And, like fowls in a farm-yard when barley is scattering, Out came the children running. the little boys and girls, With rosy cheeks and flaxen curls, And sparkling eyes and teeth like pearls, Tripping and skipping, ran merrily after The wonderful music with shouting and laughter.

XIII.

The Mayor was dumb, and the Council stood As if they were changed into blocks of wood, Unable to move a step, or cry To the children merrily skipping by, Could only follow with the eye That joyous crowd at the Piper's back. But how the Mayor was on the rack, And the wretched Council's bosoms beat, As the Piper turned from the High Street To where the Weser rolled its waters Right in the way of their sons and daughters!

However be turned from South to West, And to Koppelberg Hill his steps addressed, And after him the children pressed; Great was the joy in every breast. "He never can cross that mighty top! "He's forced to let the piping drop, "And we shall see our children stop!" When, lo, as they reached the mountain-side, A wondrous portal opened wide, As if a cavern was suddenly hollowed; And the Piper advanced and the children followed, And when all were in to the very last, door in the mountain-side shut fast.

Did I say, all No! One was lame, And could not dance the whole of the way; And in after years, if you would blame His sadness, he was used to say,—"It's dull in our town since my playmates left! "I can't forget that I'm bereft "Of all the pleasant sights they see, "Which the Piper also promised me. "For he led us, he said, to a joyous land, "Joining the town and just at hand, "Where waters gushed and fruit-trees grew "And flowers put forth a fairer hue, "And everything was strange and new; "The sparrows were brighter than peacocks here, "And their dogs outran our fallow deer, "And honey-bees had lost their stings, "And horses were born with eagles' wings: "And just as I became assured "My lame foot would be speedily cured, "The music stopped and I stood still, "And found myself outside the hill, "Left alone against my will, "To go now limping as before, "And never hear of that country more!"

XIV.

Alas, alas for Hamelin! There came into many a burgher's pate A text which says that heaven's gate Opes to the rich at as easy rate As the needle's eye takes a camel in! The mayor sent East, West, North and South, To offer the Piper, by word of mouth, Wherever it was men's lot to find him, Silver and gold to his heart's content, If he'd only return the way he went, And bring the children behind him. But when they saw 'twas a lost endeavour, And Piper and dancers were gone for ever, They made a decree that lawyers never Should think their records dated duly If, after the day of the month and year, These words did not as well appear, "And so long after what happened here "On the Twenty-second of July, "Thirteen hundred and seventy-six:" And the better in memory to fix The place of the children's last retreat, They called it, the Pied Piper's Street—Where any one playing on pipe or tabor Was sure for the future to lose his labour.

Nor suffered they hostelry or tavern To shock with mirth a street so solemn; But opposite the place of the cavern They wrote the story on a column, And on the great church-window painted The same, to make the world acquainted How their children were stolen away, And there it stands to this very day. And I must not omit to say That in Transylvania there's a tribe Of alien people who ascribe The outlandish ways and dress which their neighbours lay such stress, To their fathers and mothers having risen Out of some subterraneous prison Into which they were trepanned Long time ago in a mighty band Out of Hamelin town in Brunswick land, But how or why, they don't understand.

XV.

So, Willy, let me and you be wipers Of scores out with all menespecially pipers! And, whether they pipe us free fr<o'>m rats or fr<o'>m mice, If we've promised them aught, let us keep our promise! Pippa's Song The year's at the spring, And day's at the morn; Morning's at seven; The hill-side's dew-pearl'd; The lark's on the wing; The snail's on the thorn; God's in His heaven-All's right with the world!

Popularity

I.

Still, true poet that you are!
    I know you; let me try and draw you.
Some night you'll fail us: when afar

You rise, remember one man saw you,
Knew you, and named a star!

II.

Star, God's glow-worm! Why extend
That loving hand of his which leads you
Yet locks you safe from end to end
Of this dark world, unless he needs you,
Just saves your light to spend.

III.

Clenched hand shall unclose at last,
I know, and let out all the beauty:
My poet holds the future fast,
Accepts the coming ages' duty,
Their present for this past.

IV.

Day, the earth's feast-master's brow
Shall clear, to God the chalice raising;
"Others give best at first, but thou
"Forever set'st our table praising,
"Keep'st the good wine till now!"

V.

I'll draw you as you stand,
With few or none to watch and wonder:
I'll saya fisher, on the sand
By Tyre the old, with ocean-plunder,
A netful, brought to land.

VI.

Has not heard how Tyrian shells
Enclosed the blue, that dye of dyes
Whereof one drop worked miracles,
And coloured like Astarte's eyes
Raw silk the merchant sells

VII.

And each bystander of them all
Could criticize, and quote tradition
How depths of blue sublimed some pall
To get which, pricked a king's ambition
Worth sceptre, crown and ball.

VIII.

There's the dye, in that rough mesh,
The sea has only just o'erwhispered!
Live whelks, each lip's beard dripping fresh,
As if they still the water's lisp heard
Through foam the rock-weeds thresh.

IX.

To furnish Solomon
Such hangings for his cedar-house,
That, when gold-robed he took the throne
In that abyss of blue, the Spouse
Might swear his presence shone

X.

Like the centre-spike of gold
Which burns deep in the blue-bell's womb,
What time, with ardours manifold,
The bee goes singing to her groom,
Drunken and overbold.

XI.

Conchs! not fit for warp or woof!
Till cunning come to pound and squeeze
And clarify,refine to proof
The liquor filtered by degrees,
While the world stands aloof.

XII.

And there's the extract, flasked and fine,

And priced and saleable at last!
And Hobbs, Nobbs, Stokes and Nokes combine
To paint the future from the past,
Put blue into their line.

XIII.

Hints blue,Straight he turtle eats:
Nobbs prints blue,claret crowns his cup:
Nokes outdares Stokes in azure feats,—
Both gorge. Who fished the murex up
What porridge had John Keats The Syrian Venus.
Molluscs from which the famous
Tyrian purple dye was obtained.
Porphyria's Lover
Rain set early in to-night,
The sullen wind was soon awake,
It tore the elm-tops down for spite,
And did its worst to vex the lake:
I listened with heart fit to break.
When glided in Porphyria; straight
She shut the cold out and the storm,
And kneeled and made the cheerless grate
Blaze up, and all the cottage warm;
Which done, she rose, and from her form
Withdrew the dripping cloak and shawl,
And laid her soiled gloves by,
untied Her hat and let the damp hair fall,
And, last, she sat down by my side
And called me. When no voice replied,
She put my arm about her waist,
And made her smooth white shoulder bare,
And all her yellow hair displaced,
And, stooping, made my cheek lie there,
And spread, o'er all, her yellow hair,
Murmuring how she loved meshe
Too weak, for all her heart's endeavour,
To set its struggling passion free
From pride, and vainer ties dissever,

And give herself to me for ever.
But passion sometimes would prevail,
Nor could to-night's gay feast restrain
A sudden thought of one so pale
For love of her, and all in vain:
So, she was come through wind and rain.
Be sure I looked up at her eyes
Happy and proud; at last I knew
Porphyria worshipped me; surprise
Made my heart swell, and still it grew
While I debated what to do.
Moment she was mine, mine, fair,
Perfectly pure and good: I found
A thing to do, and all her hair
In one long yellow string I wound
Three times her little throat around,
And strangled her. No pain felt she;
I am quite sure she felt no pain.
As a shut bud that holds a bee,
I warily oped her lids: again
Laughed the blue eyes without a stain.
And I untightened next the tress
About her neck; her cheek once more
Blushed bright beneath my burning kiss:
I propped her head up as before, Only,
this time my shoulder bore
Her head, which droops upon it still:
The smiling rosy little head,
So glad it has its utmost will,
That all it scorned at once is fled, And I,
its love, am gained instead!
Porphyria's love: she guessed not how
Her darling one wish would be heard.
And thus we sit together now,
And all night long we have not stirred,
And yet God has not said a word!
Prospice
Fear deathto feel the fog in my throat,

The mist in my face,
When the snows begin, and the blasts denote
I am nearing the place,
The power of the night, the press of the storm,
The post of the foe;
Where he stands, the Arch Fear in a visible form;
Yet the strong man must go:
For the journey is done and the summit attained,
And the barriers fall,
Though a battle's to fight ere the guerdon be gained,
The reward of it all.
I was ever a fighter, soone fight more,
The best and the last!
I would hate that Death bandaged my eyes,
And forbore, And made me creep past.
No! let me taste the whole of it, fare like my peers,
The heroes of old,
Bear the brunt, in a minute pay glad life's arrears
Of pain, darkness and cold.
For sudden the worst turns the best to the brave.
The black minute's at end,
And the elements' rage, the fiend voices that rave,
Shall dwindle, shall blend,
Shall change, shall become first a peace out of pain.
Then a light, then thy breat,
O thou soul of my soul! I shall clasp thee again,
And with God be the rest!

Protus

Among these latter busts we count by scores, Half-emperors and quarter-emperors, Each with his bay-leaf fillet, loose-thonged vest, Loricand low-browed Gorgon on the breast,—One loves a baby face, with violets there, Violets instead of laurel in the hair, As those were all the little locks could bear. Now read here. "Protus ends a period "Of empery beginning with a god; "Born in the porphyry chamber at Byzant, "Queens by his cradle, proud and ministrant: "And if he quickened breath there, 'twould like fire "Pantingly through the dim vast realm transpire. "A fame that he was missing spread afar: "The world from its four corners, rose in war, "Till he was borne out on a balcony "To pacify the world when it should see. "The captains ranged before him, one, his hand "Made baby points at, gained the chief command. "And day by day more beautiful he grew "In shape, all said, in feature and in hue, "While young Greek sculptors, gazing on the child, "Because with old Greek sculptore reconciled. "Already sages laboured to condense "In easy tomes a life's experience: "And artists took grave counsel to impart "In one breath and one hand-sweep, all their art—"To make his graces prompt as blossoming "Of plentifully-watered palms in spring: "Since well beseems it, whoso mounts the throne, "For beauty, knowledge, strength, should stand alone, "And mortals love the letters of his name."

Stop! Have you turned two pages Still the same. New reign, same date. The scribe goes on to say How that same year, on such a month and day, "John the Pannonian, groundedly believed "A Blacksmith's bastard, whose hard hand reprieved "The Empire from its fate the year before,—"Came, had a mind to take the crown, and wore "The same for six years (during which the Huns "Kept off their fingers from us), till his sons "Put something in his liquor"and so forth. Then a new reign. Stay"Take at its just worth" (Subjoins an annotator) "what I give

"As hearsay. Some think, John let Protus live "And slip away. 'Tis said, he reached man's age "At some blind northern court; made, first a page, "Then tutor to the children; last, of use "About the hunting-stables. I deduce "He wrote the little tract 'On worming dogs,' "Whereof the name in sundry catalogues.

"Is extant yet. A Protus of the race "Is rumoured to have died a monk in Thrace,—"And if the same, he reached senility." Here's John the Smith's rough-hammered head. Great eye, Gross jaw and griped lips do what granite can To give you the crown-grasper. What a man!

Rabbi Ben Ezra

Grow old along with me! The best is yet to be, The last of life, for which the first was made: Our times are in His hand

Who saith 'A whole I planned, Youth shows but half; trust God: see all, nor be afraid!' Not that, amassing flowers, Youth sighed 'Which rose make ours, Which lily leave and then as best recall' Not that, admiring stars, It yearned 'Nor Jove, nor Mars; Mine be some figured flame which blends, transcends them all!' Not for such hopes and fears Annulling youth's brief years, Do I remonstrate: folly wide the mark! Rather I prize the doubt Low kinds exist without, Finished and finite clods, untroubled by a spark. Poor vaunt of life indeed, Were man but formed to feed On joy, to solely seek and find and feast: Such feasting ended, then As sure an end to men; Irks care the crop-full bird Frets doubt the maw-crammed beast Rejoice we are allied To That which doth provide And not partake, effect and not receive! A spark disturbs our clod; Nearer we hold of God Who gives, than of His tribes that take, I must believe.

Then, welcome each rebuff That turns earth's smoothness rough, Each sting that bids nor sit nor stand but go! Be our joys three-parts pain! Strive, and hold cheap the strain; Learn, nor account the pang; dare, never grudge the throe! For thence,—a paradox Which comforts while it mocks,-Shall life succeed in that it seems to fail: What I aspired to be, And was not, comforts me:

A brute I might have been, but would not sink i' the scale. What is he but a brute Whose flesh has soul to suit, Whose spirit works lest arms and legs want play To man, propose this test-Thy body at its best, How far can that project thy soul on its lone way Yet gifts should prove their use: I own the Past profuse Of power each side, perfection every turn: Eyes, ears took in their dole, Brain treasured up the whole; Should not the heart beat once 'How good to live and learn' Not once beat 'Praise be Thine! I see the whole design, I, who saw power, see now love perfect too: Perfect I call Thy plan: Thanks that I was a man! Maker, remake, complete.

I trust what Thou shalt do!' For pleasant is this flesh; Our soul, in its rose-mesh Pulled ever to the earth, still yearns for rest; Would we some prize might hold To match those manifold Possessions of the brute,—gain most, as we did best! Let us not always say, 'Spite of this flesh to-day I strove, made head, gained ground upon the whole!' As the bird wings and sings, Let us cry 'All good things Are ours, nor soul helps flesh more, now, than flesh helps soul!' Therefore I summon age To grant youth's heritage, Life's struggle having so far reached its term: Thence shall I pass, approved A man, for aye removed From the developed brute; a god though in the germ. And I shall thereupon Take rest, ere I be gone Once more on my adventure brave and new: Fearless and unperplexed, When I wage battle next, What weapons to select, what armour to indue. Youth ended, I shall try My gain or loss thereby; Leave the fire ashes, what survives is gold: And I shall weigh the same, Give life its praise or blame: Young, all lay in dispute; I shall know, being old.

For note, when evening shuts, A certain moment cuts The deed off, calls the glory from the grey: A whisper from the west Shoots—'Add this to the rest, Take it and try its worth: here dies another day.' So, still within this life, Though lifted o'er its strife, Let me discern, compare, pronounce at last, This rage was right i' the main, That acquiescence vain: The Future I may face now I have proved the Past.' For more is not reserved To man, with soul just nerved To act to-morrow what he learns to-day: Here, work enough to watch The Master work, and catch Hints of the proper craft, tricks of the tool's true play. As it was better, youth Should strive, through acts uncouth, Toward making, than repose on aught found made: So, better, age, exempt From strife, should know, than tempt Further.

Thou waitedst age: wait death nor be afraid! Enough now, if the Right And Good and Infinite Be named here, as thou callest thy hand thine own With knowledge absolute, Subject to no dispute From fools that crowded youth, nor let thee feel alone. Be there, for once and all, Severed great minds from small, Announced to each his station in the Past! Was I, the world arraigned, Were they, my soul disdained, Right Let age speak the truth and give us peace at last! Now, who shall arbitrate Ten men love what I hate, Shun what I follow, slight what I receive; Ten, who in ears and eyes Match me: we all surmise, They this thing, and I that: whom shall my soul believe Not on the vulgar mass Called 'work,' must sentence pass, Things done, that took the eye and had the price; O'er which, from level stand, The low world laid its hand, Found straightway to its mind, could value in a trice: But all, the world's coarse thumb And finger failed to plumb, So passed in making up the main account; All instincts immature, All purposes unsure, That weighed not as his work, yet swelled the man's amount: Thoughts hardly to be packed Into a narrow act, Fancies that broke through language and escaped; All I could never be, All, men ignored in me, This, I was worth to God, whose wheel the pitcher shaped.

Any, note that Potter's wheel, That metaphor! and feel Why time spins fast, why passive lies our clay,-Thou, to whom fools propound, When the wine makes its round 'Since life fleets, all is change; the Past gone, seize to-day!' Fool! All that is, at all, Lasts ever, past recall; Earth changes, but thy soul and God stand sure: What entered into thee, That was, is, and shall be: Time's wheel runs back or stops: Potter and clay endure. He fixed thee mid this dance Of plastic circumstance, This Present, thou, forsooth, wouldst fain arrest: Machinery just meant To give thy soul its bent, Try thee and turn thee forth, sufficiently impressed.

What though the earlier grooves, Which ran the laughing loves Around thy base, no longer pause and press What though, about thy rim, Skull-things in order grim Grow out, in graver mood, obey the sterner stress Look not thou down but up! To uses of a cup, The festal board, lamp's flash and trumpet's peal, The new wine's foaming flow, The Master's lips a-glow! Thou, heaven's consummate cup, what need'st thou with earth's wheel But I need, now as then, Thee, God, who mouldest men;

And since, not even while the whirl was worst, Did I,—to the wheel of life With shapes and colours rife, Bound dizzily,—mistake my end, to slake Thy thirst: So, take and use Thy work: Amend what flaws may lurk, What strain o' the stuff, what warpings past the aim! My times be in Thy hand! Perfect the cup as planned! Let age approve of youth, and death complete the same!

Respectability

I.

Had the world in its caprice
Deigned to proclaim "I know you both,
"Have recognized your plighted troth,
Am sponsor for you: live in peace!"—
How many precious months and years
Of youth had passed, that speed so fast,
Before we found it out at last,
The world, and what it fears

II.

Much of priceless life were spent
With men that every virtue decks,
And women models of their sex,
Society's true ornament,—
we dared wander, nights like this,
Thro' wind and rain, and watch the Seine,
And feel the Boulevart break again
To warmth and light and bliss

III.

I know! the world proscribes not love;
Allows my finger to caress
Your lips' contour and downiness,
Provided it supply a glove.
The world's good word!the Institute!
Guizot receives Montalembert!
Eh Down the court three lampions flare:
Put forward your best foot!

Saul

I.

Abner, "At last thou art come! Ere I tell, ere thou speak,
"Kiss my cheek, wish me well!" Then I wished it, and did kiss
his cheek. And he, "Since the King, O my friend, for thy

countenance sent, "Neither drunken nor eaten have we; nor until from his tent "Thou return with the joyful assurance the King liveth yet, "Shall our lip with the honey be bright, with the water be wet. "For out of the black mid-tent's silence, a space of three days, "Not a sound hath escaped to thy servants, of prayer nor of praise, "To betoken that Saul and the Spirit have ended their strife, "And that, faint in his triumph, the monarch sinks back upon life.

II.

"Yet now my heart leaps, O beloved! God's child with his dew "On thy gracious gold hair, and those lilies still living and blue "Just broken to twine round thy harp-strings, as if no wild beat "Were now raging to torture the desert!"

III.

Then I, as was meet, down to the God of my fathers, and rose on my feet, And ran o'er the sand burnt to powder. The tent was unlooped; I pulled up the spear that obstructed, and under I stooped Hands and knees on the slippery grass-patch, all withered and gone, That extends to the second enclosure, I groped my way on Till I felt where the foldskirts fly open. Then once more I prayed, And opened the foldskirts and entered, and was not afraid But spoke, "Here is David, thy servant!" And no voice replied. At the first I saw nought but the blackness but soon I descried A something more black than the blacknessthe vast, the upright Main prop which sustains the pavilion: and slow into sight Grew a figure against it, gigantic and blackest of all. Then a sunbeam, that burst thro' the tent-roof, showed Saul.

IV.

Stood as erect as that tent-prop, both arms stretched out wide On the great cross-support in the centre, that goes to each side; He relaxed not a muscle, but hung there as, caught in his pangs And waiting his change, the king-serpent all heavily hangs, Far away from his kind, in the pine, till deliverance come With the spring-time,so agonized Saul, drear and stark, blind and dumb.

V.

Then I tuned my harp,took off the lilies we twine round its chords Lest they snap 'neath the stress of the noon-tidethose sunbeams like swords! And I first played the tune all our sheep know, as, one after one, So docile they come to the pen-door till folding be done. They are white and untorn by the bushes, for lo, they have fed Where the long grasses stifle the water within the stream's bed; And now one after one seeks its lodging, as star follows star Into eve and the blue far above us,so blue and so far!

VI.

Then the tune, for which quails on the cornland will each leave his mate To fly after the player; then, what makes the crickets elate Till for boldr ess they fight one another: and then, what has weight To set the quick jerboa amusing outside his sand house—There are none such as he for a wonder, half bird and half mouse! God made all the creatures and gave them our love and our fear, To give sign, we and they are his children, one family here.

VII.

Then I played the help-tune of our reapers, their wine-song, when hand Grasps at hand, eye lights eye in good friendship, and great hearts expand And grow one in the sense of this world's life.And then, the last song When the dead man is praised on his journey"Bear, bear him along "With his few faults shut up like dead flowerets! Are balm-seeds not here "To console us The land has none left such as he on the bier. "Oh, would we might keep thee, my brother!"And then, the glad chaunt Of the marriage,first go the young maidens, next, she whom we vaunt As the beauty, the pride of our dwelling.And then, the great march Wherein man runs to man to assist him and buttress an arch Nought can break; who shall harm them, our friendsThen, the chorus intoned As the Levites go up to the altar in glory enthroned. But I stopped here: for here in the darkness Saul groaned.

VIII.

And I paused, held my breath in such silence, and listened apart; And the tent shook, for mighty Saul shuddered: and sparkles 'gan dart From the jewels that woke in his turban, at once with a start, All its lordly male-sapphires, and rubies courageous at heart. So the head: but the body still moved not, still hung there erect. And I bent once again to my playing, pursued it unchecked, As I sang,—

IX.

"Oh, our manhood's prime vigour! No spirit feels waste, "Not a muscle is stopped in its playing nor sinew unbraced. "Oh, the wild joys of living! the leaping from rock up to rock, "The strong rending of boughs from the fir-tree, the cool silver shock "Of the plunge in a pool's living water, the hunt of the bear, "And the sultriness showing the lion is couched in his lair. "And the meal, the rich dates yellowed over with gold dust divine, "And the locust-flesh steeped in the pitcher, the full draught of wine, "And the sleep in the dried river-channel where bulrushes tell "That the water was wont to go warbling so softly and well.

"How good is man's life, the mere living! how fit to employ "All the heart and the soul and the senses for ever in joy! "Hast thou loved the white locks of thy father, whose sword thou didst guard "When he trusted thee forth with the armies, for glorious reward "Didst thou see the thin hands of thy mother, held up as men sung "The low song of the nearly-departed, and bear her faint tongue "Joining in while it could to the witness, 'Let one more attest, " 'I have lived, seen God's hand thro'a lifetime, and all was for best' "Then they sung thro' their tears in strong triumph, not much, but the rest. "And thy brothers, the help and the contest, the working whence grew "Such result as, from seething grape-bundles, the spirit strained true:

"And the friends of thy boyhoodthat boyhood of wonder and hope, "Present promise and wealth of the future beyond the eye's scope,—"Till lo, thou art grown to a monarch; a people is thine; "And all gifts, which the world offers singly, on one head combine! "On one head, all the beauty and strength, love and rage (like the throe "That, a-work in the rock, helps its labour and lets the gold go) "High ambition and deeds which surpass it, fame crowning them,all "Brought to blaze on the head of one creatureKing Saul!"

X.

And lo, with that leap of my spirit,heart, hand, harp and voice, Each lifting Saul's name out of sorrow, each bidding rejoice Saul's fame in the light it was made foras when, dare I say, The Lord's army, in rapture of service, strains through its array, And up soareth the cherubim-chariot"Saul!" cried I, and stopped, And waited the thing that should follow. Then Saul, who hung propped By the tent's cross-support in the centre, was struck by his name. Have ye seen when Spring's arrowy summons goes right to the aim, And some mountain, the last to withstand her, that held (he alone, While the vale laughed in freedom and flowers) on a broad bust of stone A year's snow bound about for a breastplate,leaves grasp of the sheet Fold on fold all at once it crowds thunderously down to his feet, And there fronts you, stark, black, but alive yet, your mountain of old, With his rents, the successive bequeathings of ages untold—Yea, each harm got in fighting your battles, each furrow and scar Of his head thrust 'twixt you and the tempestall hail, there they are! Now again to be softened with verdure, again hold the nest.

Of the dove, tempt the goat and its young to the green on his crest For their food in the ardours of summer. One long shudder thrilled All the tent till the very air tingled, then sank and was stilled At the King's self left standing before me, released and aware. What was gone, what remained All to traverse, 'twixt hope and despair; Death was past, life not come: so he waited. Awhile his right hand Held the brow, helped the eyes left too vacant forthwith to remand To their place what new objects should enter: 'twas Saul as before. I looked up and dared gaze at those eyes, nor was hurt any more Than by slow pallid sunsets in autumn, ye watch from the shore, At their sad level gaze o'er the oceana sun's slow decline

Over hills which, resolved in stern silence, o'erlap and entwine Base with base to knit strength more intensely: so, arm folded arm O'er the chest whose slow heavings subsided.

XI.

What spell or what charm,

(For, awhile there was trouble within me) what next should I urge To sustain him where song had restored himSong filled to the verge His cup with the wine of this life, pressing all that it yields Of mere fruitage, the strength and the beauty: beyond, on what fields, Glean a vintage more potent and perfect to brighten the eye And bring blood to the lip, and commend them the cup they put by He saith, "It is good;" still he drinks not: he lets me praise life, Gives assent, yet would die for his own part.

XII.

Then fancies grew rife

Which had come long ago on the pasture, when round me the sheep Fed in silenceabove, the one eagle wheeled slow as in sleep; And I lay in my hollow and mused on the world that might lie 'Neath his ken, though I saw but the strip 'twixt the hill and the sky: And I laughed``Since my days are ordained to be passed with my flocks, ``Let me people at least, with my fancies, the plains and the rocks, ``Dream the life I am never to mix with, and image the show ``Of mankind as they live in those fashions I hardly shall know! ``Schemes of life, its best rules and right uses, the courage that gains, ``And the prudence that keeps what men strive for." And now these old trains Of vague thought came again; I grew surer; so, once more the string Of my harp made response to my spirit, as thus—

XIII.

"Yea, my King,"

I began"thou dost well in rejecting mere comforts that spring "From the mere mortal life held in common by man and by brute: "In our flesh grows the branch of this life, in our soul it bears fruit. "Thou hast marked the slow rise of the tree,how its stem trembled first "Till it passed the kid's lip, the stag's antler then safely outburst "The fan-branches all round; and thou mindest when these too, in turn "Broke a-bloom and the palm-tree seemed perfect: yet more was to learn, "E'en the good that comes in with the palm-fruit. Our dates shall we slight, "When their juice brings a cure for all sorrow or care for the plight "Of the palm's self whose slow growth produced them Not so! stem and branch "Shall decay, nor be known in their place, while the palm-wine shall staunch "Every wound of man's spirit in winter. I pour thee such wine. "Leave the flesh to the fate it was fit for! the spirit be thine! "By the spirit, when age shall o'ercome thee, thou still shalt enjoy "More indeed, than at first when inconscious, the life of a boy.

"Crush that life, and behold its wine running! Each deed thou hast done "Dies, revives, goes to work in the world; until e'en as the sun "Looking down on the earth, though clouds spoil him, though tempests efface, "Can find nothing his own deed produced not, must everywhere trace "The results of his past summer-prime'so, each ray of thy will, "Every flash of thy passion and prowess, long over, shall thrill "Thy whole people, the countless, with ardour, till they too give forth "A like cheer to their sons, who in turn, fill the South and the North "With the radiance thy deed was the germ of. Carouse in the past! "But the license of age has its limit; thou diest at last: "As the lion when age dims his eyeball, the rose at her height "So with manso his power and his beauty for ever take flight.

"No! Again a long draught of my soul-wine! Look forth o'er the years! "Thou hast done now with eyes for the actual; begin with the seer's! "Is Saul dead In the depth of the vale make his tombbid arise "A grey mountain of marble heaped four-square, till, built to the skies, "Let it mark where the great First King slumbers: whose fame would ye know "Up above see the rock's naked face, where the record shall go "In great characters cut by the scribe,Such was Saul, so he did; "With the sages directing the work, by the populace chid,—"For not half, they'll affirm, is comprised there! Which fault to amend,

"In the grove with his kind grows the cedar, whereon they shall spend "(See, in tablets 'tis level before them) their praise, and record "With the gold of the graver, Saul's story,the statesman's great word "Side by side with the poet's sweet comment. The river's a-wave "With smooth paper-reeds grazing each other when prophet-winds rave: "So the pen gives unborn generations their due and their part "In thy being! Then, first of the mighty, thank God that thou art!"

XIV.

And behold while I sang... but O Thou who didst grant me that day, And before it not seldom hast granted thy help to essay, Carry on and complete an adventure,my shield and my sword In that act where my soul was thy servant, thy word was my word,—Still be with me, who then at the summit of human endeavour And scaling the highest, man's thought could, gazed hopeless as ever On the new stretch of heaven above metill, mighty to save, Just one lift of thy hand cleared that distanceGod's throne from man's grave! Let me tell out my tale to its endingmy voice to my heart Which can scarce dare believe in what marvels last night I took part, As this morning I gather the fragments, alone with my sheep, And still fear lest the terrible glory evanish like sleep! For I wake in the grey dewy covert, while Hebron upheaves The dawn struggling with night on his shoulder, and Kidron retrieves Slow the damage of yesterday's sunshine.

XV.

I say then,my song

While I sang thus, assuring the monarch, and ever more strong Made a proffer of good to console himhe slowly resumed His old motions and habitudes kingly. The right-hand replumed His black locks to their wonted composure, adjusted the swathes Of his turban, and seethe huge sweat that his countenance bathes, He wipes off with the robe; and he girds now his loins as of yore, And feels slow for the armlets of price, with the clasp set before. He is Saul, ye remember in glory,ere error had bent The broad brow from the daily communion;

and still, though much spent Be the life and the bearing that front you, the same, God did choose, To receive what a man may waste, desecrate, never quite lose. So sank he along by the tent-prop till, stayed by the pile Of his armour and war-cloak and garments, he leaned there awhile, And sat out my singing,one arm round the tent-prop, to raise His bent head, and the other hung slacktill I touched on the praise I foresaw from all men in all time, to the man patient there; And thus ended, the harp falling forward.

Then first I was 'ware That he sat, as I say, with my head just above his vast knees Which were thrust out on each side around me, like oak-roots which please To encircle a lamb when it slumbers. I looked up to know If the best I could do had brought solace: he spoke not, but slow Lifted up the hand slack at his side, till he laid it with care Soft and grave, but in mild settled will, on my brow: thro' my hair The large fingers were pushed, and he bent back my bead, with kind power—All my face back, intent to peruse it, as men do a flower.

Held he me there with his great eyes that scrutinized mine—And oh, all my heart how it loved him! but where was the sign I yearned"Could I help thee, my father, inventing a bliss, "I would add, to that life of the past, both the future and this; "I would give thee new life altogether, as good, ages hence, "As this moment,had love but the warrant, love's heart to dispense!"

XVI.

Then the truth came upon me. No harp moreno song more! outbroke—

XVII.

"I have gone the whole round of creation: I saw and I spoke: "I, a work of God's hand for that purpose, received in my brain "And pronounced on the rest of his hand-workreturned him again "His creation's approval or censure: I spoke as I saw: "I report, as a man may of God's workall's love, yet all's law. "Now I lay down the judgeship he lent me. Each faculty tasked "To perceive him, has gained an abyss, where a dewdrop was asked. "Have I knowledge confounded it shrivels at Wisdom laid bare. "Have I forethought how purblind, how blank, to the Infinite Care! "Do I task any faculty highest, to image success "I but open my eyes,and perfection, no more and no less, "In the kind I imagined, full-fronts me, and God is seen God "In the star, in the stone, in the flesh, in the soul and the clod. "And thus looking within and around me, I ever renew "(With that stoop of the soul which in bending upraises it too) "The submission of man's nothing-perfect to God's all-complete, "As by each new obeisance in spirit, I climb to his feet. "Yet with all this abounding experience, this deity known.

"I shall dare to discover some province, some gift of my own. "There's a faculty pleasant to exercise, hard to hoodwink, "I am fain to keep still in abeyance, (I laugh as I think) "Lest, insisting to claim and parade in it, wot ye, I worst "E'en the Giver in one gift.Behold, I could love if I durst! "But I sink the pretension as fearing a man may o'ertake "God's own speed in the one way of love:

I abstain for love's sake. "What, my soul see thus far and no farther when doors great and small, "Nine-and-ninety flew ope at our touch, should the hundredth appal "In the least things have faith, yet distrust in the greatest of all "Do I find love so full in my nature, God's ultimate gift, "That I doubt his own love can compete with it Here, the parts shift "Here, the creature surpass the Creator,the end, what Began "Would I fain in my impotent yearning do all for this man.

"And dare doubt he alone shall not help him, who yet alone can "Would it ever have entered my mind, the bare will, much less power, "To bestow on this Saul what I sang of, the marvellous dower "Of the life he was gifted and filled with to make such a soul, "Such a body, and then such an earth for insphering the whole "And doth it not enter my mind (as my warm tears attest) "These good things being given, to go on, and give one more, the best "Ay, to save and redeem and restore him, maintain at the height "This perfection,succeed with life's day-spring, death's minute of night "Interpose at the difficult minute, snatch Saul the mistake, "Saul the failure, the ruin he seems now,and bid him awake "From the dream, the probation, the prelude, to find himself set "Clear and safe in new light and new life,a new harmony yet "To be run, and continued, and endedwho knowsor endure! "The man taught enough, by life's dream, of the rest to make sure; "By the pain-throb, triumphantly winning intensified bliss, "And the next world's reward and repose, by the struggles in this.

XVIII.

"I believe it! 'Tis thou, God, that givest, 'tis I who receive: "In the first is the last, in thy will is my power to believe. "All's one gift: thou canst grant it moreover, as prompt to my prayer "As I breathe out this breath, as I open these arms to the air. "From thy will, stream the worlds, life and nature, thy dread Sabaoth: "_I_ willthe mere atoms despise me! Why am I not loth "To look that, even that in the face too Why is it I dare "Think but lightly of such impuissance What stops my despair "This;'tis not what man Does which exalts him, but what man Would do! "See the KingI would help him but cannot, the wishes fall through.

"Could I wrestle to raise him from sorrow, grow poor to enrich, "To fill up his life, starve my own out, I wouldknowing which, "I know that my service is perfect. Oh, speak through me now! "Would I suffer for him that I love So wouldst thouso wilt thou! "So shall crown thee the topmost, ineffablest, uttermost crown—"And thy love fill infinitude wholly, nor leave up nor down "One spot for the creature to stand in! It is by no breath, "Turn of eye, wave of hand, that salvation joins issue with death!

"As thy Love is discovered almighty, almighty be proved "Thy power, that exists with and for it, of being Beloved! "He who did most, shall bear most; the strongest shall stand the most weak. "'Tis the weakness in strength, that I cry for! my flesh, that I seek "In the Godhead! I seek and I find it. O Saul, it shall be "A Face like my face that receives thee; a Man like to me, "Thou shalt love and be loved by, for ever: a Hand like this hand "Shall throw open the gates of new life to thee! See the Christ stand!"

XIX.

I know not too well how I found my way home in the night. There were witnesses, cohorts about me, to left and to right, Angels, powers, the unuttered, unseen, the alive, the aware: I repressed, I got through them as hardly, as strugglingly there, As a runner beset by the populace famished for news—Life or death. The whole earth was awakened, hell loosed with her crews; And the stars of night beat with emotion, and tingled and shot Out in fire the strong pain of pent knowledge: but I fainted not, For the Hand still impelled me at once and supported, suppressed All the tumult, and quenched it with quiet, and holy behest, Till the rapture was shut in itself, and the earth sank to rest.

Anon at the dawn, all that trouble had withered from earth—Not so much, but I saw it die out in the day's tender birth; In the gathered intensity brought to the grey of the hills; In the shuddering forests' held breath; in the sudden wind-thrills; In the startled wild beasts that bore off, each with eye sidling still Though averted with wonder and dread; in the birds stiff and chill That rose heavily, as I approached them, made stupid with awe: E'en the serpent that slid away silent,he felt the new law. The same stared in the white humid faces upturned by the flowers; The same worked in the heart of the cedar and moved the vine-bowers: And the little brooks witnessing murmured, persistent and low, With their obstinate, all but hushed voices"E'en so, it is so!" The jumping hare.

One of the three cities of Refuge. A brook in Jerusalem. Soliloquy Of The Spanish Cloister

I.

R-rthere go, my heart's abhorrence!
Water your damned flower-pots, do!
If hate killed men, Brother Lawrence,
God's blood, would not mine kill you!
What your myrtle-bush wants trimming
Oh, that rose has prior claims—
Needs its leaden vase filled brimming
Hell dry you up with its flames!

II.

The meal we sit together:
    Salve tibi!I must hear Wise talk of
The kind of weather, Sort of season,
    time of year: _Not a plenteous cork-crop: scarcely
Dare we hope oak-galls, I doubt:
    What's the Latin name for "parsley"_
What's the Greek name for Swine's Snout

III.

We'll have our platter burnished,
    Laid with care on our own shelf!
With a fire-new spoon we're furnished,
    And a goblet for ourself,
like something sacrificial
    Ere 'tis fit to touch our chaps—
Marked with L. for our initial!
    (He-he! There his lily snaps!)

IV.

Saint_, forsooth! While brown Dolores
    Squats outside the Convent bank
With Sanchicha, telling stories,
    Steeping tresses in the tank,
Black, lustrous, thick like horsehairs,
    Can't I see his dead eye glow,
Bright as 'twere a Barbary corsair's
    (That is, if he'd let it show!)

V.

He finishes refection,
    Knife and fork he never lays
Cross-wise, to my recollection,
    As do I, in Jesu's praise. I the
Trinity illustrate, Drinking watered orange-pulp—
    In three sips the Arian frustrate;
While he drains his at one gulp.

VI.

Those melons If he's able
We're to have a feast! so nice!
One goes to the Abbot's table,
All of us get each a slice.
Go on your flowers None double
Not one fruit-sort can you spy Strange!
And I, too, at such trouble,
Keep them close-nipped on the sly!

VII.

A great text in Galatians,
Once you trip on it, entails
Twenty-nine distinct damnations,
One sure, if another fails:
If I trip him just a-dying,
Sure of heaven as sure can be,
Spin him round and send him flying
Off to hell, a Manichee

VIII.

My scrofulous French novel
On grey paper with blunt type!
Simply glance at it, you grovel
Hand and foot in Belial's gripe:
If I double down its pages
At the woeful sixteenth print,
When he gathers his greengages,
Ope a sieve and slip it in't

IX.

There's Satan!one might venture
Pledge one's soul to him, yet leave
Such a flaw in the indenture
As he'd miss till, past retrieve,
Blasted lay that rose-acacia
We're so proud of! _Hy, Zy, Hine..._

'St, there's Vespers! _Plena grati
Ave, Virgo!_ Gr-r-ryou swine!

Song I.

But you, who do not love her,
Is she not pure gold, my mistress
Holds earth aughtspeak truthabove her
Aught like this tress, see, and this tress,
And this last fairest tress of all,
So fair, see, ere I let it fall

II.

You spend your lives in praising;
To praise, you search the wide world over:
Then why not witness, calmly gazing,
If earth holds aughtspeak truthabove her
Above this tress, and this, I touch
But cannot praise, I love so much!
Song from 'Paracelsus'
HEAP cassia, sandal-buds and stripes
Of labdanum, and aloe-balls,
D, with dull nard an Indian wipes
From out her hair: such balsam falls Down sea-side mountain pedestals, From tree-tops where tired winds are fain, Spent with the vast and howling main, To treasure half their island-gain. And strew faint sweetness from some old Egyptian's fine worm-eaten shroud Which breaks to dust when once unroll'd; Or shredded perfume, like a cloud From closet long to quiet vow'd, With moth'd and dropping arras hung, Mouldering her lute and books among, As when a queen, long dead, was young. Summum Bonum All the breath and the bloom of the year in the bag of one bee: All the wonder and wealth of the mine in the heart of one gem.

In the core of one pearl all the shade and the shine of the sea: Breath and bloom, shade and shine, wonder, wealth, and—how far above them-Truth, that's brighter than gem, Trust, that's purer than pearl,-Brightest truth, purest trust in the universe—all were for me In the kiss of one girl The Bishop

Orders His Tomb Vanity, saith the preacher, vanity! Draw round my bed: is Anselm keeping back Nephews - sons mine... ah God, I know not! Well-She, men would have to be your mother once, Old Gandolf envied me, so fair she was! What's done is done, and she is dead beside, Dead long ago, and I am Bishop since, And as she died so must we die ourselves, And thence ye may perceive the world's a dream. Life, how and what is it As here I lie.

In this state-chamber, dying by degrees, Hours and long hours in the dead night, I ask "Do I live, am I dead" Peace, peace seems all. Saint Praxed's ever was the church for peace; And so, about this tomb of mine. I fought With tooth and nail to save my niche, ye know: —Old Gandolf cozened me, despite my care; Shrewd was that snatch from out the corner South He graced his carrion with, God curse the same! Yet still my niche is not so cramped but thence One sees the pulpit o' the epistle-side, And somewhat of the choir, those silent seats, And up into the aery dome where live The angels, and a sunbeam's sure to lurk.

And I shall fill my slab of basalt there, And 'neath my tabernacle take my rest, With those nine columns round me, two and two, The odd one at my feet where Anselm stands: Peach-blossom marble all, the rare, the ripe As fresh-poured red wine of a mighty pulse. —Old Gandolf with his paltry onion-stone, Put me where I may look at him! True peach, Rosy and flawless: how I earned the prize! Draw close: that conflagration of my church —What then So much was saved if aught were missed! My sons, ye would not be my death Go dig The white-grape vineyard where the oil-press stood, Drop water gently till the surface sink.

And if ye find... Ah God, I know not, I!... Bedded in store of rotten fig-leaves soft, And corded up in a tight olive-frail, Some lump, ah God, of lapis lazuli, Big as a Jew's head cut off at the nape, Blue as a vein o'er the Madonna's breast... Sons, all have I bequeathed you, villas, all, That brave Frascati villa with its bath, So, let the blue lump poise between my knees, Like God the Father's globe on both His hands Ye worship in the Jesu Church so gay, For Gandolf shall not choose but see and burst! Swift as a weaver's shuttle fleet our years: Man goeth to the grave, and where is he Did I say basalt for my slab, sons Black-'Twas ever antique-black I meant! How else Shall ye contrast my frieze to come beneath The bas-relief in bronze ye promised me, Those Pans and Nymphs ye wot of, and perchance Some tripod, thyrsus, with a vase or so, The Saviour at his sermon on the mount, Saint Praxed in a glory, and one Pan Ready to twitch the Nymph's last garment off, And Moses with the tables... but I know Ye mark me not! What do they whisper thee, Child of my bowels, Anselm Ah, ye hope To revel down my villas while I gasp Bricked o'er with beggar's mouldy travertine Which Gandolf from his tomb-top chuckles at! Nay, boys, ye love me—all of jasper, then! 'Tis jasper ye stand pledged to, lest I grieve.

My bath must needs be left behind, alas! One block, pure green as a pistachio-nut, There's plenty jasper somewhere in the world-And have I not Saint Praxed's ear to pray Horses for ye, and brown Greek manuscripts, And mistresses with great smooth marbly limbs —That's if ye carve my epitaph aright, Choice Latin, picked phrase, Tully's every word, No gaudy ware like Gandolf's second line-Tully, my masters Ulpian serves his need! And then how I shall lie through centuries, And hear the blessed mutter of the mass, And see God made and eaten all day long, And feel the steady candle-flame, and taste Good strong thick stupefying incense-smoke! For as I lie here, hours of the dead night, Dying in state and by such slow degrees, I fold my arms as if they clasped a crook, And stretch my feet forth straight as stone can point.

And let the bedclothes, for a mortcloth, drop Into great laps and folds of sculptor's-work: And as yon tapers dwindle, and strange thoughts Grow, with a certain humming in my ears, About the life before I lived this life, And this life too, popes, cardinals and priests, Saint Praxed at his sermon on the mount, Your tall pale mother with her talking eyes, And new-found agate urns as fresh as day, And marble's language, Latin pure, discreet, —Aha, ELUCESCEBAT quoth our friend No Tully, said I, Ulpian at the best! Evil and brief hath been my pilgrimage. All lapis, all, sons! Else I give the Pope My villas! Will ye ever eat my heart Ever your eyes were as a lizard's quick, They glitter like your mother's for my soul, Or ye would heighten my impoverished frieze, Piece out its starved design, and fill my vase With grapes, and add a vizor and a Term, And to the tripod ye would tie a lynx That in his struggle throws the thyrsus down, To comfort me on my entablature Whereon I am to lie till I must ask.

Do I live, am I dead" There, leave me, there! For ye have stabbed me with ingratitude To death—ye wish it—God, ye wish it! Stone-Gritstone, a-crumble! Clammy squares which sweat As if the corpse they keep were oozing through-And no more lapis to delight the world! Well, go! I bless ye. Fewer tapers there, But in a row: and, going, turn your backs —Ay, like departing altar-ministrants, And leave me in my church, the church for peace, That I may watch at leisure if he leers-Old Gandolf, at me, from his onion-stone, As still he envied me, so fair she was! The Bishop Orders His Tomb At Saint Praxed's Church Vanity, saith the preacher, vanity! Draw round my bed: is Anselm keeping back Nephews — sons mine — ah God, I know not! Well -She, men would have to be your mother once, Old Gandolf envied me, so fair she was! What's done is done, and she is dead beside, Dead long ago, and I am Bishop since, And as she died so must we die ourselves, And thence ye may perceive the world's a dream. Life, how and what is it As here I lie.

In this state-chamber, dying by degrees, Hours and long hours in the dead night, I ask "Do I live, am I dead" Peace, peace seems all. Saint Praxed's ever was the church for peace; And so, about this tomb of mine. I fought With tooth and nail to save my niche, ye know: — Old Gandolf cozened me, despite my care; Shrewd was that snatch from out the corner South He graced his carrion with, God curse the same! Yet still my niche is not so çramped but thence One sees the pulpit o' the epistle-side, And somewhat of the choir, those silent seats, And up into the very dome where live The angels, and a sunbeam's sure to lurk: And I shall fill my slab of basalt there, And 'neath my tabernacle take my rest, With those nine columns round me, two and two, The odd one at my feet where

Anselm stands: Peach-blossom marble all, the rare, the ripe As fresh poured red wine of a mighty pulse — Old Gandolf with his paltry onion-stone, Put me where I may look at him! True peach, Rosy and flawless: how I earned the prize! Draw close: that conflagration of my church — What then So much was saved if aught were missed! My sons, ye would not be my death Go dig The white-grape vineyard where the oil-press stood, Drop water gently till the surface sink.

And if ye find — Ah God, I know not, I! -Bedded in store of rotten fig-leaves soft, And corded up in a tight olive-frail, Some lump, ah God, of lapis lazuli, Big as a Jew's head cut off at the nape, Blue as a vein o'er the Madonna's breast Sons, all have I bequeathed you, villas, all, That brave Frascati villa with its bath, So, let the blue lump poise between my knees, Like God the Father's globe on both his hands Ye worship in the Jesu Church so gay, For Gandolf shall not choose but see and burst! Swift as a weaver's shuttle fleet our years: Man goeth to the grave, and where is he Did I say basalt for my slab, sons Black -'Twas ever antique-black I meant! How else Shall ye contrast my frieze to come beneath The bas-relief in bronze ye promised me.

Those Pans and Nymphs ye wot of, and perchance Some tripod, thyrsus, with a vase or so, The Saviour at his sermon on the mount, Saint Praxed in a glory, and one Pan Ready to twitch the Nymph's last garment off, And Moses with the tables — but I know Ye mark me not! What do they whisper thee, Child of my bowels, Anselm Ah, ye hope To revel down my villas while I gasp Bricked o'er with beggar's mouldy travertine Which Gandolf from his tomb-top chuckles at! Nay, boys, ye love me — all of jasper, then! 'Tis jasper ye stand pledged to, lest I grieve. My bath must needs be left behind, alas! One block, pure green as a pistachio-nut, There's plenty jasper somewhere in the world -And have I not Saint Praxed's ear to pray Horses for ye, and brown Greek manuscripts, And mistresses with great smooth marbly limbs — That's if ye carve my epitaph aright, Choice Latin, picked phrase, Tully's every word, No gaudy ware like Gandolf's second line -Tully, my masters Ulpian serves his need! And then how I shall lie through centuries, And hear the blessed mutter of the mass, And see God made and eaten all day long, And feel the steady candle-flame, and taste Good strong thick stupefying incense-smoke! For as I lie here, hours of the dead night, Dying in state and by such slow degrees, I fold my arms as if they clasped a crook, And stretch my feet forth straight as stone can point, And let the bedclothes, for a mortcloth, drop Into great laps and folds of sculptor's work:

And as yon tapers dwindle, and strange thoughts Grow, with a certain humming in my ears, About the life before I lived this life, And this life too, popes, cardinals and priests, Saint Praxed at his sermon on the mount, Your tall pale mother with her talking eyes, And new-found agate urns as fresh as day, And marble's language, Latin pure, discreet, — Aha, ELUCESCEBAT quoth our friend No Tully, said I, Ulpian at the best! Evil and brief hath been my pilgrimage.

All lapis, all, sons! Else I give the Pope My villas! Will ye ever eat my heart Ever your eyes were as a lizard's quick, They glitter like your mother's for my soul, Or ye would heighten my impoverished frieze, Piece out its starved design, and fill my vase With grapes, and add a visor and a Term, And to the tripod ye would tie a lynx That in his struggle throws the thyrsus down, To comfort me on my entablature Whereon I am to lie till I must ask Do I live, am I dead" There, leave me, there! For ye have stabbed me with ingratitude To death — ye wish it — God, ye wish it! Stone -Gritstone, a crumble! Clammy squares which sweat As if the corpse they keep were oozing through -And no more lapis to delight the world! Well, go! I bless ye. Fewer tapers there, But in a row: and, going, turn your backs.

Ay, like departing altar-ministrants, And leave me in my church, the church for peace, That I may watch at leisure if he leers -Old Gandolf — at me, from his onion-stone, As still he envied me, so fair she was! The Bishop Orders His Tomb at Ssaint Praxed's Church, Rome Vanity, saith the preacher, vanity! Draw round my bed: is Anselm keeping back Nephews—sons mine... ah God, I know not! Well-She, men would have to be your mother once, Old Gandolf envied me, so fair she was! What's done is done, and she is dead beside, Dead long ago, and I am Bishop since, And as she died so must we die ourselves, And thence ye may perceive the world's a dream. Life, how and what is it As here I lie In this state-chamber, dying by degrees, Hours and long hours in the dead night, I ask Do I live, am I dead' Peace, peace seems all.

Saint Praxed's ever was the church for peace; And so, about this tomb of mine. I fought With tooth and nail to save my niche, ye know: —Old Gandolf cozened me, despite my care; Shrewd was that snatch from out the corner South He graced his carrion with, God curse the same! Yet still my niche is not so cramped but thence One sees the pulpit o' the epistle-side, And somewhat of the choir, those silent seats, And up into the aery dome where live The angels, and a sunbeam's sure to lurk And I shall fill my slab of basalt there, And 'neath my tabernacle take my rest, With those nine columns round me, two and two, The odd one at my feet where Anselm stands: Peach-blossom marble all, the rare, the ripe As fresh-poured red wine of a mighty pulse. —Old Gandolf with his paltry onion-stone, Put me where I may look at him! True peach, Rosy and flawless: how I earned the prize! Draw close: that conflagration of my church —What then So much was saved if aught were missed! My sons, ye would not be my death Go dig The white-grape vineyard where the oil-press stood, Drop water gently till the surface sink.

And if ye find... Ah God, I know not, I!... Bedded in store of rotten fig-leaves soft, And corded up in a tight olive-frail, Some lump, ah God, of lapis lazuli, Big as a Jew's head cut off at the nape, Blue as a vein o'er the Madonna's breast... Sons, all have I bequeathed you, villas, all, That brave Frascati villa with its bath, So, let the blue lump poise between my knees, Like God the Father's globe on both His hands Ye worship in the Jesu Church so gay, For Gandolf shall not choose but see and burst! Swift as a weaver's shuttle fleet our years: Man goeth to the grave, and where is he

Did I say basalt for my slab, sons Black-'Twas ever antique-black I meant! How else Shall ye contrast my frieze to come beneath The bas-relief in bronze ye promised me, Some tripod, thyrsus, with a vase or so, The Saviour at his sermon on the mount, Saint Praxed in a glory, and one Pan Ready to twitch the Nymph's last garment off, And Moses with the tables... but I know Ye mark me not! What do they whisper thee, Child of my bowels, Anselm Ah, ye hope To revel down my villas while I gasp Bricked o'er with beggar's mouldy travertine Which Gandolf from his tomb-top chuckles at! Nay, boys, ye love me—all of jasper, then! 'Tis jasper ye stand pledged to, lest I grieve. My bath must needs be left behind, alas! One block, pure green as a pistachio-nut, There's plenty jasper somewhere in the world-And have I not Saint Praxed's ear to pray Horses for ye, and brown Greek manuscripts, And mistresses with great smooth marbly limbs —That's if ye carve my epitaph aright.

Choice Latin, picked phrase, Tully's every word, No gaudy ware like Gandolf's second line-Tully, my masters Ulpian serves his need! And then how I shall lie through centuries, And hear the blessed mutter of the mass, And see God made and eaten all day long, And feel the steady candle-flame, and taste Good strong thick stupefying incense-smoke! For as I lie here, hours of the dead night, Dying in state and by such slow degrees, I fold my arms as if they clasped a crook, And stretch my feet forth straight as stone can point, And let the bedclothes, for a mortcloth, drop Into great laps and folds of sculptor's-work: And as yon tapers dwindle, and strange thoughts Grow, with a certain humming in my ears, About the life before I lived this life, And this life too, popes, cardinals and priests, Saint Praxed at his sermon on the mount, Your tall pale mother with her talking eyes.

And new-found agate urns as fresh as day, And marble's language, Latin pure, discreet, —Aha, ELUCESCEBAT quoth our friend No Tully, said I, Ulpian at the best! Evil and brief hath been my pilgrimage. All lapis, all, sons! Else I give the Pope My villas! Will ye ever eat my heart Ever your eyes were as a lizard's quick, They glitter like your mother's for my soul, Or ye would heighten my impoverished frieze, Piece out its starved design, and fill my vase With grapes, and add a vizor and a Term, And to the tripod ye would tie a lynx That in his struggle throws the thyrsus down, To comfort me on my entablature Whereon I am to lie till I must ask 'Do I live, am I dead' There, leave me, there! For ye have stabbed me with ingratitude To death—ye wish it—God, ye wish it! Stone-Gritstone, a-crumble! Clammy squares which sweat As if the corpse they keep were oozing through-And no more lapis to delight the world! Well, go! I bless ye. Fewer tapers there, But in a row: and, going, turn your backs —Ay, like departing altar-ministrants.

And leave me in my church, the church for peace, That I may watch at leisure if he leers-Old Gandolf, at me, from his onion-stone, As still he envied me, so fair she was! The Boy And the Angel Morning, evening, noon and night, "Praise God!; sang Theocrite. Then to his poor trade he turned, Whereby the daily meal was earned. Hard he laboured, long and well; O'er his work the boy's curls fell. But ever, at each period, He stopped and sang, "Praise God!" Then back again his curls he threw, And cheerful turned to work anew. Said Blaise, the listening monk, "Well done; "I doubt not thou art heard, my son: "As well as if thy voice to-day "Were praising God, the Pope's great way. "This Easter Day, the Pope at Rome "Praises God from Peter's dome." Said Theocrite, "Would God that I "Might praise him, that great way, and die!" Night passed, day shone.

And Theocrite was gone. With God a day endures alway, A thousand years are but a day. God said in heaven, "Nor day nor night "Now brings the voice of my delight." Then Gabriel, like a rainbow's birth, Spread his wings and sank to earth; Entered, in flesh, the empty cell, Lived there, and played the craftsman well; And morning, evening, noon and night, Praised God in place of Theocrite. And from a boy, to youth he grew: The man put off the stripling's hue: The man matured and fell away Into the season of decay: And ever o'er the trade he bent, And ever lived on earth content. (He did God's will; to him, all one If on the earth or in the sun.) God said, "A praise is in mine ear; "There is no doubt in it, no fear: "So sing old worlds, and so "New worlds that from my footstool go. "Clearer loves sound other ways: "I miss my little human praise." Then forth sprang Gabriel's wings, off fell The flesh disguise, remained the cell. 'Twas Easter Day: he flew to Rome, And paused above Saint Peter's dome.

In the tiring-room close by The great outer gallery, With his holy vestments dight, Stood the new Pope, Theocrite: And all his past career Came back upon him clear, Since when, a boy, he plied his trade, Till on his life the sickness weighed; And in his cell, when death drew near, An angel in a dream brought cheer: And rising from the sickness drear He grew a priest, and now stood here. To the East with praise he turned, And on his sight the angel burned. "I bore thee from thy craftsman's cell "And set thee here; I did not well. "Vainly I left my angel-sphere, "Vain was thy dream of many a year. "Thy voice's praise seemed weak; it dropped—"Creation's chorus stopped! "Go back and praise again "The early way, while I remain.

"With that weak voice of our disdain, "Take up creation's pausing strain. "Back to the cell and poor employ: "Resume the craftsman and the boy!" Theocrite grew old at home; A new Pope dwelt in Peter's dome. One vanished as the other died: They sought God side by side.

The Confessional

I.

Is a lietheir Priests, their Pope, Their Saints, their... all they fear or hope Are lies, and liesthere! through my door And ceiling, there! and walls and floor, There, lies, they lieshall still be hurled Till spite of them I reach the world!

II.

Think Priests just and holy men! Before they put me in this den I was a human creature too, With flesh and blood like one of you, A girl that laughed in beauty's pride Like lilies in your world outside.

III.

I had a lovershame avaunt!

This poor wrenched body, grim and gaunt, Was kissed

all over till it burned, By lips the truest, love e'er turned His heart's own tint: one night they kissed My soul out in a burning mist.

IV.

Next day when the accustomed train Of things grew round my sense again, "That is a sin," I said: and slow With downcast eyes to church I go, And pass to the confession-chair, And tell the old mild father there.

V.

When I falter Beltran's name, "Ha" quoth the father; "much I blame "The sin; yet wherefore idly grieve "Despair notstrenuously retrieve! "Nay, I will turn this love of thine "To lawful love, almost divine;

VI.

"For he is young, and led astray, "This Beltran, and he schemes, men say, "To change the laws of church and state "So, thine shall be an angel s fate, "Who, ere the thunder breaks, should roll
"Its cloud away and save his soul.

VII.

"For, when he lies upon thy breast, "Thou mayst demand and be possessed "Of all his plans, and next day steal "To me, and all those plans reveal, "That I and every priest, to purge "His soul, may fast and use the scourge."

VIII.

That father's beard was long and white, With love and truth his brow seemed bright; I went back, all on fire with joy,, that same evening, bade the boy Tell me, as lovers should, heart-free, Something to prove his love of me.

IX.

Told me what he would not tell For hope of heaven or fear of hell; And I lay listening in such pride! And, soon as he had left my side, Tripped to the church by morning-light To save his soul in his despite.

X.

I told the father all his schemes,
Were his comrades, what their dreams; "And now make haste," I said, "to pray "The one spot from his soul away; "To-night he comes, but not the same "Will look!" At night he never came.

XI.

Next night: on the after-morn, I went forth with a strength new-born. The church was empty; something drew My steps into the street; I knew It led me to the market-place: Where, lo, on high, the father's face!

XII.

That horrible black scaffold dressed, That stapled block... God sink the rest! That head strapped back, that blinding vest, Those knotted hands and naked breast, Till near one busy hangman pressed, And, on the neck these arms caressed...

XIII.

No part in aught they hope or fear! No heaven with them, no hell!and here, No earth, not so much space as pens My body in their worst of dens But shall bear God and man my cry, Lieslies, againand still, they lie! The Dtatue And The Bust

There's a palace in Florence, the world knows well, And a statue watches it from the square, And this story of both do our townsmen tell. Ages ago, a lady there, At the farthest window facing the East Asked, "Who rides by with the royal air" The bridesmaids' prattle around her ceased; She leaned forth, one on either hand.

They saw how the blush of the bride increased—They felt by its beats her heart expand—As one at each ear and both in a breath Whispered, "The Great-Duke Ferdinand." That selfsame instant, underneath, The Duke rode past in his idle way, Empty and fine like a swordless sheath. Gay he rode, with a friend as gay, Till he threw his head back"Who is she" "A bride the Riccardi brings home to-day." Hair in heaps lay heavily Over a pale brow spirit-pure—

Carved like the heart of a coal-black tree, Crisped like a war-steed's encolure—And vainly sought to dissemble her eyes of the blackest black our eyes endure. And lo, a blade for a knight's emprise Filled the fine empty sheath of a man,—The Duke grew straightway brave and wise. He looked at her, as a lover can.

She looked at him, as one who awakes: The past was a sleep, and her life began. Now, love so ordered for both their sakes, A feast was held that selfsame night In the pile which the mighty shadow makes. (For Via Larga is three-parts light, But the palace overshadows one, Because of a crime which may God requite! To Florence and God the wrong was done, Through the first republic's murder there By Cosimo and his cursed son.)

The Duke (with the statue's face in the square) Turned in the midst of his multitude At the bright approach of the bridal pair. Face to face the lovers stood A single minute and no more, While the bridegroom bent as a man subdued—Bowed till his bonnet brushed the floor—For the Duke on the lady a kiss conferred, As the courtly custom was of yore. In a minute can lovers exchange a word If a word did pass, which I do not think, Only one out of the thousand heard. That was the bridegroom. At day's brink He and his bride were alone at last In a bedchamber by a taper's blink. Calmly he said that her lot was cast, That the door she had passed was shut on her Till the final catafalk repassed. The world meanwhile, its noise and stir, Through a certain window facing the East, She could watch like a convent's chronicler. Since passing the door might lead to a feast, And a feast might lead to so much beside, He, of many evils, chose the least. "Freely I choose too," said the bride—"Your window and its world suffice," Replied the tongue, while the heart replied—"If I spend the night with that devil twice, "May his window serve as my loop of hell

"Whence a damned soul looks on paradise! "I fly to the Duke who loves me well, "Sit by his side and laugh at sorrow "Ere I count another ave-bell. "'Tis only the coat of a page to borrow, "And tie my hair in a horse-boy's trim, "And I save my soulbut not to-morrow"—(She checked herself and her eye grew dim) "My father tarries to bless my state: "I must keep it one day more for him.

"Is one day more so long to wait "Moreover the Duke rides past, I know; "We shall see each other, sure as fate." She turned on her side and slept. Just so! So we resolve on a thing and sleep: So did the lady, ages ago.

That night the Duke said, "Dear or cheap "As the cost of this cup of bliss may prove "To body or soul, I will drain it deep." And on the morrow, bold with love, He beckoned the bridegroom (close on call, As his duty bade, by the Duke's alcove) And smiled "'Twas a very funeral, "Your lady will think, this feast of ours,—"A shame to efface, whate'er befall! "What if we break from the Arno bowers, "And try if Petraja, cool and green,"Cure last night's fault with this morning's flowers" The bridegroom, not a thought to be seen On his steady brow and quiet mouth, Said, "Too much favour for me so mean! "But, alas! my lady leaves the South; "Each wind that comes from the Apennine "Is a menace to her tender youth: "Nor a way exists, the wise opine, "If she quits her palace twice this year, "To avert the flower of life's decline." Quoth the Duke, "A sage and a kindly fear. "Moreover Petraja is cold this spring: "Be our feast to-night as usual here!" And then to himself"Which night shall bring Thy bride to her lover's embraces, fool—Or I am the fool, and thou art the king! "Yet my passion must wait a night, nor cool—"For to-night the Envoy arrives from France "Whose heart I unlock with thyself, my tool. "I need thee still and might miss perchance. "To-day is not wholly lost, beside, "With its hope of my lady's countenance.

For I ridewhat should I do but ride "And passing her palace, if I list, "May glance at its windowwell betide!" So said, so done: nor the lady missed One ray that broke from the ardent brow, Nor a curl of the lips where the spirit kissed. Be sure that each renewed the vow, No morrow's sun should ariseand set And leave them then as it left them now. But next day passed, and next day yet, With still fresh cause to wait one day more Ere each leaped over the parapet. And still, as love's brief morning wore, With a gentle start, half smile, half sigh, They found love not as it seemed before. They thought it would work infallibly, But not in despite of heaven and earth: The rose would blow when the storm passed by. Meantime they could profit in winter's dearth By store of fruits that supplant the rose: The world and its ways have a certain worth: And to press a point while these oppose Were simple policy; better wait: We lose no friends and we gain no foes. Meantime, worse fates than a lover's fate, Who daily may ride and pass and look Where his lady watches behind the grate! And sheshe watched the square like a book holding one picture and only one.

Which daily to find she undertook: When the picture was reached the book was done, And she turned from the picture at night to scheme Of tearing it out for herself next sun. So weeks grew months, years; gleam by gleam The glory dropped from their youth and love, And both perceived they had dreamed a dream; Which hovered as dreams do, still above: But who can take a dream for a truth Oh, hide our eyes from the next remove! One day as the lady saw her youth Depart, and the silver thread that streaked Her hair, and, worn by the serpent's tooth, The brow so puckered, the chin so peaked,— And wondered who the woman was, Hollow-eyed and haggard-cheeked, Fronting her silent in the glass—"Summon here," she suddenly said, "Before the rest of my old self pass, "Him, the Carver, a hand to aid, "Who fashions the clay no love will change, "And fixes a beauty never to fade. "Let Robbia's craft so apt and strange "Arrest the remains of young and fair, "And rivet them while the seasons range. "Make me a face on the window there, "Waiting as ever, mute the while, "My love to pass below in the square! "And let me think that it may beguile "Dreary days which the dead must spend "Down in their darkness under the aisle, "To say, 'What matters it at the end " 'I did no more while my heart was warm

" 'Than does that image, my pale-faced friend.' "Where is the use of the lip's red charm, "The heaven of hair, the pride of the brow, "And the blood that blues the inside arm—"Unless we turn as the soul knows how, "The earthly gift to an end divine "A lady of clay is as good, I trow."

But long ere Robbia's cornice, fine, With flowers and fruits which leaves enlace, Was set where now is the empty shrine—(And, leaning out of a bright blue space, As a ghost might lean from a chink of sky, The passionate pale lady's face—Eyeing ever, with earnest eye And quick-turned neck at its breathless stretch, Some one who ever is passing by) The Duke had sighed like the simplest wretch In Florence, "Youthmy dream escapes! Will its record stay" And he bade them fetch Some subtle moulder of brazen shapes—"Can the soul, the will, die out of a man "Ere his body find the grave that gapes "John of Douay shall effect my plan, "Set me on horseback herc aloft, "Alive, as the crafty sculptor can, "In the very square I have crossed so oft: "That men may admire, when future suns "Shall touch the eyes to a purpose soft, "While the mouth and the brow stay brave in bronze—"Admire and say, 'When he was alive 'How he would take his pleasure once!' "And it shall go hard but I contrive "To listen the while, and laugh in my tomb "At idleness which aspires to strive."

So! While these wait the trump of doom, How do their spirits pass, I wonder, Nights and days in the narrow room Still, I suppose, they sit and ponder What a gift life was, ages ago, Six steps out of the chapel yonder. Only they see not God, I know, Nor all that chivalry of his, The soldier-saints who, row on row, Burn upward each to his point of bliss—Since, the end of life being manifest, He had burned his way thro' the world to this. I hear you reproach, "But delay was best, For their end was a crime."Oh, a crime will do As well, I reply, to serve for a test, As a virtue golden through and through, Sufficient to vindicate itself And prove its worth at a moment's view! Must a game be played for the sale of pelf Where a button goes, 'twere an epigram To offer the stamp of the very Guelph.

The true has no value beyond the sham: As well the

counter as coin, I submit, When your table's a hat, and your prize a dram. Stake your counter as boldly every whit, Venture as warily, use the same skill, Do your best, whether winning or losing it, If you choose to play!is my principle. Let a man contend to the uttermost For his life's set prize, be it what it will! The counter our lovers staked was lost As surely as if it were lawful coin: And the sin I impute to each frustrate ghost Isthe unlit lamp and the ungirt loin, Though the end in sight was a vice, I say. You of the virtue (we issue join) How strive you _De te, fabula!_ Neck and shoulder of a horse.

The stage or scaffolding for a coffin whilst in the church. Giovanni of Bologna, a sculptor. The Englishman In Italy PIANO DI SORRENTO Fort,

Fort, my beloved one,
Sit here by my side,
On my knees put up both little feet!
I was sure, if I tried,
I could make you laugh spite of Scirocco.
Now, open your eyes,
Let me keep you amused till he vanish
In black from the skies,
With telling my memories over
As you tell your beads;
All the Plain saw me gather, I garland
The flowers or the weeds.
Time for rain! for your long hot dry Autumn
Had net-worked with brown
The white skin of each grape on the bunches,
Marked like a quail's crown,
Those creatures you make such account of,
Whose heads,speckled white
Over brown like a great spider's back,
As I told you last night,—
Your mother bites off for her supper.
Red-ripe as could be,
Pomegranates were chapping and splitting
In halves on the tree:
And betwixt the loose walls of great flint-stone,

Or in the thick dust
On the path, or straight out of the rock-side,
Wherever could thrust
Some burnt sprig of bold hardy rock-flower
Its yellow face up,
For the prize were great butterflies fighting,
Some five for one cup.
So, I guessed, ere I got up this morning,
What change was in store,
By the quick rustle-down of the quail-nets
Which woke me before
I could open my shutter, made fast
With a bough and a stone,
And look thro' the twisted dead vine-twigs,
Sole lattice that's known.
Quick and sharp rang the rings down the net-poles,
While, busy beneath,
Your priest and his brother tugged at them,
The rain in their teeth.
And out upon all the flat house-roofs
Where split figs lay drying,
The girls took the frails under cover:
Nor use seemed in trying
To get out the boats and go fishing,
For, under the cliff,
Fierce the black water frothed o'er the blind-rock.
No seeing our skiff
Arrive about noon from Amalfi,
Our fisher arrive
And pitch down his basket before us,
All trembling alive
With pink and grey jellies, your sea-fruit;
You touch the strange lumps,
And mouths gape there, eyes open, all manner
Of horns and of humps,
Which only the fisher looks grave at,
While round him like imps
Cling screaming the children as naked

And brown as his shrimps;
Himself too as bare to the middle
You see round his neck
The string and its brass coin suspended,
That saves him from wreck.
But to-day not a bout reached Salerno,
So back, to a man,
Came our friends, with whose help in the vineyards
Grape-harvest began.
In the vat, halfway up in our house-side,
Like blood the juice spins,
While your brother all bare-legged is dancing
Till breathless he grins
Dead-beaten in effort on effort
To keep the grapes under,
Since still when he seems all but master,
In pours the fresh plunder
From girls who keep coming and going
With basket on shoulder,
And eyes shut against the rain's driving;
Your girls that are older,—
For under the hedges of aloe,
And where, on its bed
Of the orchard's black mould, the love-apple
Lies pulpy and red,
All the young ones are kneeling and filling
Their laps with the snails
Tempted out by this first rainy weather,—
Your best of regales,
As to-night will be proved to my sorrow,
When, supping in state,
We shall feast our grape-gleaners (two dozen,
Three over one plate)
With lasagne so tempting to swallow
In slippery ropes,
And gourds fried in great purple slices,
That colour of popes.
Meantime, see the grape bunch they've brought you:

The rain-water slips
O'er the heavy blue bloom on each globe
Which the wasp to your lips
Still follows with fretful persistence:
Nay, taste, while awake,
This half of a curd-white smooth cheese-ball
That peels, flake by flake,
Like an onion, each smoother and whiter;
Next, sip this weak wine
From the thin green glass flask, with its stopper,
A leaf of the vine;
And end with the prickly-pear's red flesh
That leaves thro' its juice
The stony black seeds on your pearl-teeth.
Scirocco is loose!
Hark, the quick, whistling pelt of the olives
Which, thick in one's track,
Tempt the stranger to pick up and bite them,
Tho' not yet half black!
How the old twisted olive trunks shudder,
The medlars let fall
Their hard fruit, and the brittle great fig-trees
Snap off, figs and all,
For here comes the whole of the tempest!
No refuge, but creep
Back again to my side and my shoulder,
And listen or sleep.
O how will your country show next week,
When all the vine-boughs
Have been stripped of their foliage to pasture
The mules and the cows
Last eve, I rode over the mountains;
Your brother, my guide,
Soon left me, to feast on the myrtles
That offered, each side,
Their fruit-balls, black, glossy and luscious,—
Or strip from the sorbs
A treasure, or, rosy and wondrous,

Those hairy gold orbs!
But my mule picked his sure sobre path out,
Just stopping to neigh
When he recognized down in the valley
His mates on their way
With the faggots and barrels of water;
And soon we emerged
From the plain, where the woods could scarce follow;
And still as we urged
Our way, the woods wondered, and left us,
As up still we trudged
Though the wild path grew wilder each instant,
And place was e'en grudged
'Mid the rock-chasms and piles of loose stones
Like the loose broken teeth
Of some monster which climbed there to die
From the ocean beneath—
Place was grudged to the silver-grey fume-weed
That clung to the path,
And dark rosemary ever a-dying
That, 'spite the wind's wrath,
So loves the salt rock's face to seaward,
And lentisks as staunch
To the stone where they root and bear berries,
And... what shows a branch
Coral-coloured, transparent, with circlets
Of pale seagreen leaves;
Over all trod my mule with the caution
Of gleaners o'er sheaves,
Still, foot after foot like a lady,
Till, round after round,
He climbed to the top of Calvano,
And God's own profound
Was above me, and round me the mountains,
And under, the sea,
And within me my heart to bear witness
What was and shall be.
Oh, heaven and the terrible crystal!

No rampart excludes
Your eye from the life to be lived
In the blue solitudes.
Oh, those mountains, their infinite movement!
Still moving with you;
For, ever some new head and breast of them
Thrusts into view
To observe the intruder; you see it
If quickly you turn
And before they escape you surprise them.
They grudge you should learn
How the soft plains they look on, lean over
And love (they pretend)
Cower beneath them, the flat sea-pine crouches,
The wild fruit-trees bend,
E'en the myrtle-leaves curl, shrink and shut:
All is silent and grave:
'Tis a sensual and timorous beauty,
How fair! but a slave.
So, I turned to the sea; and there slumbered
As greenly as ever
Those isles of the siren, your Galli;
No ages can sever
The Three, nor enable their sister
To join them,halfway
On the voyage, she looked at Ulysses—
No farther to-day,
Tho' the small one, just launched in the wave,
Watches breast-high and steady
From under the rock, her bold sister
Swum halfway already.
Fort, shall we sail there together
And see from the sides
Quite new rocks show their faces, new haunts
Where the siren abides
Shall we sail round and round them, close over
The rocks, tho' unseen,
That ruffle the grey glassy water

To glorious green
Then scramble from splinter to splinter,
Reach land and explore,
On the largest, the strange square black turret
With never a door,
Just a loop to admit the quick lizards;
Then, stand there and hear
The birds' quiet singing, that tells us
What life is, so clear
The secret they sang to Ulysses
When, ages ago,
He heard and he knew this life's secret
I hear and I know.
Ah, see! The sun breaks o'er Calvano;
He strikes the great gloom
And flutters it o'er the mount's summit
In airy gold fume.
All is over. Look out, see the gipsy,
Our tinker and smith,
Has arrived, set up bellows and forge,
And down-squatted forthwith
To his hammering, under the wall there;
One eye keeps aloof
The urchins that itch to be putting
His jews'-harps to proof,
While the other, thro' locks of curled wire,
Is watching how sleek
Shines the hog, come to share in the windfall
Chew, abbot's own cheek!
All is over. Wake up and come out now,
And down let us go,
And see the fine things got in order
At church for the show
Of the Sacrament, set forth this evening.
To-morrow's the Feast
Of the Rosary's Virgin, by no means
Of Virgins the least,
As you'll hear in the off-hand discourse

Which (all nature, no art)
The Dominican brother, these three weeks,
Was getting by heart.
Not a pillar nor post but is dizened
With red and blue papers;
All the roof waves with ribbons, each altar
A-blaze with long tapers;
But the great masterpiece is the scaffold
Rigged glorious to hold
All the fiddlers and fifers and drummers
And trumpeters bold,
afraid of Bellini nor Auber,
Who, when the priest's hoarse,
Will strike us up something that's brisk
For the feast's second course.
And then will the flaxen-wigged Image
Be carried in pomp
Thro' the plain, while in gallant procession
The priests mean to stomp.
All round the glad church lie old bottles
With gunpowder stopped,
Which will be, when the Image re-enters,
Religiously popped;
And at night from the crest of Calvano
Great bonfires will hang,
On the plain will the trumpets join chorus,
And more poppers bang.
At all events, cometo the garden
As far as the wall;
See me tap with a hoe on the plaster
Till out there shall fall
scorpion with wide angry nippers!
"Such trifles!" you say Fort, in my England at home,
Men meet gravely to-day
And debate, if abolishing Corn-laws
Be righteous and wise
If 'twere proper, Scirocco should vanish
In black from the skies!

The mastic tree (resinous).

The Flight Of The Duchess

I.

You're my friend: I was the man the Duke spoke to; I helped the Duchess to cast off his yoke, too; So here's the tale from beginning to end, My friend!

II.

Is a great wild country: If you climb to our castle's top, I don't see where your eye can stop; For when you've passed the cornfield country, Where vineyards leave off, flocks are packed, And sheep-range leads to cattle-tract, And cattle-tract to open-chase, And open-chase to the very base Of the mountain where, at a funeral pace, Round about, solemn and slow, One by one, row after row, Up and up the pine-trees go, So, like black priests up, and so Down the other side again To another greater, wilder country, That's one vast red drear burnt-up plain, Branched through and through with many a vein Whence iron's dug, and copper's dealt; Look right, look left, look straight before,—Beneath they mine, above they smelt, Copper-ore and iron-ore, And forge and furnace mould and melt, And so on, more and ever more, Till at the last, for a bounding belt, Comes the salt sand hoar of the great sea-shore, And the whole is our Duke's country.

III.

Was born the day this present Duke was—(And O, says the song, ere I was old!) In the castle where the other Duke was—(When I was happy and young, not old!) I in the kennel, he in the bower: We are of like age to an hour. My father was huntsman in that day; Who has not heard my father say That, when a boar was brought to bay, Three times, four times out of five, With his huntspear he'd contrive To get the killing-place transfixed, And pin him true, both eyes betwixt And that's why the old Duke would rather He lost a salt-pit than my father, And loved to have him ever in call; That's why my father stood in the hall When the old Duke brought his infant out To show the people, and while they passed The wondrous bantling round about, Was first to start at the outside blast As the Kaiser's courier blew his horn Just a month after the babe was born.

"And," quoth the Kaiser's courier, "since "The Duke has got an heir, our Prince "Needs the Duke's self at his side: " The Duke looked down and seemed to wince, But he thought of wars o'er the world wide, Castles a-fire, men on their march, The toppling tower, the crashing arch; And up he looked, and awhile he eyed The row of crests and shields and banners Of all achievements after all manners, And "ay," said the Duke with a surly pride.

The more was his comfort when he died At next year's end, in a velvet suit, With a gilt glove on his hand, his foot In a silken shoe for a leather boot, Petticoated like a herald, In a chamher next to an ante-room, Where he breathed the breath of page and groom, What he called stink, and they, perfume: They should have set him on red Berold Mad with pride, like fire to manage.

They should have got his cheek fresh tannage Such a day as to-day in the merry sunshine! Had they stuck on his fist a rough-foot merlin! (Hark, the wind's on the heath at its game! Oh for a noble falcon-lanner flap each broad wing like a banner, And turn in the wind, and dance like flame!) Had they broached a white-beer cask from Berlin Or if you incline to prescribe mere wine Put to his lips, when they saw him pine, A cup of our own Moldavia fine, Cotnar for instance, green as May sorrel And ropy with sweet,we shall not quarrel.

IV.

At home, the sick tall yellow Duchess Was left with the infant in her clutches, She being the daughter of God knows who: And now was the time to revisit her tribe. Abroad and afar they went, the two, And let our people rail and gibe At the empty hall and extinguished fire, As loud as we liked, but ever in vain, Till after long years we had our desire, And back came the Duke and his mother again.

V.

He came back the pertest little ape That ever affronted human shape; Full of his travel, struck at himself. You'd say, he despised our bluff old ways Not he! For in Paris they told the elf Our rough North land was the Land of Lays, The one good thing left in evil days; Since the Mid-Age was the Heroic Time, And only in wild nooks like ours Could you taste of it yet as in its prime, And see true castles, with proper towers, Young-hearted women, old-minded men, And manners now as manners were then.

So, all that the old Dukes had been, without knowing it, This Duke would fain know he was, without being it; 'Twas not for the joy's self, but the joy of his showing it, Nor for the pride's self, but the pride of our seeing it, He revived all usages thoroughly worn-out, The souls of them fumed-forth, the hearts of them torn-out: And chief in the chase his neck he perilled a lathy horse, all legs and length, With blood for bone, all speed, no strength; They should have set him on red Berold With the red eye slow consuming in fire, And the thin stiff ear like an abbey-spire!.

VI.

Well, such as he was, he must marry, we heard: And out of a convent, at the word, the lady, in time of spring. Oh, old thoughts they cling, they cling! That day, I know, with a dozen oaths I clad myself in thick hunting-clothes Fit for the chase of urochs or buffle In winter-time when you need to muffle. But the Duke had a mind we should cut a figure, And so we saw the lady arrive: My friend, I have seen a white crane bigger! She was the smallest lady alive in a piece of nature's madness, Too small, almost, for the life and gladness That over-filled her, as some hive Out of the bears' reach on the high trees Is crowded with its safe merry bees:

In truth, she was not hard to please! she looked, down

she looked, round at the mead, Straight at the castle, that's best indeed To look at from outside the walls: As for us, styled the "serfs and thralls," She as much thanked me as if she had said it, (With her eyes, do you understand) Because I patted her horse while I led it; And Max, who rode on her other hand, Said, no bird flew past but she inquired What its true name was, nor ever seemed tired—If that was an eagle she saw hover, And the green and grey bird on the field was the plover. When suddenly appeared the Duke: And as down she sprung, the small foot pointed On to my hand,as with a rebuke, And as if his backbone were not jointed, The Duke stepped rather aside than forward, And welcomed her with his grandest smile; And, mind you, his mother all the while Chilled in the rear, like a wind to Nor'ward; And up, like a weary yawn, with its pullies Went, in a shriek, the rusty portcullis; And, like a glad sky the north-wind sullies, The lady's face stopped its play, As if her first hair had grown grey; For such things must begin some one day.

VII.

In a day or two she was well again; As who should say, "You labour in vain! "This is all a jest against God, who meant "I should ever be, as I am, content " And glad in his sight; therefore, glad I will be." So, smiling as at first went she.

VIII.

Was active, stirring, all fire—Could not rest, could not tire—To a stone she might have given life! (I myself loved once, in my day) For a shepherd's, miner's, huntsman's wife, (I had a wife, I know what I say) Never in all the world such an one! And here was plenty to be done, And she that could do it, great or small, She was to do nothing at all.

There was already this man in his post,
This in his station, and that in his office,
And the Duke's plan admitted a wife, at most,
To meet his eye, with the other trophies,

Now outside the hall, now in it,
To sit thus, stand thus, see and be seen,
At the proper place in the proper minute,
And die away the life between.
It was amusing enough, each infraction
Of rule(but for after-sadness that came)
To hear the consummate self-satisfaction
With which the young Duke and the old dame Would let her advise, and criticise, And, being a fool, instruct the wise, And, child-like, parcel out praise or blame: They bore it all in complacent guise, As though an artificer, after contriving A wheel-work image as if it were living, Should find with delight it could motion to strike him! So found the Duke, and his mother like him: The lady hardly got a rebuff—had not been contemptuous enough, With his cursed smirk, as he nodded applause, And kept off the old mother-cat's claws.

IX.

So, the little lady grew silent and thin,
Paling and ever paling,
As the way is with a hid chagrin;
And the Duke perceived that she was ailing, And said in his heart, "'Tis done to spite me, "But I shall find in my power to right me!" Don't swear, friend! The old one, many a year, Is in hell, and the Duke's self... you shall hear.

X.

Well, early in autumn, at first winter-warning, When the stag had to break with his foot, of a morning, A drinking-hole out of the fresh tender ice That covered the pond till the sun, in a trice, Loosening it, let out a ripple of gold, And another and another, and faster and faster, Till, dimpling to blindness, the wide water rolled: Then it so chanced that the Duke our master Asked himself what were the pleasures in season, And found, since the calendar bade him be hearty, He should do the Middle Age no treason In resolving on a hunting-party.

Always provided, old books showed the way of it! What meant old poets by their strictures And when old poets had said their say of it, How taught old painters in their pictures We must revert to the proper channels, Workings in tapestry, paintings on panels, And gather up woodcraft's authentic traditions: Here was food for our various ambitions, As on each case, exactly stated—To encourage your dog, now, the properest chirrup, Or best prayer to Saint Hubert on mounting your stirrup—We of the house hold took thought and debated. Blessed was he whose back ached with the jerkin His sire was wont to do forest-work in; Blesseder he who nobly sunk "ohs" And "ahs" while he tugged on his grand-sire's trunk-hose; What signified hats if they had no rims on, Each slouching before and behind like the scallop, And able to serve at sea for a shallop, Loaded with lacquer and looped with crimson So that the deer now, to make a short rhyme on't, What with our Venerers, Prickers and Yerderers, Might hope for real hunters at length and not murderers, And oh the Duke's tailor, he had a hot time on't!

XI.

You must know that when the first dizziness Of flap-hats and buff-coats and jack-boots subsided, The Duke put this question, "The Duke's part provided, "Had not the Duchess some share in the business" For out of the mouth of two or three witnesses Did he establish all fit-or-unfitnesses: And, after much laying of heads together, Somebody's cap got a notable feather By the announcement with proper unction That he had discovered the lady's function; Since ancient authors gave this tenet, "When horns wind a mort and the deer is at siege, "Let the dame of the castle prick forth on her jennet, "And, with water to wash the hands of her liege "In a clean ewer with a fair toweling, " Let her preside at the disemboweling."

Now, my friend, if you had so little religion As to catch a hawk, some falcon-lanner, And thrust her broad wings like a banner Into a coop for a vulgar pigeon; And if day by day and week by week You cut her claws, and sealed her eyes, And clipped her wings, and tied her beak, Would it cause you any great surprise If, when you decided to give her an airing, You found she needed a little preparing I say, should you be such a curmudgeon, If she clung to the perch, as to take it in dudgeon Yet when the Duke to his lady signified, Just a day before, as he judged most dignified, In what a pleasure she was to participate,—And, instead of leaping wide in flashes, Her eyes just lifted their long lashes, if pressed by fatigue even he could not dissipate.

And duly acknowledged the Duke's forethought, But spoke of her health, if her health were worth aught, Of the weight by day and the watch by night, And much wrong now that used to be right, So, thanking him, declined the hunting,—Was conduct ever more affronting With all the ceremony settled—With the towel ready, and the sewer Polishing up his oldest ewer, And the jennet pitched upon, a piebald, Black-barred, cream-coated and pink eye-balled,—No wonder if the Duke was nettled when she persisted nevertheless,—Well, I suppose here's the time to confess That there ran half round our lady's chamber A balcony none of the hardest to clamber; And that Jacynth the tire-woman, ready in waiting, Stayed in call outside, what need of relating And since Jacynth was like a June rose, why, a fervent Adorer of Jacynth of course was your servant; And if she had the habit to peep through the casement, How could I keep at any vast distance And so, as I say, on the lady's persistence, The Duke, dumb-stricken with amazement, Stood for a while in a sultry smother, And then, with a smile that partook of the awful, Turned her over to his yellow mother To learn what was held decorous and lawful; And the mother smelt blood with a cat-like instinct, As her cheek quick whitened thro' all its quince-tinct.

Oh, but the lady heard the whole truth at once! What meant she—Who was sheHer duty and station, The wisdom of age and the folly of youth, at once, Its decent regard and its fitting relation—In brief, my friend, set all the devils in hell free And turn them out to carouse in a belfry And treat the priests to a fifty-part canon, And then you may guess how that tongue of hers ran on! Well, somehow or other it ended at last, licking her whiskers, out she passed; And after her,making (he hoped) a face Like Emperor Nero or Sultan Saladin, Stalked the Duke's self with the austere grace Of ancient hero or modern paladin, From door to staircaseoh such a solemn Unbending of the vertebral column!

XII.

At sunrise our company mustered; And here was the huntsman bidding unkennel, And there 'neath his bonnet the pricker blustered, With feather dank as a bough of wet fennel; For the court-yard walls were filled with fog You might have cut as an axe chops a log—Like so much wool for colour and bulkiness; And out rode the Duke in a perfect sulkiness, Since, before breakfast, a man feels but queasily, And a sinking at the lower abdomen Begins the day with indifferent omen. And lo, as he looked around uneasily, The sun ploughed the fog up and drove it asunder This way and that from the valley under; And, looking through the court-yard arch, Down in the valley, what should meet him But a troop of Gipsies on their march No doubt with the annual gifts to greet him.

XIII.

Now, in your land, Gipsies reach you, only
After reaching all lands beside;
North they go, South they go, trooping or lonely,
And still, as they travel far and wide,

They and keep now a trace here, trace there, That puts you in mind of a place here, a place there. But with us, I believe they rise out of the ground, And nowhere else, I take it, are found With the earth-tint yet so freshly embrowned: Born, no doubt, like insects which breed on The very fruit they are meant to feed on. For the earthnot a use to which they don't turn it, The ore that grows in the mountain's womb, Or the sand in the pits like a honeycomb, They sift and soften it, bake it and burn it—Whether they weld you, for instance, a snaffle With side-bars never a brute can baffle; Or a lock that's a puzzle of wards within wards; Or, if your colt's fore-foot inclines to curve inwards, Horseshoes they hammer which turn on a swivel And won't allow the hoof to shrivel.

Then they cast bells like the shell of the winkle That keep a stout heart in the ram with their tinkle; But the sandthey pinch and pound it like otters; Commend me to Gipsy glass-makers and potters! Glasses they'll blow you, crystal-clear, Where just a faint cloud of rose shall appear, As if in pure water you dropped and let die A bruised black-blooded mulberry; And that other sort, their crowning pride, With long white threads distinct inside, Like the lake-flower's fibrous roots which dangle Loose such a length and never tangle, Where the bold sword-lily cuts the clear waters, And the cup-lily couches with all the white daughters: Such are the works they put their hand to, The uses they turn and twist iron and sand to. And these made the troop, which our Duke saw sally Toward his castle from out of the valley, Men and women, like new-hatched spiders, Come out with the morning to greet our riders.

And up they wound till they reached the ditch, Whereat all stopped save one, a witch That I knew, as she hobbled from the group, By her gait directly and her stoop, I, whom Jacynth was used to importune To let that same witch tell us our fortune. The oldest Gipsy then above ground; And, sure as the autumn season came round, She paid us a visit for profit or pastime, And every time, as she swore, for the last time. And presently she was seen to sidle Up to the Duke till she touched his bridle, So that the horse of a sudden reared up As under its nose the old witch peered up With her worn-out eyes, or rather eye-holes Of no use now but to gather brine, And began a kind of level whine Such as they used to sing to their viols When their ditties they go grinding Up and down with nobody minding: And then, as of old, at the end of the humming Her usual presents were forthcoming A dog-whistle blowing the fiercest of trebles, (Just a sea-shore stone holding a dozen fine pebbles,) Or a porcelain mouth-piece to screw on a pipe-end,—And so she awaited her annual stipend.

But this time, the Duke would scarcely vouchsafe A word

in reply; and in vain she felt With twitching fingers at her belt For the purse of sleek pine-martin pelt, Ready to ptlt what he gave in her pouch safe,—Till, either to quicken his apprehension, Or possibly with an after-intention, She was come, she said, to pay her duty To the new Duchess, the youthful beauty. No sooner had she named his lady, Than a shine lit up the face so shady, And its smirk returned with a novel meaning—For it struck him, the babe just wanted weaning; If one gave her a taste of what life was and sorrow, She, foolish to-day, would be wiser tomorrow; And who so fit a teacher of trouble this sordid crone bent well-nigh double So, glancing at her wolf-skin vesture, (If such it was, for they grow so hirsute That their own fleece serves for natural fur-suit.

He was contrasting, 'twas plain from his gesture, The life of the lady so flower-like and delicate With the loathsome squalor of this helicat. I, in brief, was the man the Duke beckoned From out of the throng, and while I drew near He told the croneas I since have reckoned By the way he bent and spoke into her ear With circumspection and mystery—The main of the lady's history, Her frowardness and ingratitude: And for all the crone's submissive attitude I could see round her mouth the loose plaits tightening, And her brow with assenting intelligence brightening, As though she engaged with hearty good-will Whatever he now might enjoin to fulfil, And promised the lady a thorough frightening. And so, just giving her a glimpse a purse, with the air of a man who imps The wing of the hawk that shall fetch the hernshaw, He bade me take the Gipsy mother And set her telling some story or other Of hill or dale, oak-wood or fernshaw, To wile away a weary hour the lady left alone in her bower, Whose mind and body craved exertion And yet shrank from all better diversion.

XIV.

Then clapping heel to his horse, the mere curveter,
Out rode the Duke, and after his hollo
And hounds swept, huntsman and servitor,
And back I turned and bade the crone follow.

And what makes me confident what's to be told you
Had all along been of this crone's devising,
Is, that, on looking round sharply, behold you,
There was a novelty quick as surprising:
For first, she had shot up a full head in stature,
And her step kept pace with mine nor faltered,
As if age had foregone its usurpature,
And the ignoble mien was wholly altered, And the face looked quite of another nature, And the change reached too, whatever the change meant, Her shaggy wolf-skin cloak's arrangement: For where its tatters hung loose like sedges, Gold coins were glittering on the edges, Like the band-roll strung with tomans Which proves the veil a Persian woman's. And under her brow, like a snail's horns newly Come out as after the rain he paces, Two unmistakeable eye-points duly Live and aware looked out of their places. So, we went and found Jacynth at the entry Of the lady's chamber standing sentry; I told the command and produced my companion, And Jacynth rejoiced to admit any one, For since last night, by the same token, Not a single word had the lady spoken: They went in both to the presence together, While I in the balcony watched the weather.

XV.

Now, what took place at the very first of all, I cannot tell, as I never could learn it: Jacynth constantly wished a curse to fall On that little head of hers and burn it If she knew how she came to drop so soundly Asleep of a sudden and there continue The whole time sleeping as profoundly As one of the boars my father would pin you 'Twixt the eyes where life holds garrison, Jacynth forgive me the comparison! But where I begin asy own narration Is a little after I took my station To breathe the fresh air from the balcony, And, having in those days a falcon eye, To follow the hunt thro' the open country, From where the bushes thinlier crested The hillocks, to a plain where's not one tree. When, in a moment, my ear was arrested Bywas it singing, or was it saying, Or a strange musical instrument playing In the chamberand to be certain I pushed the lattice, pulled the curtain, And there lay Jacynth asleep, Yet as if a watch she tried to keep, In a rosy sleep along the floor With her head against the door; While in the midst, on the seat of state, Was a queenthe Gipsy woman late, With head and face downbent On the lady's head and face intent: For, coiled at her feet like a child at ease, The lady sat between her knees And o'er them the lady's clasped hands met, And on those hands her chin was set, And her upturned face met the face of the crone Wherein the eyes had grown and grown As if she could double and quadruple At pleasure the play of either pupil Very like, by her hands' slow fanning, As up and down like a gor-crow's flappers They moved to measure, or bell-clappers.

I said "Is it blessing, is it banning, "Do they applaud you or burlesque you—"Those hands and fingers with no flesh on" But, just as I thought to spring in to the rescue, At once I was stopped by the lady's expression: For it was life her eyes were drinking From the crone's wide pair above unwinking, Life's pure fire received without shrinking, Into the heart and breast whose heaving Told you no single drop they were leaving, Life, that filling her, passed redundant Into her very hair, back swerving Over each shoulder, loose and abundant, As her head thrown back showed the white throat curving; And the very tresses shared in the pleasure, Moving to the mystic measure, Bounding as the bosom bounded. I stopped short, more and more confounded, As still her cheeks burned and eyes glistened, As she listened and she listened: all at once a hand detained me, The selfsame contagion gained me, And I kept time to the wondrous chime, Making out words and prose and rhyme, Till it seemed that the music furled Its wings like a task fulfilled, and dropped From under the words it first had propped, And left them midway in the world: Word took word as hand takes hand, I could hear at last, and understand, And when I held the unbroken thread, The Gipsy said:—

"And so at last we find my tribe.

"And so I set thee in the midst,

"And to one and all of them describe
"What thou saidst and what thou didst,
"Our long and terrible journey through,
"And all thou art ready to say and do
"In the trials that remain:
"I trace them the vein and the other vein
"That meet on thy brow and part again,
"Making our rapid mystic mark;
"And I bid my people prove and probe
"Each eye's profound and glorious globe
"Till they detect the kindred spark
"In those depths so dear and dark,
"Like the spots that snap and burst and flee,
"Circling over the midnight sea.
"And on that round young cheek of thine
"I make them recognize the tinge,
"As when of the costly scarlet wine
"They drip so much as will impinge
"And spread in a thinnest scale afloat
"One thick gold drop from the olive's coat
"Over a silver plate whose sheen
"Still thro' the mixture shall be seen.
"For so I prove thee, to one and all,
"Fit, when my people ope their breast,
"To see the sign, and hear the call,
"And take the vow, and stand the test
"Which adds one more child to the rest—
"When the breast is bare and the arms are wide,
"And the world is left outside.
"For there is probation to decree,
"And many and long must the trials be
"Thou shalt victoriously endure,
"If that brow is true and those eyes are sure;
"Like a jewel-finder's fierce assay
"Of the prize he dug from its mountain-tomb—
"Let once the vindicating ray
"Leap out amid the anxious gloom,
"And steel and fire have done their part

"And the prize falls on its finder's heart;
"So, trial after trial past,
"Wilt thou fall at the very last
"Breathless, half in trance
"With the thrill of the great deliverance,
"Into our arms for evermore;
"And thou shalt know, those arms once curled
"About thee, what we knew before,
"How love is the only good in the world.
"Henceforth be loved as heart can love,
"Or brain devise, or hand approve!
"Stand up, look below,
"It is our life at thy feet we throw
"To step with into light and joy;
"Not a power of life but we employ
"To satisfy thy nature's want;
"Art thou the tree that props the plant,
"Or the climbing plant that seeks the tree—
"Canst thou help us, must we help thee
"If any two creatures grew into one,
"They would do more than the world has done.
"Though each apart were never so weak,
"Ye vainly through the world should seek
"For the knowledge and the might
"Which in such union grew their right:
"So, to approach at least that end,
"And blend,as much as may be, blend
"Thee with us or us with thee,—
"As climbing plant or propping tree,
"Shall some one deck thee, over and down,
"Up and about, with blossoms and leaves
"Fix his heart's fruit for thy garland crown,
"Cling with his soul as the gourd-vine cleaves,
"Die on thy boughs and disappear
"While not a leaf of thine is sere
"Or is the other fate in store,
"And art thou fitted to adore,
"To give thy wondrous self away,

"And take a stronger nature's sway
"I foresee and could foretell
"Thy future portion, sure and well:
"But those passionate eyes speak true, speak true,
"Let them say what thou shalt do!
"Only be sure thy daily life,
"In its peace or in its strife,
"Never shall be unobserved:
"We pursue thy whole career,
"And hope for it, or doubt, or fear,—
"Lo, hast thou kept thy path or swerved,
"We are beside thee in all thy ways,
"With our blame, with our praise,
"Our shame to feel, our pride to show,
"Glad, angrybut indifferent, no!
"Whether it be thy lot to go,

"For the good of us all, where the haters meet "In the crowded city's horrible street; "Or thou step alone through the morass "Where never sound yet was "Save the dry quick clap of the stork's bill, "For the air is still, and the water still, "When the blue breast of the dipping coot "Dives under, and all is mute.

"So, at the last shall come old age, "Decrepit as befits that stage; "How else wouldst thou retire apart "With the hoarded memories of thy heart, "And gather all to the very least "Of the fragments of life's earlier feast, "Let fall through eagerness to find "The crowning dainties yet behind "Ponder on the entire past "Laid together thus at last, "When the twilight helps to fuse "The first fresh with the faded hues, "And the outline of the whole, "As round eve's shades their framework roll, "Grandly fronts for once thy soul.

"And then as, 'mid the dark, a glean "Of yet another morning breaks, "And like the hand which ends a dream, "Death, with the might of his sunbeam, "Touches the flesh and the soul awakes, "Then" Ay, then indeed something would happen! But what For here her voice changed like a bird's; There grew more of the music and less of the words; Had Jacynth only been by me to clap pen To paper and put you down every syllable With those clever clerkly fingers, All I've forgotten as well as what lingers In this old brain of mine that's but ill able To give you even this poor version Of the speech I spoil, as it were, with stammering More fault of those who had the hammering Of prosody into me and syntax, And did it, not with hobnails but tintacks! But to return from this excursion.—

Just, do you mark, when the song was sweetest, The peace most deep and the charm completest, There came, shall I say, a snap—And the charm vanished! And my sense returned, so strangely banished, And, starting as from a nap, knew the crone was bewitching my lady, With Jacynth asleep; and but one spring made I Down from the casement, round to the portal, Another minute and I had entered,—When the door opened, and more than mortal Stood, with a face where to my mind centred All beauties I ever saw or shall see, The Duchess: I stopped as if struck by palsy. She was so different, happy and beautiful, I felt at once that all was best, And that I had nothing to do, for the rest, But wait her commands, obey and be dutiful. Not that, in fact, there was any commanding; I saw the glory of her eye, And the brow's height and the breast's expanding, And I was hers to live or to die.

As for finding what she wanted, You know God Almighty granted little signs should serve wild creatures To tell one another all their desires, So that each knows what his friend requires, And does its bidding without teachers. I preceded her; the crone Followed silent and alone; I spoke to her, but she merely jabbered In the old style; both her eyes had slunk Back to their pits; her stature shrunk; In short, the soul in its body sunk Like a blade sent home to its scabbard. We descended, I preceding; Crossed the court with nobody heeding, All the world was at the chase, The courtyard like a desert-place, The stable emptied of its small fry; I saddled myself the very palfrey I remember patting while it carried her, The day she arrived and the Duke married her.

And, do you know, though it's easy deceiving Oneself in such matters, I can't help believing The lady had not forgotten it either, And knew the poor devil so much beneath her Would have been only too glad for her service To dance on hot ploughshares like a Turk dervise, But, unable to pay proper duty where owing it, Was reduced to that pitiful method of showing it: For though the moment I began setting His saddle on my own nag of Berold's begetting, (Not that I meant to be obtrusive) She stopped me, while his rug was shifting, By a single rapid finger's lifting, And, with a gesture kind but conclusive, And a little shake of the head, refused me,—I say, although she never used me, Yet when she was mounted, the Gipsy behind her, And I ventured to remind her, suppose with a voice of less steadiness Than usual, for my feeling exceeded me, Something to the effect that I was in readiness Whenever God should please she needed me,—Then, do you know, her face looked down on me With a look that placed a crown on me, And she felt in her bosom,mark, her bosom—And, as a flower-tree drops its blossom, Dropped me... ah, had it been a purse Of silver, my friend, or gold that's worse, Why, you see, as soon as I found myself So understood,that a true heart so may gain Such a reward,I should have gone home again, Kissed Jacynth, and soberly drowned myself! It was a little plait of hair Such as friends in a convent make To wear, each for the other's sake,—This, see, which at my breast I wear, Ever did (rather to Jacynth's grudgment), And ever shall, till the Day of Judgment. And then,and then,to cut short,this is idle, These are feelings it is not good to foster,—I pushed the gate wide, she shook the bridle, And the palfrey bounded,and so we lost her.

XVI.

When the liquor's out why clink the cannikin I did think to describe you the panic in redoubtable breast of our master the mannikin, And what was the pitch of his mother's yellowness, How she turned as a shark to snap the spare-rib Clean off, sailors say, from a pearl-diving Carib, When she heard, what she called the flight of the feloness But it seems such child's play, What they said and did with the lady away! And to dance on, when we've lost the music, Always made meand no doubt makes yousick. Nay, to my mind, the world's face looked so stern As that sweet form disappeared through the postern, She that kept it in constant good humour.

It ought to have stopped; there seemed nothing to do more. But the world thought otherwise and went on, And my head's one that its spite was spent on: Thirty years are fled since that morning, And with them all my head's adorning. Nor did the old Duchess die outright, As you expect, of suppressed spite, The natural end of every adder suffered to empty its poison-bladder: But she and her son agreed, I take it, That no one should touch on the story to wake it, For the wound in the Duke's pride rankled fiery, So, they made no search and small inquiry—And when fresh Gipsies have paid us a visit, I've Noticed the couple were never inquisitive, But told them they're folks the Duke don't want here, And bade them make haste and cross the frontier. Brief, the Duchess was gone and the Duke was glad of it, And the old one was in the young one's stead, And took, in her place, the household's head, And a blessed time the household had of it! And were I not, as a man may say, cautious How I trench, more than needs, on the nauseous, I could favour you with sundry touches Of the paint-smutches with which the Duchess Heightened the mellowness of her cheek's yellowness (To get on faster) until at last her Cheek grew to be one master-plaster Of mucus and focus from mere use of ceruse: In short, she grew from scalp to udder Just the object to make you shudder.

XVII.

You're my friend—

A thing friendship is, world without end! How it gives the heart and soul a stir-up As if somebody broached you a glorious runlet, And poured out, all lovelily, sparklingly, sunlit, Our green Moldavia, the streaky syrup, Cotnar as old as the time of the Druids—Friendship may match with that monarch of fluids; Each supples a dry brain, fills you its ins-and-outs, Gives your life's hour-glass a shake when the thin sand doubts Whether to run on or stop short, and guarantees Age is not all made of stark sloth and arrant ease. I have seen my little lady once more, Jacynth, the Gipsy, Berold, and the rest of it, For to me spoke the Duke, as I told you before; I always wanted to make a clean breast of it:

And now it is madewhy, my heart's blood, that went trickle, Trickle, but anon, in such muddy driblets, pumped up brisk now, through the main ventricle, And genially floats me about the giblets. I'll tell you what I intend to do: I must see this fellow his sad life through—He is our Duke, atter all, I, as he says, but a serf and thrall. My father was born here, and I inherit His fame, a chain he bound his son with; Could I pay in a lump I should prefer it, But there's no mine to blow up and get done with: So, I must stay till the end of the chapter. For, as to our middle-age-manners-adapter, Be it a thing to be glad on or sorry on, Some day or other, his head in a morion And breast in a hauberk, his heels he'll kick up, Slain by an onslaught fierce of hiccup.

Then, when red doth the sword of our Duke rust, And its leathern sheath lie o'ergrown with a blue crust, Then I shall scrape together my earnings; For, you see, in the churchyard Jacynth reposes, And our children all went the way of the roses: It's a long lane that knows no turnings. One needs but little tackle to travel in; So, just one stout cloak shall I indue: And for a stall, what beats the javelin With which his boars my father pinned you And then, for a purpose you shall hear presently, Taking some Cotnar, a tight plump skinful, I shall go journeying, who but I, pleasantly! Sorrow is vain and despondency sinful.

A man's age He must hurry more, that's all; Cram in a day, what his youth took a year to hold. When we mind labour, then only, we're too old—What age had Methusalem when he begat Saul And at last, as its haven some buffeted ship sees, (Come all the way from the north-parts with sperm oil) I hope to get safely out of the turmoil And arrive one day at the land of the Gipsies, And find my lady, or hear the last news of her From some old thief and son of Lucifer, His forehead chapleted green with wreathy hop, Sunburned all over like an thiop.

And when my Cotnar begins to operate And the tongue of the rogue to run at a proper rate, And our wine-skin, tight once, shows each flaccid dent, I shall drop in withas if by accident—"You never knew, then, how it all ended, "What fortune good or bad attended "The little lady your Queen befriended" And when that's told me, what's remaining This world's too hard for my explaining. The same wise judge of matters equine Who still preferred some slim four-year-old To the big-boned stock of mighty Berold, And, fur strong Cotnar, drank French weak wine, He also umst be such a lady's scorner! Smooth Jacob still rubs homely Esau: Now up, now down, the world's one see-saw.

So, I shall find out some snug corner Under a hedge, like Orson the wood-knight, Turn myself round and bid the world good night; And sleep a sound sleep till the trumpet's blowing Wakes me (unless priests cheat us laymen) To a world where will be no furtiner throwing Pearls befare swine that Can't value them. Amen!

The Glove

PETER RONSARD loquitur.)

"Heigho!" yawned one day King Francis, "Distance all value enhances! "When a man's busy, why, leisure "Strikes him as wonderful pleasure: " 'Faith, and at leisure once is he "Straightway he wants to be busy. "Here we've got peace; and aghast I'm "Caught thinking war the true pastime. "Is there a reason in metre "Give us your speech, master Peter!" I who, if mortal dare say so, Ne'er am at loss with my Naso, "Sire," I replied, "joys prove cloudlets: "Men are the merest Ixions"—Here the King whistled aloud, "Let's "Heighogo look at our lions!" Such are the sorrowful chances If you talk fine to King Francis. And so, to the courtyard proceeding, Our company, Francis was leading, Increased by new followers tenfold Before be arrived at the penfold; Lords, ladies, like clouds which bedizen At sunset the western horizon.

And Sir De Lorge pressed 'mid the foremost With the dame he professed to adore most. Oh, what a face! One by fits eyed Her, and the horrible pitside; For the penfold surrounded a hollow Which led where the eye scarce dared follow, And shelved to the chamber secluded Where Bluebeard, the great lion, brooded. The King bailed his keeper, an Arab As glossy and black as a scarab, And bade him make sport and at once stir Up and out of his den the old monster. They opened a hole in the wire-work Across it, and dropped there a firework, And fled: one's heart's beating redoubled; A pause, while the pit's mouth was troubled, The blackness and silence so utter, By the firework's slow sparkling and sputter; Then earth in a sudden contortion Gave out to our gaze her abortion. Such a brute! Were I friend Clement Marot (Whose experience of nature's but narrow, And whose faculties move in no small mist When he versifies David the Psalmist) I should study that brute to describe you Illim Juda Leonem de Tribu.

One's whole blood grew curdling and creepy To see the black mane, vast and heapy, The tail in the air stiff and straining, The wide eyes, nor waxing nor waning, As over the barrier which bounded His platform, and us who surrounded The barrier, they reached and they rested On space that might stand him in best stead: For who knew, he thought, what the amazement, The eruption of clatter and blaze meant, And if, in this minute of wonder, No outlet, 'mid lightning and thunder, Lay broad, and, his shackles all shivered, The lion at last was delivered Ay, that was the open sky o'erhead! And you saw by the flash on his forehead, By the hope in those eyes wide and steady, He was leagues in the desert already, Driving the flocks up the mountain, Or catlike couched hard by the fountain To waylay the date-gathering negress: So guarded he entrance or egress.

"How he stands!" quoth the King: "we may well swear, ("No novice, we've won our spurs elsewhere "And so can afford the confession,) "We exercise wholesome discretion "In keeping aloof from his threshold; "Once hold you, those jaws want no fresh hold, "Their first would too pleasantly purloin "The visitor's brisket or surloin: "But who's he would prove so fool-hardy "Not the best man of Marignan, pardie!" The sentence no sooner was uttered, Than over the rails a glove flattered, Fell close to the lion, and rested:

The dame 'twas, who flung it and jested With life so, De Lorge had been wooing For months past; he sat there pursuing His suit, weighing out with nonchalance Fine speeches like gold from a balance. Sound the trumpet, no true knight's a tarrier! De Lorge made one leap at the barrier, Walked straight to the glove,while the lion Neer moved, kept his far-reaching eye on The palm-tree-edged desert-spring's sapphire, And the musky oiled skin of the Kaffir,—Picked it up, and as calmly retreated, Leaped back where the lady was seated, And full in the face of its owner Flung the glove.

"Your heart's queen, you dethrone her "So should I!"cried the King"'twas mere vanity, "Not love, set that task to humanity!" Lords and ladies alike turned with loathing From such a proved wolf in sheep's clothing. Not so, I; for I caught an expression In her brow's undisturbed self-possession Amid the Court's scoffing and merriment,—As if from no pleasing experiment She rose, yet of pain not much heedful So long as the process was needful,—As if she had tried in a crucible, To what "speeches like gold" were reducible, And, finding the finest prove copper, Felt the smoke in her face was but proper; To know what she had _not_ to trust to, Was worth all the ashes and dust too. She went out 'mid hooting and laughter; Clement Marot stayed; I followed after, And asked, as a grace, what it all meant If she wished not the rash deed's recalment "For I" so I spoke "am a poet: "Human nature,behoves that I know it!" She told me.

"Too long had I heard "Of the deed proved alone by the word: "For my lovewhat De Lorge would not dare! "With my scornwhat De Lorge could compare! "And the endless descriptions of death "He would brave when my lip formed a breath, "I must reckon as braved, or, of course, "Doubt his wordand moreover, perforce, "For such gifts as no lady could spurn, "Must offer my love in return. "When I looked on your lion, it brought "All the dangers at once to my thought, "Encountered by all sorts of men, "Before he was lodged in his den,—"From the poor slave whose club or bare hands "Dug the trap, set the snare on the sands, "With no King and no Court to applaud, "By no shame, should he shrink, overawed, "Yet to capture the creature made shift, "That his rude boys might laugh at the gift, "To the page who last leaped o'er the fence "Of the pit, on no greater pretence "Than to get back the bonnet he dropped, "Lest his pay for a week should be stopped. "So, wiser I judged it to make.

"One trial what 'death for my sake' "Really meant, while the power was yet mine, "Than to wait until time should define "Such a phrase not so simply as I, "Who took it to mean just 'to die.' "The blow a glove gives is but weak: "Does the mark yet discolour my cheek "But when the heart suffers a blow, "Will the pain pass so soon, do you know" I looked, as away she was sweeping, And saw a youth eagerly keeping As close as he dared to the doorway. No doubt that a noble should more weigh His life than befits a plebeian; And yet, had our brute been Nemean—(I judge by a certain calm fervour The youth stepped with, forward to serve her) He'd have scarce thought you did him the worst turn If you whispered "Friend, what you'd get, first earn!" And when, shortly after, she carried Her shame from the Court, and they married, To that marriage some happiness, maugre The voice of the Court, I dared augur.

For De Lorge, he made women with men vie, Those in wonder and praise, these in envy; And in short stood so plain a head taller That he wooed and won... how do you call her The beauty, that rose in the sequel To the King's love, who loved her a week well. And 'twas noticed he never would honour De Lorge (who looked daggers upon her) With the easy commission of stretching His legs in the service, and fetching His wife, from her chamber, those straying Sad gloves she was always mislaying, While the King took the closet to chat in,—But of course this adventure came pat in. And never the King told the story, How bringing a glove brought such glory, But the wife smiled"His nerves are grown firmer: "Mine he brings now and utters no murmur." _Venienti occurrite morbo! With which moral I drop my theorbo. A beetle.

The Guardian-Angel A PICTURE AT FANO.

I.

And great Angel, wouldst thou only leave That child, when thou hast done with him, for me! Let me sit all the day here, that when eve Shall find performed thy special ministry, And time come for departure, thou, suspending Thy flight, mayst see another child for tending, Another still, to quiet and retrieve.

II.

I shall feel thee step one step, no more, From where thou standest now, to where I gaze, And suddenly my head is covered o'er With those wings, white above the child who prays Now on that tomband I shall feel thee guarding Me, out of all the world; for me, discarding Yon heaven thy home, that waits and opes its door.

III.

Would not look up thither past thy head Because the door opes, like that child, I know, For I should have thy gracious face instead, Thou bird of God! And wilt thou bend me low Like him, and lay, like his, my hands together, And lift them up to pray, and gently tether Me, as thy lamb there, with thy garment's spread

IV.

This was ever granted, I would rest My bead beneath thine, while thy healing hands Close-covered both my eyes beside thy breast, Pressing the brain, which too much thought expands, Back to its proper size again, and smoothing Distortion down till every nerve had soothing, And all lay quiet, happy and suppressed.

V.

Soon all worldly wrong would be repaired! I think how I should view the earth and skies And sea, when once again my brow was bared After thy healing, with such different eyes. O world, as God has made it! All is beauty: And knowing this, is love, and love is duty. What further may be sought for or declared

VI.

Drew this angel I saw teach (Alfred, dear friend!)that little child to pray, Holding the little hands up, each to each Pressed gently,with his own head turned away Over the earth where so much lay before him Of work to do, though heaven was opening o'er him, And he was left at Fano by the beach.

VII.

Were at Fano, and three times we went To sit and see him in his chapel there, And drink his beauty to our soul's content My angel with me too: and since I care For dear Guercino's fame (to which in power And glory comes this picture for a dower, Fraught with a pathos so magnificent)—

VIII.

Since he did not work thus earnestly At all times, and has else endured some wrong—I took one thought his picture struck from me, And spread it out, translating it to song. My love is here. Where are you, dear old friend How rolls the Wairoa at your world's far end This is Ancona, yonder is the sea.

The Heretic's Tragedy

I.

PREADMONISHETH THE ABBOT DEODAET.

The Lord, we look to once for all, Is the Lord we should look at, all at once: He knows not to vary, saith Saint Paul, Nor the shadow of turning, for the nonce. See him no other than as he is! Give both the infinitudes their due—Infinite mercy, but, I wis, As infinite a justice too. [_Organ: plagal-cadence._As infinite a justice too.

II.

ONE SINGETH.

Master of the Temple of God, Falling to sin the Unknown Sin, What he bought of Emperor Aldabrod, He sold it to Sultan Saladin:, caught by Pope Clement, a-buzzing there, Hornet-prince of the mad wasps' hive, And clipt of his wings in Paris square, They bring him now to be burned alive.

And wanteth there grace of lute or clavicithern, ye shall say to confirm him who singeth_ We bring John now to be burned alive.

III.

The midst is a goodly gallows built; 'Twixt fork and fork, a stake is stuck; But first they set divers tumbrils a-tilt, Make a trench all round with the city muck; Inside they pile log upon log, good store; Faggots no few, blocks great and small, Reach a man's mid-thigh, no less, no more,— For they mean he should roast in the sight of all. CHORUS. We mean he should roast in the sight of all.

IV.

Good sappy bavins that kindle forthwith;
Billets that blaze substantial and slow;
Pine-stump split deftly, dry as pith;
Larch-heart that chars to a chalk-white glow:
Then up they hoist me John in a chafe,
Sling him fast like a hog to scorch,
Spit in his face, then leap back safe,
Sing "Laudes" and bid clap-to the torch. CHORUS.
_Laus Deo_who bids clap-to the torch.

V.

John of the Temple, whose fame so bragged,
    Is burning alive in Paris square!
can he curse, if his mouth is gagged
    Or wriggle his neck, with a collar there
Or heave his chest, which a band goes round
    Or threat with his fist, since his arms are spliced
Or kick with his feet, now his legs are bound
    Thinks John, I will call upon Jesus Christ.
[_Here one crosseth himself_

VI.

ChristJohn had bought and sold,
    Jesus ChristJohn had eaten and drunk;
To him, the Flesh meant silver and gold.
    (_Salv reverenti._)
Now it was, "Saviour, bountiful lamb,
    "I have roasted thee Turks, though men roast me!

"See thy servant, the plight wherein I am!
"Art thou a saviour Save thou me!" CHORUS.
'Tis John the mocker cries, "Save thou me!"

VII.

Maketh God's menace an idle word
Saith, it no more means what it proclaims,
Than a damsel's threat to her wanton bird—
For she too prattles of ugly names.
Saith, he knoweth but one thing,what he knows
That God is good and the rest is breath;
Why else is the same styled Sharon's rose
Once a rose, ever a rose, he saith. CHORUS.
O, John shall yet find a rose, he saith!

VIII.

There be roses and roses, John!
Some, honied of taste like your leman's tongue:
Some, bitter; for why (roast gaily on!)
Their tree struck root in devil's-dung.
When Paul once reasoned of righteousness
And of temperance and of judgment to come,
Good Felix trembled, he could no less:
John, snickering, crook'd his
Wicked thumb. CHORUS.
What cometh to John of the wicked thumb

IX.

Ha, John plucketh now at his rose
To rid himself of a sorrow at heart!
Lo,petal on petal, fierce rays unclose;
Anther on anther, sharp spikes outstart;
And with blood for dew, the bosom boils;
And a gust of sulphur is all its smell;
And lo, he is horribly in the toils
Of a coal-black giant flower of hell! CHORUS.
What maketh heaven, That maketh hell.

X.

As John called now, through the fire amain.
On the Name, he had cursed with, all his life—
To the Person, he bought and sold again—
For the Face, with his daily buffets rife—
Feature by feature It took its place:
And his voice, like a mad dog's choking bark,
At the steady whole of the Judge's face—
Died. Forth John's soul flared into the dark.
SUBJOINETH THE ABBOT DEODAET.
God help all poor souls lost in the dark!

Fagots.

A MIDDLE-AGE INTERLUDE.

Rosa mundi; seu, fulcite me floribus. a conceit of master gysbrecht, canon-regular of said jodocus-by-the-bar, ypres city. cantuque, _virgilius._ and hath often been sung at hock-tide and festivales. gavisus eram, _jessides._ (it would seem to be a glimpse from the burning of jacques du bourg-mulay, at paris, a. d.; as distorted by the refraction from flemish brain to brain, during the course of a couple of centuries.) [Molay was Grand Master of the Templars when that order was suppressed in.

The Italian In England

That second time they hunted me From hill to plain, from shore to sea, And Austria, hounding far and wide Her blood-hounds thro' the country-side, Breathed hot and instant on my trace,—I made six days a hiding-place Of that dry green old aqueduct Where I and Charles, when boys, have plucked The fire-flies from the roof above, Bright creeping thro' the moss they love: How long it seems since Charles was lost! Six days the soldiers crossed and crossed The country in my very sight; And when that peril ceased at night.

The sky broke out in red dismay With signal fires; well, there I lay Close covered o'er in my recess, Up to the neck in ferns and cress, Thinking on Metternich our friend, And Charles's miserable end, And much beside, two days; the third, Hunger o'ercame me when I heard The peasants from the village go To work among the maize; you know, With us in

Lombardy, they bring Provisions packed on mules, a string With little bells that cheer their task, And casks, and boughs on every cask To keep the sun's heat from the wine; These I let pass in jingling line, And, close on them, dear noisy crew, The peasants from the village, too; For at the very rear would troop Their wives and sisters in a group To help, I knew.

When these had passed, I threw my glove to strike the last, Taking the chance: she did not start, Much less cry out, but stooped apart, One instant rapidly glanced round, And saw me beckon from the ground. A wild bush grows and hides my crypt; She picked my glove up while she stripped A branch off, then rejoined the rest With that; my glove lay in her breast. Then I drew breath; they disappeared: It was for Italy I feared.

An hour, and she returned alone Exactly where my glove was thrown. Meanwhile came many thoughts: on me Rested the hopes of Italy.

I had devised a certain tale Which, when 'twas told her, could not fail Persuade a peasant of its truth; I meant to call a freak of youth This hiding, and give hopes of pay, And no temptation to betray. But when I saw that woman's face, Its calm simplicity of grace, Our Italy's own attitude In which she walked thus far, and stood, Planting each naked foot so firm, To crush the snake and spare the worm—At first sight of her eyes, I said, "I am that man upon whose head "They fix the price, because I hate "The Austrians over us: the State "Will give you goldoh, gold so much!—"If you betray me to their clutch, "And be your death, for aught I know, "If once they find you saved their foe.

"Now, you must bring me food and drink, "And also paper, pen and ink, "And carry safe what I shall write "To Padua, which you'll reach at night "Before the duomo shuts; go in, "And wait till Tenebr begin; "Walk to the third confessional, "Between the pillar and the wall, "And kneeling whisper, _Whence comes peace_ "Say it a second time, then cease; "And if the vo'ce inside returns, "_From Christ and Freedom; what concerns "The cause of Peace_for answer, slip "My letter where you placed your lip; "Then come back happy we have done "Our mother serviceI, the son, "As you the daughter of our land!" Three mornings more, she took her stand In the same place, with the same eyes: I was no surer of sun-rise That of her coming.

We conferred Of her own prospects, and I heard She had a loverstout and tall, She saidthen let her eyelids fall, "He could do much"as if some doubt Entered her heart,then, passing out, "She could not speak for others, who "Had other thoughts; herself she knew:" And so she brought me drink and food. After four days, the scouts pursued Another path; at last arrived The help my Paduan friends contrived To furnish me: she brought the news. For the first time I could not choose But kiss her hand, and lay my own Upon her head"This faith was shown "To Italy, our mother; she "Uses my hand and blesses thee." She followed down to the sea-shore; I left and never saw her more.

How very long since I have thought Concerningmuch less wished foraught Beside the good of Italy, For which I live and mean to die! I never was in love; and since Charles proved false, what shall now convince. My inmost heart I have a friend However, if I pleased to spend Real wishes on myselfsay, three—I know at least what one should be. I would grasp Metternich until I felt his red wet throat distil In blood thro' these two hands. And next, Nor much for that am I perplexed—Charles, perjured traitor, for his part, Should die slow of a broken heart Under his new employer.

Last Ah, there, what should I wish For fast Do I grow old and out of strength. If I resolved to seek at length My father's house again, how scared They all would look, and unprepared! My brothers live in Austria's pay Disowned me long ago, men say; And all my early mates who used To praise me soperhaps induced More than one early step of mine—Are turning wise: while some opine "Freedom grows license," some suspect "Haste breeds delay," and recollect They always said, such premature Beginnings never could endure! So, with a sullen "All's for best," The land seems settling to its rest. I think then, I should wish to stand This evening in that dear, lost land, Over the sea the thousand miles, And know if yet that woman smiles With the calm smile; some little farm She lives in there, no doubt: what harm If I sat on the door-side bench, And, while her spindle made a trench Fantastically in the dust, Inquired of all her fortunesjust Her children's ages and their names, And what may be the husband's aims For each of them. I'd talk this out, And sit there, for an hour about, Then kiss her hand once more, and lay Mine on her head, and go my way.

So much for idle wishinghow It steals the time! To business now.

The Laboratory ANCIEN RGIME.

I.

That I, tying thy glass mask tightly, May gaze thro' these faint smokes curling whitely, As thou pliest thy trade in this devil's-smithy—Which is the poison to poison her, prithee.

II.

He is with her, and they know that I know they are, what they do: they believe my tears flow While they laugh, laugh at me, at me fled to the drear Empty church, to pray God in, for them!I am here.

III.

Away, moisten and mash up thy paste, Pound at thy powder,I am not in haste! Better sit thus, and observe thy strange things, Than go where men wait me and dance at the King's.

IV.

That in the mortaryou call it a gum, the brave tree whence such gold oozings come! And yonder soft phial, the exquisite blue, Sure to taste sweetly,is that poison too.

V.

I but all of them, thee and thy treasures, What a wild crowd of invisible pleasures! To carry pure death in an earring, a casket, A signet, a fan-mount, a filigree basket!

VI.

Soon, at the King's, a mere lozenge to give, And Pauline should have just thirty minutes to live! But to light a pastile, and Elise, with her head And her breast and her arms and her hands, should drop dead!

VII.

Quickis it finished The colour's too grim! Why not soft like the phial's, enticing and dim Let it brighten her drink, let her turn it and stir, And try it and taste, ere she fix and prefer!

VIII.

What a drop! She's not little, no minion like me! That's why she ensnared him: this never will free The soul from those masculine eyes,Say, "no!" To that pulse's magnificent come-and-go.

IX.

Only last night, as they whispered, I brought My own eyes to bear on her so, that I thought Could I keep them one half minute fixed, she would fall Shrivelled; she fell not; yet this does it all!

X.

That I bid you spare her the pain; Let death be felt and the proof remain: Brand, burn up, bite into its grace—He is sure to remember her dying face!

XI.

It done Take my mask off! Nay, be not morose; It kills her, and this prevents seeing it close; The delicate droplet, my whole fortune's fee! If it hurts her, beside, can it ever hurt me

XII.

Now, take all my jewels, gorge gold to your fill, You may

kiss me, old man, on my mouth if you will! But brush this dust off me, lest horror it brings Ere I know itnext moment I dance at the King's!

The Laboratory-Ancien Régime

I.

Now that I, tying thy glass mask tightly, May gaze thro' these faint smokes curling whitely, As thou pliest thy trade in this devil's-smithy—Which is the poison to poison her, prithee

II.

He is with her, and they know that I know Where they are, what they do: they believe my tears flow While they laugh, laugh at me, at me fled to the drear Empty church, to pray God in, for them!I am here.

III.

Grind away, moisten and mash up thy paste, Pound at thy powder,I am not in haste! Better sit thus, and observe thy strange things, Than go where men wait me and dance at the King's.

IV.

That in the mortaryou call it a gum Ah, the brave tree whence such gold oozings come! And yonder soft phial, the exquisite blue, Sure to taste sweetly,is that poison too

V.

Had I but all of them, thee and thy treasures, What a wild crowd of invisible pleasures! To carry pure death in an earring, a casket, A signet, a fan-mount, a filigree basket!

VI.

Soon, at the King's, a mere lozenge to give, And Pauline should have just thirty minutes to live! But to light a pastile, and Elise, with her head And her breast and her arms and her hands, should drop dead!

VII.

Quickis it finished The colour's too grim! Why not soft like the phial's, enticing and dim Let it brighten her drink, let her turn it and stir, And try it and taste, ere she fix and prefer!

VIII.

What a drop! She's not little, no minion like me! That's why she ensnared him: this never will free The soul from those masculine eyes,Say, "no!" To that pulse's magnificent come-and-go.

IX.

For only last night, as they whispered, I brought My own eyes to bear on her so, that I thought Could I keep them one half minute fixed, she would fall Shrivelled; she fell not; yet this does it all!

X.

Not that I bid you spare her the pain; Let death be felt and the proof remain: Brand, burn up, bite into its grace— He is sure to remember her dying face!

XI.

Is it done Take my mask off! Nay, be not morose; It kills her, and this prevents seeing it close; The delicate droplet, my whole fortune's fee! If it hurts her, beside, can it ever hurt me

XII.

Now, take all my jewels, gorge gold to your fill, You may kiss me, old man, on my mouth if you will! But brush this dust off me, lest horror it brings Ere I know itnext moment I dance at the King's!

The Last Ride Together

I.

SaidThen, dearest, since 'tis so, Since now at length my

fate I know, Since nothing all my love avails, Since all, my life seemed meant for, fails, Since this was written and needs must be—My whole heart rises up to bless name in pride and thankfulness! Take back the hope you gave,I claim Only a memory of the same, And this beside, if you will not blame, Your leave for one more last ride with me.

II.

Mistress bent that brow of hers; Those deep dark eyes where pride demurs When pity would be softening through, Fixed me, a breathing-while or two, With life or death in the balance: right! The blood replenished me again; My last thought was at least not vain: I and my mistress, side by side Shall be together, breathe and ride, So, one day more am I deified. Who knows but the world may end tonight

III.

Hush! if you saw some western cloud All billowy-bosomed, over-bowed By many benedictionssun's moon's and evening-star's at once—And so, you, looking and loving best, Conscious grew, your passion drew Cloud, sunset, moonrise, star-shine too, Down on you, near and yet more near, Till flesh must fade for heaven was here!—Thus leant she and lingeredjoy and fear! Thus lay she a moment on my breast.

IV.

Then we began to ride. My soul itself out, a long-cramped scroll Freshening and fluttering in the wind. Past hopes already lay behind. What need to strive with a life awry Had I said that, had I done this, So might I gain, so might I miss. Might she have loved me just as well She might have hated, who can tell! Where had I been now if the worst befell And here we are riding, she and I.

V.

I alone, in words and deeds Why, all men strive and who

succeeds We rode; it seemed my spirit flew, Saw other regions, cities new, As the world rushed by on either side. I thought,All labour, yet no less Bear up beneath their unsuccess. Look at the end of work, contrast The petty done, the undone vast, This present of theirs with the hopeful past! I hoped she would love me; here we ride.

VI.

Hand and brain went ever paired What heart alike conceived and dared What act proved all its thought had been What will but felt the fleshly screen We ride and I see her bosom heave. There's many a crown for who can reach, Ten lines, a statesman's life in each! The flag stuck on a heap of bones, A soldier's doing! what atones scratch his name on the Abbey-stones. My riding is better, by their leave.

VII.

Does it all mean, poet Well, Your brains beat into rhythm, you tell What we felt only; you expressed You hold things beautiful the best, And pace them in rhyme so, side by side. 'Tis something, nay 'tis much: but then, Have you yourself what's best for men Are youpoor, sick, old ere your time—Nearer one whit your own sublime Than we who never have turned a rhyme Sing, riding's a joy! For me, I ride.

VIII.

And you, great sculptorso, you gave A score of years to Art, her slave, And that's your Venus, whence we turn To yonder girl that fords the burn! You acquiesce, and shall I repine What, man of music, you grown grey With notes and nothing else to say, Is this your sole praise from a friend, "Greatly his opera's strains intend, "Put in music we know how fashions end!" I gave my youth; but we ride, in fine.

IX.

Knows what's fit for us Had fate Proposed bliss here

should sublimate My beinghad I signed the bond—Still one must lead some life beyond, Have a bliss to die with, dim-descried. This foot once planted on the goal, This glory-garland round my soul, Could I descry such Try and test! I sink back shuddering from the quest. Earth being so good, would heaven seem best Now, heaven and she are beyond this ride.

X.

Yetshe has not spoke so long! What if heaven be that, fair and strong At life's best, with our eyes upturned Whither life's flower is first discerned, We, fixed so, ever should so abide What if we still ride on, we two With life for ever old yet new, Changed not in kind but in degree, The instant made eternity,—And heaven just prove that I and she Ride, ride together, for ever ride

The Lost Leader

I.

For a handful of silver he left us,
Just for a riband to stick in his coat—
Found the one gift of which fortune bereft us,
Lost all the others she lets us devote;
They, with the gold to give, doled him out silver,
So much was theirs who so little allowed:
How all our copper had gone for his service!
Ragswere they purple, his heart had been proud!
We that had loved him so, followed him, honoured him,
Lived in his mild and magnificent eye,
Learned his great language, caught his clear accents,
Made him our pattern to live and to die!
Shakespeare was of us, Milton was for us,
Burns, Shelley, were with us,they watch from their
Graves! He alone breaks from the van and the free-men,
He alone sinks to the rear and the slaves!

II.

Shall march prospering,not thro' his presence;

Songs may inspirit us,not from his lyre;
Deeds will be done,while he boasts his quiescence,
Still bidding crouch whom the rest bade aspire:
Blot out his name, then, record one lost soul more,
One task more declined, one more foot-path untrod,
One more devils'-triumph and sorrow for angels,
One wrong more to man, one more insult to God!
Life's night begins: let him never come back to us!
There would be doubt, hesitation and pain,
Forced praise on our partthe glimmer of twilight,
Never glad confident morning again!
fight on well, for we taught himstrike gallantly,
Menace our heart ere we master his own;
Then let him receive the new knowledge and wait us,
Pardoned in heaven, the first by the throne!

The Lost Mistress

I.

All's over, then: does truth sound bitter
As one at first believes
Hark, 'tis the sparrows' good-night twitter
About your cottage eaves!

II.

And the leaf-buds on the vine are woolly,
I noticed that, to-day;
day more bursts them open fully
You know the red turns grey. III.
To-morrow we meet the same then, dearest
May I take your hand in mine
Mere friends are we,well, friends the merest
Keep much that I resign:

IV.

Each glance of the eye so bright and black,
Though I keep with heart's endeavour,—
Your voice, when you wish the snowdrops back,
Though it stay in my soul for ever!—

V.

Yet I will but say what mere friends say,
Or only a thought stronger;
I will hold your hand but as long as all may,
Or so very little longer!
The Patriot AN OLD STORY.

I.

Was roses, roses, all the way,
With myrtle mixed in my path like mad:
The house-roofs seemed to heave and sway,
The church-spires flamed, such flags they had,
A year ago on this very day.

II.

Air broke into a mist with bells,
The old walls rocked with the crowd and cries.
Had I said, "Good folk, mere noise repels—
But give me your sun from yonder skies!"
They had answered, "And afterward, what else"

III.

It was I who leaped at the sun
To give it my loving friends to keep!
Nought man could do, have I left undone:
And you see my harvest, what I reap
This very day, now a year is run.

IV.

Nobody on the house-tops now—
Just a palsied few at the windows set;
For the best of the sight is, all allow,
At the Shambles' Gateor, better yet,
By the very scaffold's foot, I trow.

V.

Go in the rain, and, more than needs,
A rope cuts both my wrists behind;

And I think, by the feel, my forehead bleeds,
For they fling, whoever has a mind,
Stones at me for my year's misdeeds.

VI.

Thus I entered, and thus I go!
In triumphs, people have dropped down dead.
"Paid by the world, what dost thou owe
"Me"God might question; now instead,
'Tis God shall repay: I am safer so.

The Pied Piper Of Hamelin

I.

Town's in Brunswick, By famous Hanover city; The river Weser, deep and wide, Washes its wall on the southern side; A pleasanter spot you never spied; But, when begins my ditty, Almost five hundred years ago, To see the townsfolk suffer so From vermin, was a pity.

II.

Rats! fought the dogs and killed the cats, And bit the babies in the cradles, And ate the cheeses out of the vats, And licked the soup from the cooks' own ladles, Split open the kegs of salted sprats, Made nests inside men's Sunday hats, And even spoiled the women's chats By drowning their speaking With shrieking and squeaking In fifty different sharps and flats.

III.

At last the people in a body To the Town Hall came flocking: "'Tis clear," cried they, "our Mayor's a noddy; "And as for our Corporationshocking. "To think we buy gowns lined with ermine "For dolts that can't or won't determine "What's best to rid us of our vermin! "You hope, because you're old and obese, "To find in the furry civic robe ease "Rouse up, sirs! Give your brains a racking "To find the remedy we're lacking, "Or, sure as fate, we'll send you packing!" At this the Mayor and Corporation Quaked with a mighty consternation.

IV.

Hour they sat in council,
At length the Mayor broke silence:
"For a guilder I'd my ermine gown sell,
"I wish I were a mile hence!

"It's easy to bid one rack one's brain—"I'm sure my poor head aches again, "I've scratched it so, and all in vain. "Oh for a trap, a trap, a trap!" Just as he said this, what should hap At the chamber door but a gentle tap "Bless us," cried the Mayor, "what's that" (With the Corporation as he sat, Looking little though wondrous fat; Nor brighter was his eye, nor moister Than a too-long-opened oyster, when at noon his paunch grew mutinous For a plate of turtle green and glutinous) "Only a scraping of shoes on the mat "Anything like the sound of a rat "Makes my heart go pit-a-pat!"

V.

"Come in!"the Mayor cried, looking bigger: And in did come the strangest figure! His queer long coat from heel to head Was half of yellow and half of red, And he himself was tall and thin, With sharp blue eyes, each like a pin, And light loose hair, yet swarthy skin, No tuft on cheek nor beard on chin, But lips where smiles went out and in; There was no guessing his kith and kin: And nobody could enough admire The tall man and his quaint attire. Quoth one: "It's as my great-grandsire, "Starting up at the Trump of Doom's tone, "Had walked this way from his painted tombstone!"

VI.

He advanced to the council-table, "Please your honours," said he, "I'm able, "By means of a secret charm, to draw "All creatures living beneath the sun, "That creep or swim or fly or run, "After me so as you never saw! "And I chiefly use my charm "On creatures that do people harm, "The mole and toad and newt and viper; "And people call me the Pied Piper." (And here they noticed round his neck A scarf of red and yellow stripe, To match with his coat of the self-same cheque; And at the scarf's end hung a pipe;

And his fingers, they noticed, were ever straying As if impatient to be playing Upon this pipe, as low it dangled Over his vesture so old-fangled.) "Yet," said he, "poor piper as I am, "In Tartary I freed the Cham, "Last June, from his huge swarms of gnats; "I eased in Asia the Nizam "Of a monstrous brood of vampyre-bats: "And as for what your brain bewilders, "If I can rid your town of rats

"Will you give me a thousand guilders" "One fifty thousand!"was the exclamation Of the astonished Mayor and Corporation.

VII.

The street the Piper stept, Smiling first a little smile, As if he knew what magic slept In his quiet pipe the while; Then, like a musical adept, blow the pipe his lips he wrinkled, And green and blue his sharp eyes twinkled, Like a candle-flame where salt is sprinkled; And ere three shrill notes the pipe uttered, You heard as if an army muttered; And the muttering grew to a grumbling; And the grumbling grew to a mighty rumbling; And out of the houses the rats came tumbling. Great rats, small rats, lean rats, brawny rats, Brown rats, black rats, grey rats, tawny rats, Grave old plodders, gay young friskers, Fathers, mothers, uncles, cousins, Cocking tails and pricking whiskers, Families by tens and dozens, Brothers, sisters, husbands, wives—Followed the Piper for their lives. From street to street he piped advancing, And step for step they followed dancing, Until they came to the river Weser, Wherein all plunged and perished! Save one who, stout as Julius Csar, Swam across and lived to carry (As he, the manuscript he cherished) To Rat-land home his commentary: Which was, "At the first shrill notes of the pipe, "I heard a sound as of scraping tripe, "And putting apples, wondrous ripe, "Into a cider-press's gripe:

"And a moving away of pickle-tub-boards, "And a leaving ajar of conserve-cupboards, "And a drawing the corks of train-oil-flasks, "And a breaking the hoops of butter-casks: "And it seemed as if a voice "(Sweeter far than b harp or b psaltery "Is breathed) called out, 'Oh rats, rejoice! " 'The world is grown to one vast drysaltery! " 'So munch on, crunch on, take your nuncheon, " 'Breakfast, supper, dinner, luncheon!' "And just as a bulky sugar-puncheon, "All ready staved, like a great sun shone "Glorious scarce an inch before me, "Just as methought it said, 'Come, bore me!' "I found the Weser rolling o'er me."

VIII.

should have heard the Hamelin people ringing the bells till they rocked the steeple. "Go," cried the Mayor, "and get long poles, "Poke out the nests and block up the holes! "Consult with carpenters and builders, "And leave in our town not even a trace "Of the rats!"when suddenly, up the face Of the Piper perked in the market-place, With a, "First, if you please, my thousand guilders!"

IX.

A thousand guilders! The Mayor looked blue; So did the Corporation too. For council dinners made rare havoc With Claret, Moselle, Vin-de-Grave, Hock; And half the money would replenish Their cellar's biggest butt with Rhenish. To pay this sum to a wandering fellow With a gipsy coat of red and yellow! "Beside," quoth the Mayor with a knowing wink, "Our business was done at the river's brink; "We saw with our eyes the vermin sink, "And what's dead can't come to life, I think. "So, friend, we're not the folks to shrink "From the duty of giving you something for drink, "And a matter of money to put in your poke; "But as for the guilders, what we spoke "Of them, as you very well know, was in joke. "Beside, our losses have made us thrifty. "A thousand guilders! Come, take fifty!"

X.

The Piper's face fell, and he cried "No trifling! I can't wait, beside! "I've promised to visit by dinnertime "Bagdat, and accept the prime "Of the Head-Cook's pottage, all he's rich in, "For having left, in the Caliph's kitchen, "Of a nest of scorpions no survivor: "With him I proved no bargain-driver, "With you, don't think I'll bate a stiver! "And folks who put me in a passion "May find me pipe after another fashion."

XI.

"How" cried the Mayor, "d'ye think I brook "Being worse treated than a Cook "Insulted by a lazy ribald "With idle pipe and vesture piebald "You threaten us, fellow Do your worst, "Blow your pipe there till you burst!"

XII.

Once more he stept into the street And to his lips again Laid his long pipe of smooth straight cane; And ere he blew three notes (such sweet Soft notes as yet musician's cunning Never gave the enraptured air) There was a rustling that seemed like a bustling Of merry crowds justling at pitching and hustling, Small feet were pattering, wooden shoes clattering, Little hands clapping and little tongues chattering, And, like fowls in a farm-yard when barley is scattering, Out came the children running.

The little boys and girls, With rosy cheeks and flaxen curls, And sparkling eyes and teeth like pearls, Tripping and skipping, ran merrily after The wonderful music with shouting and laughter.

XIII.

The Mayor was dumb, and the Council stood As if they were changed into blocks of wood, Unable to move a step, or cry To the children merrily skipping by, Could only follow with the eye That joyous crowd at the Piper's back. But how the Mayor was on the rack, And the wretched Council's bosoms beat, As the Piper turned from the High Street To where the Weser rolled its waters Right in the way of their sons and daughters! However be turned from South to West, And to Koppelberg Hill his steps addressed, And after him the children pressed; Great was the joy in every breast.

"He never can cross that mighty top! "He's forced to let the piping drop, "And we shall see our children stop!" When, lo, as they reached the mountain-side, A wondrous portal opened wide, As if a cavern was suddenly hollowed; And the Piper advanced and the children followed, And when all were in to the very last, door in the mountain-side shut fast. Did I say, all No! One was lame, And could not dance the whole of the way; And in after years, if you would blame His sadness, he was used to say,—"It's dull in our town since my playmates left! "I can't forget that I'm bereft "Of all the pleasant sights they see, "Which the Piper also promised me.

"For he led us, he said, to a joyous land, "Joining the town and just at hand, "Where waters gushed and fruit-trees grew "And flowers put forth a fairer hue, "And everything was strange and new; "The sparrows were brighter than peacocks here, "And their dogs outran our fallow deer, "And honey-bees had lost their stings, "And horses were born with eagles' wings: "And just as I became assured "My lame foot would be speedily cured, "The music stopped and I stood still, "And found myself outside the hill, "Left alone against my will, "To go now limping as before, "And never hear of that country more!"

XIV.

Alas, alas for Hamelin! There came into many a burgher's pate A text which says that heaven's gate Opes to the rich at as easy rate As the needle's eye takes a camel in! The mayor sent East, West, North and South, To offer the Piper, by word of mouth, Wherever it was men's lot to find him, Silver and gold to his heart's content, If he'd only return the way he went, And bring the children behind him. But when they saw 'twas a lost endeavour, And Piper and dancers were gone for ever, They made a decree that lawyers never Should think their records dated duly If, after the day of the month and year.

These words did not as well appear, "And so long after what happened here "On the Twenty-second of July, "Thirteen hundred and seventy-six:" And the better in memory to fix The place of the children's last retreat, They called it, the Pied Piper's Street—Where any one playing on pipe or tabor Was sure for the future to lose his labour. Nor suffered they hostelry or tavern To shock with mirth a street so solemn; But opposite the place of the cavern They wrote the story on a column, And on the great church-window painted The same, to make the world acquainted How their children were stolen away, And there it stands to this very day.

And I must not omit to say That in Transylvania there's a tribe Of alien people who ascribe The outlandish ways and dress which their neighbours lay such stress, To their fathers and mothers having risen Out of some subterraneous prison Into which they were trepanned Long time ago in a mighty band Out of Hamelin town in Brunswick land, But how or why, they don't understand.

XV.

So, Willy, let me and you be wipers Of scores out with all menespecially pipers! And, whether they pipe us free frm rats or frm mice, If we've promised them aught, let us keep our promise! The Statue and the Bust There's a palace in Florence, the world knows well, And a statue watches it from the square, And this story of both do our townsmen tell. Ages ago, a lady there, At the farthest window facing the East, Asked, "Who rides by with the royal air" The bridesmaids' prattle around her ceased; She leaned forth, one on either hand; They saw how the blush of the bride increased -They felt by its beats her heart expand -As one at each ear and both in a breath Whispered, "The Great-Duke Ferdinand." That self-same instant, underneath, The Duke rode past in his idle way, Empty and fine like a swordless sheath. Gay he rode, with a friend as gay, Till he threw his head back — "Who is she" — "A bride the Riccardi brings home today." Hair in heaps lay heavily Over a pale brow spirit-pure -

Carved like the heart of the coal-black tree, Crisped like a war-steed's encolure -And vainly sought to dissemble her eyes Of the blackest black our eyes endure. And lo, a blade for a knight's emprise Filled the fine empty sheath of a man, -The Duke grew straightway brave and wise. He looked at her, as a lover can; She looked at him, as one who awakes: The past was a sleep, and their life began. Now, love so ordered for both their sakes, A feast was held that selfsame night In the pile which the mighty shadow makes. (For Via Larga is three-parts light, But the palace overshadows one, Because of a crime which may God requite! To Florence and God the wrong was done, Through the first republic's murder there By Cosimo and his cursèd son.)

The Duke (with the statue's face in the square) Turned in the midst of his multitude At the bright approach of the bridal pair. Face to face the lovers stood A single minute and no more, While the bridegroom bent as a man subdued -Bowed till his bonnet brushed the floor -For the Duke on the lady a kiss conferred, As the courtly custom was of yore. In a minute can lovers exchange a word If a word did pass, which I do not think, Only one out of the thousand heard. That was the bridegroom. At day's brink He and his bride were alone at last In a bedchamber by a taper's blink. Calmly he said that her lot was cast, That the door she had passed was shut on her Till the final catafalque repassed.

The world meanwhile, its noise and stir, Through a certain window facing the East, She could watch like a convent's chronicler. Since passing the door might lead to a feast, And a feast might lead to so much beside, He, of many evils, chose the least. "Freely I choose too," said the bride -"Your window and its world suffice," Replied the tongue, while the heart replied -"If I spend the night with that devil twice, May his window serve as my loop of hell Whence a damned soul looks on paradise! "I fly to the Duke who loves me well, Sit by his side and laugh at sorrow Ere I count another ave-bell.

"'Tis only the coat of a page to borrow, And tie my hair in a horse-boy's trim, And I save my soul — but not tomorrow" -(She checked herself and her eye grew dim) "My father tarries to bless my state: I must keep it one day more for him.

"Is one day more so long to wait Moreover the Duke rides past, I know; We shall see each other, sure as fate." She turned on her side and slept. Just so! So we resolve on a thing and sleep: So did the lady, ages ago.

That night the Duke said, "Dear or cheap As the cost of this cup of bliss may prove To body or soul, I will drain it deep." And on the morrow, bold with love, He beckoned the bridegroom (close on call, As his duty bade, by the Duke's alcove) And smiled "'Twas a very funeral, Your lady will think, this feast of ours, -A shame to efface, whate'er befall! "What if we break from the Arno bowers, And try if Petraja, cool and green,

Cure last night's fault with this morning's flowers" The bridegroom, not a thought to be seen On his steady brow and quiet mouth, Said, "Too much favour for me so mean! "But, alas! my lady leaves the South; Each wind that comes from the Apennine Is a menace to her tender youth: "Nor a way exists, the wise opine, If she quits her palace twice this year, To avert the flower of life's decline." Quoth the Duke, "A sage and a kindly fear. Moreover Petraja is cold this spring: Be our feast tonight as usual here!" And then to himself — "Which night shall bring Thy bride to her lover's embraces, fool -Or I am the fool, and thou art the king! "Yet my passion must wait a night, nor cool -For tonight the Envoy arrives from France Whose heart I unlock with thyself, my tool. "I need thee still and might miss perchance. Today is not wholly lost, beside, With its hope of my lady's countenance:

"For I ride — what should I do but ride And passing her palace, if I list, May glance at its window — well betide!" So said, so done: nor the lady missed One ray that broke from the ardent brow, Nor a curl of the lips where the spirit kissed. Be sure that each renewed the vow, No morrow's sun should arise and set And leave them then as it left them now. But next day passed, and next day yet, With still fresh cause to wait one day more Ere each leaped over the parapet. And still, as love's brief morning wore, With a gentle start, half smile, half sigh, They found love not as it seemed before. They thought it would work infallibly, But not in despite of heaven and earth: The rose would blow when the storm passed by. Meantime they could profit in winter's dearth By store of fruits that supplant the rose: The world and its ways have a certain worth: And to press a point while these oppose Were simple policy; better wait: We lose no friends and we gain no foes.

Meantime, worse fates than a lover's fate, Who daily may ride and pass and look Where his lady watches behind the grate! And she — she watched the square like a book Holding one picture and only one, Which daily to find she undertook: When the picture was reached the book was done, And she turned from the picture at night to scheme Of tearing it out for herself next sun.

So weeks grew months, years; gleam by gleam The glory dropped from their youth and love, And both perceived they had dreamed a dream; Which hovered as dreams do, still above: But who can take a dream for a truth Oh, hide our eyes from the next remove! One day as the lady saw her youth Depart, and the silver thread that streaked Her hair, and, worn by the serpent's tooth, The brow so puckered, the chin so peaked, -And wondered who the woman was, Hollow-eyed and haggard-cheeked, Fronting her silent in the glass - "Summon here," she suddenly said, "Before the rest of my old self pass, "Him, the Carver, a hand to aid, Who fashions the clay no love will change, And fixes a beauty never to fade.

"Let Robbia's craft so apt and strange Arrest the remains of young and fair, And rivet them while the seasons range. "Make me a face on the window there, Waiting as ever, mute the while, My love to pass below in the square! "And let me think that it may beguile Dreary days which the dead must spend Down in their darkness under the aisle, "To say, 'What matters it at the end I did no more while my heart was warm Than does that image, my pale-faced friend.' "Where is the use of the lip's red charm, The heaven of hair, the pride of the brow, And the blood that blues the inside arm -"Unless we turn, as the soul knows how, The earthly gift to an end divine A lady of clay is as good, I trow.

" But long ere Robbia's cornice, fine, With flowers and fruits which leaves enlace, Was set where now is the empty shrine -(And, leaning out of a bright blue space, As a ghost might lean from a chink of sky, The passionate pale lady's face -Eyeing ever, with earnest eye And quick-turned neck at its breathless stretch, Some one who ever is passing by —) The Duke had sighed like the simplest wretch In Florence, "Youth — my dream escapes! Will its record stay" And he bade them fetch Some subtle moulder of brazen shapes -"Can the soul, the will, die out of a man Ere his body find the grave that gapes "John of Douay shall effect my plan, Set me on horseback here aloft, Alive, as the crafty sculptor can, "In the very square I have crossed so oft: That men may admire, when future suns Shall touch the eyes to a purpose soft, "While the mouth and the brow stay brave in bronze -Admire and say, 'When he was alive How he would take his pleasure once!' "And it shall go hard but I contrive To listen the while, and laugh in my tomb At idleness which aspires to strive."

So! While these wait the trump of doom, How do their spirits pass, I wonder, Nights and days in the narrow room Still, I suppose, they sit and ponder What a gift life was, ages ago, Six steps out of the chapel yonder. Only they see not God, I know, Nor all that chivalry of his, The soldier-saints who, row on row, Burn upward each to his point of bliss -Since, the end of life being manifest, He had burned his way through the world to this. I hear you reproach, "But delay was best, For their end was a crime." — Oh, a crime will do As well, I reply, to serve for a test, As a virtue golden through and through, Sufficient to vindicate itself And prove its worth at a moment's view! Must a game be played for the sake of pelf Where a button goes, 'twere an epigram To offer the stamp of the very Guelph.

The true has no value beyond the sham: As well the counter as coin, I submit, When your table's a hat, and your prize a dram. Stake your counter as boldly every whit, Venture as warily, use the same skill, Do your best, whether winning or losing it, If you choose to play! — is my principle. Let a man contend to the uttermost For his life's set prize, be it what it will! The counter our lovers staked was lost As surely as if it were lawful coin: And the sin I impute to each frustrate ghost Is — the unlit lamp and the ungirt loin, Though the end in sight was a vice, I say. You of the virtue (we issue join) How strive you De te, fabula.

The Twins

Give" and "It-shall-be-given-unto-you."

I.

Rough old Martin Luther Bloomed fablesflowers on furze, The better the uncouther: Do roses stick like burrs

II.

A beggar asked an alms

One day at an abbey-door,
Luther; but, seized with qualms,
The abbot replied, "We're poor!

III.

"Poor, who had plenty once,
"When gifts fell thick as rain:
"But they give us nought, for the nonce,
"And how should we give again"

IV.

Then the beggar, "See your sins!
"Of old, unless I err,
"Ye had brothers for inmates, twins,
"Date and Dabitur.

V.

"While Date was in good case
"Dabitur flourished too:
"For Dabitur's lenten face
"No wonder if Date rue.

VI.

"Would ye retrieve the one
"Try and make plump the other!
"When Date's penance is done,
"Dabitur helps his brother.

VII.

"Only, beware relapse!"
The Abbot hung his head.
This beggar might be perhaps
An angel, Luther said.
The Wanderers the sea our galleys went,
With cleaving prows in order brave
To a speeding wind and a bounding wave-
A gallant armament: bark built out of a forest-tree
Left leafy and rough as first it grew, And nail'd all over

the gaping sides, Within and without, with black bull-hides, Seethed in fat and suppled in flame, To bear the playful billows' game; So, each good ship was rude to see, Rude and bare to the outward view. But each upbore a stately tent Where cedar pales in scented row Kept out the flakes of the dancing brine, And an awning droop'd the mast below, In fold on fold of the purple fine, That neither noontide nor star-shine Nor moonlight cold which maketh mad, Might pierce the regal tenement. When the sun dawn'd, O, gay and glad We set the sail and plied the oar; But when the night-wind blew like breath, For joy of one day's voyage more, We sang together on the wide sea, Like men at peace on a peaceful shore; Each sail was loosed to the wind so free, Each helm made sure by the twilight star.

And in a sleep as calm as death, We, the voyagers from afar, Lay stretch'd along, each weary crew In a circle round its wondrous tent gleam'd soft light and curl'd rich scent, And with light and perfume, music too: So the stars wheel'd round, and the darkness past, And at morn we started beside the mast, And still each ship was sailing fast! Now, one morn, land appear'd—a speck Dim trembling betwixt sea and sky-'Avoid it,' cried our pilot, 'check The shout, restrain the eager eye!' But the heaving sea was black behind For many a night and many a day, And land, though but a rock, drew nigh; So we broke the cedar pales away, Let the purple awning flap in the wind, And a statue bright was on every deck! We shouted, every man of us, And steer'd right into the harbour thus, With pomp and paean glorious.

A hundred shapes of lucid stone! All day we built its shrine for each, A shrine of rock for ever one, Nor paused till in the westering sun We sat together on the beach To sing because our task was done; When lo! what shouts and merry songs! What laughter all the distance stirs! A loaded raft with happy throngs Of gentle islanders! 'Our isles are just at hand,' they cried, 'Like cloudlets faint in even sleeping; Our temple-gates are open'd wide, Our olive-groves thick shade are keeping For these majestic forms'—they cried. O, then we awoke with sudden start From our deep dream, and knew, too late, How bare the rock, how desolate, Which had received our precious freight: Yet we call'd out—'Depart! gifts, once given, must here abide: Our work is done; we have no heart To mar our work,'—we cried.

The Year's at the Spring The year's at the spring, And day's at the morn; Morning's at seven; The hill-side's dew-pearled; The lark's on the wing; The snail's on the thorn; God's in his Heaven— All's right with the world! Through The Metidja To Abd-El-Kadr Abd-el-Kadr was an Arab Chief of Algiers who resisted the French in.]

I.

As I ride, as I ride, With a full heart for my guide, So its tide rocks my side, As I ride, as I ride, That, as I were double-eyed, He, in whom our Tribes confide, Is descried, ways untried As I ride, as I ride.

II.

As I ride, as I ride To our Chief and his Allied, Who dares chide my heart's pride As I ride, as I ride Or are witnesses denied—Through the desert waste and wide Do I glide unespied As I ride, as I ride

III.

As I ride, as I ride, When an inner voice has cried, The sands slide, nor abide (As I ride, as I ride) O'er each visioned homicide That came vaunting (has he lied) To residewhere he died, As I ride, as I ride.

IV.

As I ride, as I ride, Ne'er has spur my swift horse plied, Yet his hide, streaked and pied, As I ride, as I ride, Shows where sweat has sprung and dried, Zebra-footed, ostrich-thighed—How has vied stride with stride As I ride, as I ride!

V.

As I ride, as I ride, Could I loose what Fate has tied, Ere I pried, she should hide (As I ride, as I ride) All that's meant mesatisfied When the Prophet and the Bride Stop veins I'd have subside As I ride, as I ride!

I.

Through The Metodja To Abd-El-Kadr I As I ride, as I ride, With a full heart for my guide, So its tide rocks my side, As I ride, as I ride, That, as I were double-eyed, He, in whom our Tribes confide, Is descried, ways untried As I ride, as I ride.

II.

As I ride, as I ride

To our Chief and his Allied, Who dares chide my heart's pride As I ride, as I ride Or are witnesses denied— Through the desert waste and wide Do I glide unespied As I ride, as I ride

III.

As I ride, as I ride, When an inner voice has cried, The sands slide, nor abide (As I ride, as I ride) O'er each visioned Homicide That came vaunting (has he lied) To reside—where he died, As I ride, as I ride.

IV.

As I ride, as I ride, Ne'er has spur my swift horse plied, Yet his hide, streaked and pied, As I ride, as I ride, Shows where sweat has sprung and dried, —Zebra-footed, ostrich-thighed— How has vied stride with stride As I ride, as I ride!

V.

As I ride, as I ride, Could I loose what Fate has tied, Ere I pried, she should hide As I ride, as I ride, All that's meant me: satisfied When the Prophet and the Bride Stop veins I'd have subside As I ride, as I ride! Thus the Mayne glideth THUS the Mayne glideth Where my Love abideth; Sleep 's no softer: it proceeds On through lawns, on through meads, On and on, whate'er befall, and musical, Though the niggard pasturage Bears not on its shaven ledge Aught but weeds and waving grasses To view the river as it passes, Save here and there a scanty patch Of primroses too faint to catch A weary bee.... And scarce it pushes Its gentle way through strangling rushes Where the glossy kingfisher Flutters when noon-heats are near, Glad the shelving banks to shun, Red and steaming in the sun, Where the shrew-mouse with pale throat Burrows, and the speckled stoat; Where the quick sandpipers flit In and out the marl and grit That seems to breed them, brown as they: Naught disturbs its quiet way, Save some lazy stork that springs, Trailing it with legs and wings, Whom the shy fox from the hill Rouses, creep he ne'er so still.

Time's Revenges

I've a Friend, over the sea; I like him, but he loves me. It all grew out of the books I write; They find such favour in his sight That he slaughters you with savage looks Because you don't admire my books. He does himself though,and if some vein Were to snap to-night in this heavy brain, To-morrow month, if I lived to try, Round should I just turn quietly, Or out of the bedclothes stretch my hand Till I found him, come from his foreign land To be my nurse in this poor place, And make my broth and wash my face And light my fire and, all the while, Bear with his old good-humoured smile That I told him "Better have kept away "Than come and kill me, night and day, "With, worse than fever throbs and shoots, "The creaking of his clumsy boots."

I am as sure that this he would do As that Saint Paul's is striking two. And I think I rather... woe is me! Yes, rather would see him than not see, If lifting a hand could seat him there Before me in the empty chair To-night, when my head aches indeed, And I can neither think nor read Nor make these purple fingers hold The pen; this garret's freezing cold! And I've a Ladythere he wakes, The laughing fiend and prince of snakes Within me, at her name, to pray Fate send some creature in the way Of my love for her, to be down-torn, Upthrust and outward-borne, So I might prove myself that sea Of passion which I needs must be! Call my thoughts false and my fancies quaint And my style infirm and its figures faint, All the critics say, and more blame yet, And not one angry word you get. But, please you, wonder I would put My cheek beneath that lady's foot Rather than trample under mine The laurels of the Florentine, And you shall see how the devil spends A fire God gave for other ends! I tell you, I stride up and down This garret, crowned with love's best crown, And feasted with love's perfect feast.

To think I kill for her, at least, Body and soul and peace and fame, Alike youth's end and manhood's aim, So is my spirit, as flesh with sin, Filled full, eaten out and in With the face of her, the eyes of her, The lips, the little chin, the stir Of shadow round her month; and she I'll tell you,calmly would decree That I should roast at a slow fire, If that would compass her desire And make her one whom they invite To the famous ball to-morrow night. There may be heaven; there must be hell; Meantime, there is our earth herewell!

To Edward Fitzgerald

I chanced upon a new book yesterday; I opened it, and, where my finger lay 'Twixt page and uncut page, these words I read Some six or seven at most - and learned thereby That you, Fitzgerald, whom by ear and eye She never knew, "thanked God my wife was dead." Aye, dead! and were yourself alive, good Fitz, How to return you thanks would task my wits. Kicking you seems the common lot of curs While more appropriate greeting lends you grace, Surely to spit there glorifies your face Spitting from lips once sanctified by hers.

Twins, The

"Give" and "It-shall-be-given-unto-you."

I.

Rough old Martin Luther
    Bloomed fablesflowers on furze,
The better the uncouther:
    Do roses stick like burrs

II.

A beggar asked an alms
    One day at an abbey-door,
Luther; but, seized with qualms,
    The abbot replied, "We're poor!

III.

"Poor, who had plenty once,
"When gifts fell thick as rain:
"But they give us nought, for the nonce,
"And how should we give again"

IV.

Then the beggar, "See your sins!
"Of old, unless I err,
"Ye had brothers for inmates, twins,
"Date and Dabitur.

V.

"While Date was in good case
"Dabitur flourished too:
"For Dabitur's lenten face
"No wonder if Date rue.

VI.

"Would ye retrieve the one
"Try and make plump the other!
"When Date's penance is done,
"Dabitur helps his brother.

VII.

"Only, beware relapse!"
The Abbot hung his head.
This beggar might be perhaps
An angel, Luther said.

I.

Two In The Campagna
I wonder do you feel to-day
As I have felt since, hand in hand,
We sat down on the grass, to stray
In spirit better through the land,
This morn of Rome and May

II.

Me, I touched a thought, I know,
    Has tantalized me many times,
(Like turns of thread the spiders throw
    Mocking across our path) for rhymes
To catch at and let go.

III.

Me to hold it! First it left
    The yellowing fennel, run to seed
There, branching from the brickwork's cleft,
    Some old tomb's ruin: yonder weed
Took up the floating wet,

IV.

One small orange cup amassed
    Five beetles,blind and green they grope
Among the honey-meal: and last,
    Everywhere on the grassy slope I traced it.
Hold it fast!

V.

Champaign with its endless fleece
    Of feathery grasses everywhere!
Silence and passion, joy and peace,
    An everlasting wash of air—
Rome's ghost since her decease.

VI.

Such life here, through such lengths of hours,
    Such miracles performed in play,
primal naked forms of flowers,
    Such letting nature have her way
While heaven looks from its towers!

VII.

How say you Let us, O my dove,
    Let us be unashamed of soul,

As earth lies bare to heaven above!
How is it under our control To love or not to love

VIII.

Would that you were all to me,
You that are just so much, no more.
Nor yours nor mine, nor slave nor free!
Where does the fault lie What the core
O' the wound, since wound must be

IX.

Would I could adopt your will,
See with your eyes, and set my heart
Beating by yours, and drink my fill
At your soul's springs,your part my part
In life, for good and ill.

X.

I yearn upward, touch you close,
Then stand away. I kiss your cheek,
Catch your soul's warmth,I pluck the rose
And love it more than tongue can speak—
Then the good minute goes.

XI.

how am I so far
Out of that minute Must I go
Still like the thistle-ball, no bar,
Onward, whenever light winds blow,
Fixed by no friendly star

XII.

When I seemed about to learn!
Where is the thread now Off again!
The old trick! Only I discern—
Infinite passion, and the pain
Of finite hearts that yearn.
Herb with yellow flowers and seeds supposed to be

medicinal. Up at a Villa — Down in the City (As Distinguished by an Italian Person of Quality)

I.

Had I but plenty of money, money enough and to spare,
The house for me, no doubt, were a house in the city-square;
Ah, such a life, such a life, as one leads at the window there!

II.

Something to see, by Bacchus, something to hear, at least!
There, the whole day long, one's life is a perfect feast; While
up at a villa one lives, I maintain it, no more than a beast.

III.

Well now, look at our villa! stuck like the horn of a bull
Just on a mountain's edge as bare as the creature's skull, Save
a mere shag of a bush with hardly a leaf to pull! - I scratch my
own, sometimes, to see if the hair's turned wool.

IV.

But the city, oh the city—the square with the houses! Why
They are stone-faced, white as a curd, there's something to take
the eye! Houses in four straight lines, not a single front awry!
You watch who crosses and gossips, who saunters, who hurries
by: Green blinds, as a matter of course, to draw when the sun
gets high; And the shops with fanciful signs which are painted
properly.

V.

What of a villa Though winter be over in March by rights,
'Tis May perhaps ere the snow shall have withered well off
the heights: You've the brown ploughed land before, where
the oxen steam and wheeze, And the hills over-smoked behind
by the faint grey olive trees.

VI.

Is it better in May, I ask you You've summer all at once;
In a day he leaps complete with a few strong April suns. 'Mid

the sharp short emerald wheat, scarce risen three fingers well, The wild tulip, at end of its tube, blows out its great red bell Like a thin clear bubble of blood, for the children to pick and sell.

VII.

Is it ever hot in the square There's a fountain to spout and splash! In the shade it sings and springs; in the shine such foam-bows flash On the horses with curling fish-tails, that prance and paddle and pash Round the lady atop in her conch—fifty gazers do not abash, Though all that she wears is some weeds round her waist in a sort of sash!

VIII.

All the year long at the villa, nothing to see though you linger, Except yon cypress that points like Death's lean lifted forefinger. Some think fireflies pretty, when they mix in the corn and mingle, Or thrid the stinking hemp till the stalks of it seem a-tingle. Late August or early September, the stunning cicala is shrill, And the bees keep their tiresome whine round the resinous firs on the hill. Enough of the seasons,—I spare you the months of the fever and chill.

IX.

Ere opening your eyes in the city, the blessed church-bells begin: No sooner the bells leave off than the diligence rattles in: You get the pick of the news, and it costs you never a pin. By and by there's the travelling doctor gives pills, lets blood, draws teeth; Or the Pulcinello-trumpet breaks up the market beneath. At the post-office such a scene-picture—the new play, piping hot! And a notice how, only this morning, three liberal thieves were shot. Above it, behold the Archbishop's most fatherly of rebukes, And beneath, with his crown and his lion, some little new law of the Duke's! Or a sonnet with flowery marge, to the Reverend Don So-and-so Who is Dante, Boccaccio, Petrarca, Saint Jerome, and Cicero, "And moreover," (the sonnet goes rhyming,) "the skirts of Saint Paul has reached, Having preached us those six Lent-lectures more unctuous than ever he preached." Noon strikes,—here sweeps the procession! our Lady borne smiling and smart With a pink gauze gown all spangles, and seven swords stuck in her heart! Bang, whang, whang goes the drum, tootle-te-tootle the fife; No keeping one's haunches still: it's the greatest pleasure in life.

X.

But bless you, it's dear—it's dear! fowls, wine, at double the rate. They have clapped a new tax upon salt, and what oil pays passing the gate It's a horror to think of. And so, the villa for me, not the city! Beggars can scarcely be choosers: but still—ah, the pity, the pity! Look, two and two go the priests, then the monks with cowls and sandals, And the penitents dressed in white shirts, a-holding the yellow candles; One, he carries a flag up straight, and another a cross with handles, And the Duke's guard brings up the rear, for the better prevention of scandals.

Bang, whang, whang goes the drum, tootle-te-tootle the fife. Oh, a day in the city-square, there is no such pleasure in life!

Up At A Villa Down In The City

AS DISTINGUISHED BY AN ITALIAN PERSON OF QUALITY.)

I.

I but plenty of money, money enough and to spare, The house for me, no doubt, were a house in the city-square; Ah, such a life, such a life, as one leads at the window there!

II.

To see, by Bacchus, something to hear, at least! There, the whole day long, one's life is a perfect feast; While up at a villa one lives, I maintain it, no more than a beast.

III.

Now, look at our villa! stuck like the horn of a bull Just on a mountain-edge as bare as the creature's skull, Save a mere shag of a bush with hardly a leaf to pull! I scratch my own, sometimes, to see if the hair's turned wool.

IV.

But the city, oh the citythe square with the houses! Why They are stone-faced, white as a curd, there's something to take the eye! Houses in four straight lines, not a single front awry;

Watch who crosses and gossips, who saunters, who hurries by; Green blinds, as a matter of course, to draw when the sun gets high; And the shops with fanciful signs which are painted properly.

V.

Of a villa Though winter be over in March by rights, 'Tis May perhaps ere the snow shall have withered well off the heights: You've the brown ploughed land before, where the oxen steam and wheeze, And the hills over-smoked behind by the faint grey olive-trees.

VI.

It better in May, I ask you You've summer all at once; In a day he leaps complete with a few strong April suns. 'Mid the sharp short emerald wheat, scarce risen three fingers well, The wild tulip, at end of its tube, blows out its great red bell Like a thin clear bubble of blood, for the children to pick and sell.

VII.

Is it ever hot in the square There's a fountain to spout and splash! In the shade it sings and springs; in the shine such foam-bows flash On the horses with curling fish-tails, that prance and paddle and pash Round the lady atop in her conchfifty gazers do not abash, Though all that she wears is some weeds round her waist in a sort of sash.

VIII.

The year at the villa, nothing to see though you linger, Except yon cypress that points like a death's lean lifted forefinger. Some think fireflies pretty, when they mix i' the corn and mingle, Or thrid the stinking hemp till the stalks of it seem a-tingle. Late August or early September, the stunning cicala is shrill, And the bees keep their tiresome whine round the resinous firs on the hill. Enough of the seasons,I spare you the months of the fever and chill.

IX.

Ere you open your eyes in the city, the blessed church-bells begin: No sooner the bells leave off than the diligence rattles in: You get the pick of the news, and it costs you never a pin. By-and-by there's the travelling doctor gives pills, lets blood, draws teeth; Or the Pulcinello-trumpet breaks up the market beneath.

At the post-office such a scene-picturethe new play, piping hot! And a notice how, only this morning, three liberal thieves were shot. Above it, behold the Archbishop's most fatherly of rebukes, And beneath, with his crown and his lion, some little new law of the Duke's! Or a sonnet with flowery marge, to the Reverend Don So-and-so Who is Dante, Boccaccio, Petrarca, Saint Jerome and Cicero,

"And moreover," (the sonnet goes rhyming,) "the skirts of Saint Paul has reached, "Having preached us those six Lent-lectures more unctuous than ever he preached." Noon strikes,here sweeps the procession! our Lady borne smiling and smart With a pink gauze gown all spangles, and seven swords stuck in her heart! _Bang-whang-whang_ goes the drum, _tootle-to-tootle_ the fife; No keeping one's haunches still: it's the greatest pleasure in life.

X.

But bless you, it's dearit's dear! fowls, wine, at double the rate. They have clapped a new tax upon salt, and what oil pays passing the gate It's a horror to think of. And so, the villa for me, not the city! Beggars can scarcely be choosers: but stillah, the pity, the pity! Look, two and two go the priests, then the monks with cowls and sandals, And the penitents dressed in white shirts, a-holding the yellow candles; One' he carries a flag up straight, and another a cross with handles, And the Duke's guard brings up the rear, for the better prevention of scandals: Bang-whang-whang_ goes the drum, tootle te tootle the fife.

Oh, a day in the city-square, there is no such pleasure in life! Up At A Villa— Down In The City (As Distinguished by an Italian Person of Quality)

I.

Had I but plenty of money, money enough and to spare, The house for me, no doubt, were a house in the city-square; Ah, such a life, such a life, as one leads at the window there!

II.

Something to see, by Bacchus, something to hear, at least! There, the whole day long, one's life is a perfect feast; While up at a villa one lives, I maintain it, no more than a beast.

III.

Well now, look at our villa! stuck like the horn of a bull Just on a mountain's edge as bare as the creature's skull, Save a mere shag of a bush with hardly a leaf to pull! - I scratch my own, sometimes, to see if the hair's turned wool.

IV.

But the city, oh the city—the square with the houses! Why They are stone-faced, white as a curd, there's something to take the eye! Houses in four straight lines, not a single front awry! You watch who crosses and gossips, who saunters, who hurries by: Green blinds, as a matter of course, to draw when the sun gets high; And the shops with fanciful signs which are painted properly.

V.

What of a villa Though winter be over in March by rights, 'Tis May perhaps ere the snow shall have withered well off the heights: You've the brown ploughed land before, where the oxen steam and wheeze, And the hills over-smoked behind by the faint grey olive trees.

VI.

Is it better in May, I ask you You've summer all at once; In a day he leaps complete with a few strong April suns. 'Mid the sharp short emerald wheat, scarce risen three fingers well, The wild tulip, at end of its tube, blows out its great red bell Like a thin clear bubble of blood, for the children to pick and sell.

VII.

Is it ever hot in the square There's a fountain to spout and splash! In the shade it sings and springs; in the shine such foam-bows flash On the horses with curling fish-tails, that prance and paddle and pash Round the lady atop in her conch—fifty gazers do not abash, Though all that she wears is some weeds round her waist in a sort of sash!

VIII.

All the year long at the villa, nothing to see though you linger, Except yon cypress that points like Death's lean lifted forefinger. Some think fireflies pretty, when they mix in the corn and mingle, Or thrid the stinking hemp till the stalks of it seem a-tingle. Late August or early September, the stunning cicala is shrill, And the bees keep their tiresome whine round the resinous firs on the hill. Enough of the seasons,—I spare you the months of the fever and chill.

IX.

Ere opening your eyes in the city, the blessed church-bells begin: No sooner the bells leave off than the diligence rattles in: You get the pick of the news, and it costs you never a pin. By and by there's the travelling doctor gives pills, lets blood, draws teeth; Or the Pulcinello-trumpet breaks up the market beneath. At the post-office such a scene-picture—the new play, piping hot! And a notice how, only this morning, three liberal thieves were shot.

Above it, behold the Archbishop's most fatherly of rebukes, And beneath, with his crown and his lion, some little new law of the Duke's! Or a sonnet with flowery marge, to the Reverend Don So-and-so Who is Dante, Boccaccio, Petrarca, Saint Jerome, and Cicero, "And moreover," (the sonnet goes rhyming,) "the skirts of Saint Paul has reached,

Having preached us those six Lent-lectures more unctuous than ever he preached." Noon strikes,—here sweeps the procession! our Lady borne smiling and smart With a pink gauze gown all spangles, and seven swords stuck in her heart! Bang, whang, whang goes the drum, tootle-te-tootle the fife; No keeping one's haunches still: it's the greatest pleasure in life.

X.

But bless you, it's dear—it's dear! fowls, wine, at double the rate. They have clapped a new tax upon salt, and what oil pays passing the gate It's a horror to think of. And so, the villa for me, not the city! Beggars can scarcely be choosers: but still—ah, the pity, the pity! Look, two and two go the priests, then the monks with cowls and sandals, And the penitents dressed in white shirts, a-holding the yellow candles; One, he carries a flag up straight, and another a cross with handles, And the Duke's guard brings up the rear, for the better prevention of scandals. Bang, whang, whang goes the drum, tootle-te-tootle the fife. Oh, a day in the city-square, there is no such pleasure in life!

Up at a Villa—Down in the City

I but plenty of money, money enough and to spare,

The house for me, no doubt, were a house in the city-square; Ah, such a life, such a life, as one leads at the window there! Something to see, by Bacchus, something to hear, at least! There, the whole day long, one's life is a perfect feast; While up at a villa one lives, I maintain it, no more than a beast.

Well now, look at our villa! stuck like the horn of a bull Just on a mountain-edge as bare as the creature's skull, Save a mere shag of a bush with hardly a leaf to pull! —I scratch my own, sometimes, to see if the hair's turned wool. But the city, oh the city—the square with the houses! Why They are stone-faced, white as a curd, there's something to take the eye! Houses in four straight lines, not a single front awry; watch who crosses and gossips, who saunters, who hurries by; Green blinds, as a matter of course, to draw when the sun gets high; And the shops with fanciful signs which are painted properly.

What of a villa Though winter be over in March by rights, 'Tis May perhaps ere the snow shall have withered well off the heights: You've the brown ploughed land before, where the oxen steam and wheeze, And the hills over-smoked behind by the faint gray olive-trees.

Is it better in May, I ask you You've summer all at once; In a day he leaps complete with a few strong April suns. 'Mid the sharp short emerald wheat, scarce risen three fingers well, The wild tulip, at end of its tube, blows out its great red bell Like a thin clear bubble of blood, for the children to pick and sell. Is it ever hot in the square There's a fountain to spout and splash! In the shade it sings and springs: in the shine such foambows flash On the horses with curling fish-tails, that prance and paddle and pash Round the lady atop in her conch—fifty gazers do not abash, Though all that she wears is some weeds round her waist in a sort of sash.

All the year long at the villa, nothing to see though you linger, Except yon cypress that points like death's lean lifted forefinger. Some think fireflies pretty, when they mix in the corn and mingle, Or thrid the stinking hemp till the stalks of it seem a-tingle. Late August or early September, the stunning cicala is shrill, And the bees keep their tiresome whine round the resinous firs on the hill. Enough of the seasons,—I spare you the months of the fever and chill.

Ere you open your eyes in the city, the blessed church-bells begin: No sooner the bells leave off than the diligence rattles in: You get the pick of the news, and it costs you never a pin. By and by there's the travelling doctor gives pills, lets blood, draws teeth; Or the Pulcinello-trumpet breaks up the market beneath. At the post-office such a scene-picture—the new play, piping hot! And a notice how, only this morning, three liberal thieves were shot.

Above it, behold the Archbishop's most fatherly of rebukes, And beneath, with his crown and his lion, some little new law of the Duke's! Or a sonnet with flowery marge, to the Reverend Don So-and so, Who is Dante, Boccaccio, Petrarca, Saint Jerome and Cicero,

"And moreover," (the sonnet goes rhyming,) "the skirts

of Saint Paul has reached, Having preached us those six Lent-lectures more unctuous than ever he preached." Noon strikes,—here sweeps the procession! our Lady borne smiling and smart With a pink gauze gown all spangles, and seven swords stuck in her heart! Bang-whang-whang goes the drum, tootle-te-tootle the fife. No keeping one's haunches still: it's the greatest pleasure in life.

But bless you, it's dear—it's dear! fowls, wine, at double the rate. They have clapped a new tax upon salt, and what oil pays passing the gate It's a horror to think of. And so, the villa for me, not the city! Beggars can scarcely be choosers: but still—ah, the pity, the pity! Look, two and two go the priests, then the monks with cowls and sandals, And the penitents dressed in white shirts a-holding the yellow candles; One, he carries a flag up straight, and another a cross with handles. And the Duke's guard brings up the rear, for the better prevention of scandals: Bang-whang-whang goes the drum, tootle-te-tootle the fife; Oh, a day in the city-square, there is no such pleasure in life! Verse-Making Was Least of My Virtues Verse-making was least of my virtues: I viewed with despair Wealth that never yet was but might be—all that verse-making were If the life would but lengthen to wish, let the mind be laid bare. So I said, "To do little is bad, to do nothing is worse"-And made verse. Love-making,—how simple a matter! No depths to explore, No heights in a life to ascend! No disheartening Before, No affrighting Hereafter,—love now will be love ever more. So I felt "To keep silence were folly:"—all language above, I made love.

Waring

Mr. Alfred Domett, C.M.G., author of Ranolf and Amohia, "full of descriptions of New Zealand scenery.]

I.

Become of Waring Since he gave us all the slip, Chose land-travel or seafaring, Boots and chest or staff and scrip, Rather than pace up and down Any longer London town

II.

Who'd have guessed it from his lip Or his brow's

accustomed bearing, On the night he thus took ship Or started landwardlittle caring For us, it seems, who supped together (Friends of his too, I remember) And walked home thro' the merry weather, The snowiest in all December.

I left his arm that night myself For what's-his-name's, the new prose-poet Who wrote the book there, on the shelf—How, forsooth, was I to know it Waring meant to glide away Like a ghost at break of day Never looked he half so gay!

III.

He was prouder than the devil: How he must have cursed our revel! Ay and many other meetings, Indoor visits, outdoor greetings, As up and down he paced this London, With no work done, but great works undone, Where scarce twenty knew his name. Why not, then, have earlier spoken, Written, bustled Who's to blame If your silence kept unbroken "True, but there were sundry jottings, "Stray-leaves, fragments, blurts and blottings, "Certain fixst steps were achieved.

"Already which"(is that your meaning) "Had well borne out whoe'er believed "In more to come!" But who goes gleaning Hedgeside chance-glades, while full-sheaved Stand cornfields by him Pride, o'erweening Pride alone, puts forth such claims O'er the day's distinguished names.

IV.

Meantime, how much I loved him, I find out now I've lost him. I who cared not if I moved him, Who cou!d so carelessly accost him, Henceforth never shall get free Of his ghostly company, His eyes that just a little wink As deep I go into the merit Of this and that distinguished spirit—His cheeks' raised colour, soon to sink, As long I dwell on some stupendous And tremendous (Heaven defend us!) Monstr'-inform'-ingens-horrend-ous Demoniaco-seraphic Penman's latest piece of graphic. Nay, my very wrist grows warm With his dragging weight of arm. E'en so, swimmingly appears, Through one's after-supper musings, Some lost lady of old years her beauteous vain endeavour And goodness unrepaid as ever; The face, accustomed to refusings.

We, puppies that we were... Oh never Surely, nice of conscience, scrupled Being aught like false, forsooth, to Telling aught but honest truth to What a sin, had we centupled Its possessor's grace and sweetness No! she heard in its completeness Truth, for truth's a weighty matter, And truth, at issue, we can't flatter! Well, 'tis done with; she's exempt From damning us thro' such a sally; And so she glides, as down a valley, Taking up with her contempt, Past our reach; and in, the flowers Shut her unregarded hours.

V.

Oh, could I have him back once more, This Waring, but one half-day more! Back, with the quiet face of yore, So hungry for acknowledgment Like mine! I'd fool him to his bent. Feed, should not he, to heart's content I'd say, "to only have conceived, "Planned your great works, apart from progress, "Surpasses little works achieved!" I'd lie so, I should be believed. I'd make such havoc of the claims Of the day's distinguished names To feast him with, as feasts an ogress Her feverish sharp-toothed gold-crowned child! Or as one feasts a creature rarely Captured here, unreconciled To capture; and completely gives its pettish humours license, barely Requiring that it lives.

VI.

Ichabod, Ichabod, The glory is departed! Travels Waring East away Who, of knowledge, by hearsay, Reports a man upstarted Somewhere as a god, Hordes grown European-hearted, Millions of the wild made tame On a sudden at his fame In Vishnu-land what Avatar Or who in Moscow, toward thc Czar, With the demurest of footfalls Over the Kremlin's pavement bright With serpentine and syenite, Steps, with five other Generals That simultaneously take snuff, For each to have pretext enough And kerchiefwise unfold his sash Which, softness' self, is yet the stuff To hold fast where a steel chain snaps, And leave the grand white neck no gash Waring in Moscow. to those rough Cold northern natures born perhaps, Like the lambwhite maiden dear From the circle of mute kings

Unable to repress the tear, Each as his sceptre down he flings, To Dian's fane at Taurica.

Where now a captive priestess, she alway Mingles her tender grave Hellenic speech With theirs, tuned to the hailstone-beaten beach As pours some pigeon, from the myrrhy lands Rapt by the whirlblast to fierce Scythian strands Where breed the swallows, her melodious cry Amid their barbarous twitter! In Russia Never! Spain were fitter! Ay, most likely 'tis in Spain That we and Waring meet again Now, while he turns down that cool narrow lane Into the blackness, out of grave Madrid All fire and shine, abrupt as when there's slid Its stiff gold blazing pall From some black coffin-lid. Or, best of all,

I love to think

The leaving us was just a feint; Back here to London did he slink, And now works on without a wink Of sleep, and we are on the brink Of something great in fresco-pain: Some garret's ceiling, walls and floor, Up and down and o'er and o'er He splashes, as none splashed before Since great Caldera Polidore. Or Music means this land of ours Some favour yet, to pity won By Purcell from his Rosy Bowers,—"Give me my so-long promised son, "Let Waring end what I begun!" Then down he creeps and out he steals Only when the night conceals His face; in Kent 'tis cherry-time, Or hops are picking: or at prime Of March he wanders as, too happy, Years ago when he was young, Some mild eve when woods grew sappy And the early moths had sprung To life from many a trembling sheath Woven the warm boughs beneath; While small birds said to themselves What should soon be actual song, And young gnats, by tens and twelves.

Made as if they were the throng That crowd around and carry aloft The sound they have nursed, so sweet and pure, Out of a myriad noises soft, Into a tone that can endure Amid the noise of a July noon When all God's creatures crave their boon, All at once and all in tune, And get it, happy as Waring then, Having first within his ken What a man might do with men: And far too glad, in the even-glow, To mix with the world he meant to take Into his hand, he told you, so—And out of it his world to make, To contract and to expand.

As he shut or oped his hand. Oh Waring, what's to really be A clear stage and a crowd to see! Some Garrick, say, out shall not he The heart of Hamlet's mystery pluck Or, where most unclean beasts are rife, Some Juniusam I rightshall tuck His sleeve, and forth with flaying-knife! Some Chatterton shall have the luck Of calling Rowley into life! Some one shall somehow run a muck With this old world for want of strife Sound asleep. Contrive, contrive To rouse us, Waring! Who's alive Our men scarce seem in earnest now. Distinguished names!but 'tis, somehow, As if they played at being names Still more distinguished, like the games Of children. Turn our sport to earnest With a visage of the sternest! Bring the real times back, confessed Still better than our very best!

I.

"When I last saw Waring..." (How all turned to him who spoke! You saw Waring Truth or joke In land-travel or sea-faring)

II.

"We were sailing by Triest "Where a day or two we harboured: "A sunset was in the West, "When, looking over the vessel's side, "One of our company espied "A sudden speck to larboard. "And as a sea-duck flies and swims "At once, so came the light craft up, "With its sole lateen sail that trims "And turns (the water round its rims "Dancing, as round a sinking cup) "And by us like a fish it curled, "And drew itself up close beside, "Its great sail on the instant furled, "And o'er its thwarts a shrill voice cried, "(A neck as bronzed as a Lascar's) " 'Buy wine of us, you English Brig " 'Or fruit, tobacco and cigars " 'A pilot for you to Triest " 'Without one, look you ne'er so big, " 'They'll never let you up the bay! " 'We natives should know best.' "I turned, and 'just those fellows' way,' "Our captain said, 'The 'long-shore thieves " 'Are laughing at us in their sleeves.'

III.

"In truth, the boy leaned laughing back; "And one, half-hidden by his side "Under the furled sail, soon I spied, "With great grass hat and kerchief black, "Who looked up with his kingly throat, "Said somewhat, while the other shook "His hair back from his eyes to look "Their longest at us; then the boat, "I know not how, turned sharply round, "Laying her whole side on the sea "As a leaping fish does; from the lee "Into the weather, cut somehow "Her sparkling path beneath our bow "And so went off, as with a bound, "Into the rosy and golden half "O' the sky, to overtake the sun "And reach the shore, like the sea-calf "Its singing cave; yet I caught one "Glance ere away the boat quite passed, "And neither time nor toil could mar "Those features: so I saw the last "Of Waring!"You Oh, never star Was lost here but it rose afar! Look East, where whole new thousands are! In Vishnu-land what Avatar Egyptian granite.

Surnamed da Caravaggio. A pupil of Raphael. Why I Am a Liberal "Why" Because all I haply can and do, All that I am now, all I hope to be,-Whence comes it save from fortune setting free Body and soul the purpose to pursue, God traced for both If fetters, not a few, Of prejudice, convention, fall from me, These shall I bid men—each in his degree Also God-guided—bear, and gayly, too But little do or can the best of us: That little is achieved through Liberty. Who, then, dares hold, emancipated thus, His fellow shall continue bound Not I, Who live, love, labour freely, nor discuss A brother's right to freedom. That is "Why."

Women And Roses

I.

Dream of a red-rose tree. And which of its roses three Is the dearest rose to me

II.

Round and round, like a dance of snow In a dazzling drift, as its guardians, go Floating the women faded for ages, Sculptured in stone, on the poet's pages. Then follow women fresh and gay, Living and loving and loved to-day.

In the rear, flee the multitude of maidens, Beauties yet

unborn. And all, to one cadence, They circle their rose on my rose tree.

III.

Rose, thy term is reached, Thy leaf hangs loose and bleached: Bees pass it unimpeached.

IV.

Stay then, stoop, since I cannot climb, You, great shapes of the antique time! How shall I fix you, fire you, freeze you, Break my heart at your feet to please you Oh, to possess and be possessed! Hearts that beat 'neath each pallid breast! Once but of love, the poesy, the passion, Drink but once and die!In vain, the same fashion, They circle their rose on my rose tree.

V.

Dear rose, thy joy's undimmed, Thy cup is ruby-rimmed, Thy cup's heart nectar-brimmed.

VI.

Deep, as drops from a statue's plinth The bee sucked in by the hyacinth, So will I bury me while burning, Quench like him at a plunge my yearning, Eyes in your eyes, lips on your lips! Fold me fast where the cincture slips, Prison all my soul in eternities of pleasure, Girdle me for once! But nothe old measure, They circle their rose on my rose tree.

VII.

Rose without a thorn, Thy bud's the babe unborn: First streak of a new morn.

VIII.

Wings, lend wings for the cold, the clear! What is far conquers what is near. Roses will bloom nor want beholders, Sprung from the dust where our flesh moulders. What shall arrive with the cycle's change A novel grace and a beauty strange.

I will make an Eve, be the artist that began her, Shaped

her to his mind!Alas! in like manner They circle their rose on my rose tree.

You'll Love Me Yet

- You'll love me yet!—and I can tarry Your love's protracted growing:
- June reared that bunch of flowers you carry From seeds of April's sowing.
- I plant a heartful now: some seed At least is sure to strike,
- And yield—what you'll not pluck indeed, Not love, but, may be, like!
- You'll look at least on love's remains, A grave's one violet:
- Your look—that pays a thousand pains. What's death—You'll love me yet!
- You'll love me yet!—and I can tarry You'll love me yet!—and I can tarry Your love's protracted growing:
- June reared that bunch of flowers you carry From seeds of April's sowing.
- I plant a heartful now: some seed At least is sure to strike,
- And yield—what you'll not pluck indeed, Not love, but, may be, like!
- You'll look at least on love's remains, A grave's one violet:
- Your look—that pays a thousand pains. What's death—You'll love me yet!

Youth and Art

It once might have been, once only:
We lodged in a street together,
You, a sparrow on the housetop lonely,
I, a lone she-bird of his feather.
Your trade was with sticks and clay,
You thumbed, thrust, patted and polished,
Then laughed 'They will see some day
Smith made, and Gibson demolished.'
My business was song, song, song;

I chirped, cheeped, trilled and twittered,
'Kate Brown's on the boards ere long,
And Grisi's existence embittered!'
I earned no more by a warble
Than you by a sketch in plaster;
You wanted a piece of marble,
I needed a music-master.
We studied hard in our styles,
Chipped each at a crust like Hindoos,
For air looked out on the tiles,
For fun watched each other's windows.
You lounged, like a boy of the South,
Cap and blouse—nay, a bit of beard too;
Or you got it, rubbing your mouth
With fingers the clay adhered to.
And I—soon managed to find
Weak points in the flower-fence facing,
Was forced to put up a blind
And be safe in my corset-lacing.
No harm! It was not my fault
If you never turned your eye's tail up
As I shook upon E in alt,
Or ran the chromatic scale up:
For spring bade the sparrows pair,
And the boys and girls gave guesses,
And stalls in our street looked rare
With bulrush and watercresses.
Why did not you pinch a flower
In a pellet of clay and fling it
Why did not I put a power
Of thanks in a look, or sing it
I did look, sharp as a lynx,
(And yet the memory rankles,)
When models arrived, some minx
Tripped up-stairs, she and her ankles.
But I think I gave you as good!
'That foreign fellow,—who can know
How she pays, in a playful mood,

For his tuning her that piano'
Could you say so, and never say
'Suppose we join hands and fortunes,
And I fetch her from over the way,
Her, piano, and long tunes and short tunes'
No, no: you would not be rash,
Nor I rasher and something over:
You've to settle yet Gibson's hash,
And Grisi yet lives in clover.
But you meet the Prince at the Board,
I'm queen myself at bals-paré,
I've married a rich old lord,
And you're dubbed knight and an R.A.
Each life unfulfilled, you see;
It hangs still, patchy and scrappy:
We have not sighed deep, laughed free,
Starved, feasted, despaired,—been happy.
And nobody calls you a dunce,
And people suppose me clever:
This could but have happened once,
And we missed it, lost it for ever.

Bibliography

Poetry

Asolando: Fancies and Facts (1889)

Christmas-*Eve and Easter-Day* (1850)

Complete Poetic and Dramatic Works of Robert Browning (1895)

Dramatic Idyls (1879)

Dramatic Idyls: Second Series (1880)

Ferishtah's Fancies (1884)

Jocoseria (1883)

La Saisiaz, and *The Two Poets of Croisicv* (1878)

Men and Women (1855)

New Poems by *Robert Browning and Elizabeth Barrett Browning* (1914)

Pacchiarotto and How He Worked in Distemper, with Other Poems (1876)

Paracelsus (1835)

Parleyings with Certain People of Importance in Their Day (1887)

Pauline: *A Fragment of a Confession* (1833)

Red Cotton Night-Cap Country; or, *Turf and Towers* (1873)

Robert Browning: The Poems (1981)

Robert Browning: The Ring and the Book (1971)

Sordell (1840)

The Brownings to the Tennysons (1971)

The Complete Works of Robert Browning (1898)

The Inn Album (1875)

The Poetical Works of Robert Browning (1868)
The Ring and the Book (1868)
The Works of Robert Browning (1912)
Two Poems (1854)

Prose

Browning to His American Friends (1965)
Dearest Isa: Browning's Letters to Isa Blagden (1951)
Learned Lady: *Letters from Robert Browning to Mrs. Thomas FitzGerald* 1876-1889 (1966)
Letters of Robert Browning Collected by Thomas J. Wise (1933)
New Letters of Robert Browning (1950)
Robert Browning and *Julia Wedgwood*: A Broken Friendship as Revealed in Their Letters (1937)
The Letters of Robert Browning and Elizabeth Barrett, 1845-1846 (1969)
Thomas Jones, The Divine Order: *Sermons* (1884)